IX 185 TIN

Patient Safety, Law Policy and Practice

Patient safety is an issue which in recent years has grown to prominence in a number of countries' political and health service agendas. The World Health Organization has launched the World Alliance for Patient Safety. Millions of patients, according to the Alliance, endure prolonged ill-health, disability and death caused by unreliable practices, services, and poor health care environments. At any given time 1.4 million people worldwide are suffering from an infection acquired in a health facility.

Patient Safety, Law Policy and Practice explores the impact of legal systems on patient safety initiatives. It asks whether legal systems are being used in appropriate ways to support state and local managerial systems in developing patient safety procedures, and what alternative approaches can and should be utilized. The chapters in this collection explore the patient safety managerial structures that exist in countries where there is a developed patient safety infrastructure and culture. The legal structures of these countries are explored and related to major in-country patient safety issues such as consent to treatment protocols and guidelines, complaint handling, adverse incident reporting systems, and civil litigation systems, in order to draw comparisons and conclusions on patient safety.

John Tingle is Reader in Health Law at Nottingham Trent University, UK.

Pippa Bark is Principal Research Fellow at CHIME, University College London, UK.

Patient Safety, Law Policy and Practice

Edited by
John Tingle and Pippa Bark

Routledge
Taylor & Francis Group

LONDON AND NEW YORK

First published 2011
by Routledge
2 Park Square, Milton Park, Abingdon, Oxon, OX14 4RN

Simultaneously published in the USA and Canada
by Routledge
711 Third Avenue, New York, NY 10017

Routledge is an imprint of the Taylor & Francis Group, an informa business

British Library Cataloguing in Publication Data
A catalogue record for this book is available
from the British Library

Library of Congress Cataloging in Publication Data
A catalog record for this book has been requested
      p. cm.
   ISBN 978-0-415-55731-3 (hbk)—ISBN 978-0-203-83073-4 (ebk)
   1. Medical errors–Prevention–Law and legislation–Great Britain.
   2. Medical errors–Prevention–Law and legislation.   I. Tingle, John.
   II. Bark, Pippa.
KD3395.P375 2011
344.04'1—dc22

                                          2010037173

ISBN: 978-0-415-55731-3 (hbk)
ISBN: 978-0-203-83073-4 (ebk)

Typeset in Garamond
by RefineCatch Limited, Bungay, Suffolk
Printed and bound in Great Britain by
CPI Antony Rowe, Chippenham, Wiltshire

Contents

Notes on contributors

Pippa Bark is Principal Research Fellow at CHIME, University College London, UK.

Charles Foster is a Barrister at Outer Temple Chambers, London, and teaches medical law and ethics at the University of Oxford, UK.

Barry R. Furrow is Professor of Law and Director of the Health Law Program in the Earle Mack School of Law at Drexel University, Philadelphia, USA.

Dr Joan M. Gilmour is Professor of Law and Director of the Master's Program in Health Law at Osgoode Hall Law School, York University, in Toronto, Canada.

Stephen Heasell is Principal Lecturer at Nottingham Business School, School of Business, Law and Social Sciences, Nottingham Trent University, UK.

Dr Nils Hoppe leads the Medical Law and Bioethics Group at the Centre for Ethics and Law in the Life Sciences, Leibniz Universität Hannover, Germany.

Dr James Houston is Senior Lecturer in Psychology at Nottingham Trent University, UK.

Professor Johan Legemaate is Professor of Health Law, Academic Medical Center/University of Amsterdam.

Professor Jean V. McHale is Professor of Health Care Law and Director of the Institute of Medical Law, Birmingham Law School, University of Birmingham

Dr José Miola is a Senior Lecturer in Law in the Faculty of Law, University of Leicester, UK.

Dr Jamie Murphy is Senior Lecturer in Psychology at Nottingham Trent University, UK.

Dr Ash Samanta is a Consultant Rheumatologist at the University Hospitals of Leicester NHS Trust, UK.

Mrs Jo Samanta is a Solicitor and Principal Lecturer in Law at De Montfort University, Leicester, UK.

Ronni P. Solomon is Executive Vice President and General Counsel, ECRI Institute, USA.

Dr Marc Stauch is a member of the Medical Law and Bioethics Group at the Centre for Ethics and Law in the Life Sciences, Leibniz Universität Hannover, Germany.

Eva Sundin is Reader in Psychology at Nottingham Trent University, UK.

John Tingle is a Barrister and Reader in Health Law at Nottingham Law School, Nottingham Trent University, UK.

Merrilyn Walton is Associate Professor and Director Patient Safety in the Office of Postgraduate Medical Education, Faculty of Medicine, at the University of Sydney, Australia.

Preface

As a mixture of law, policy and practice, we hope this book provides the reader with a unique perspective on the international problems, solutions and challenges in patient safety. It is designed to provide the context that is currently missing from legal discussions of clinical negligence and other related areas of tort law. Our aim is to introduce the reader to 'behind the scenes', the numerous patient safety organisations, policies, tensions that exist and the general field of literature. It is clear that many avoidable clinical errors are being made and that the legal infrastructure for resolving disputes is unsatisfactory in many respects.

We have cast our net widely and have invited international academic colleagues in other jurisdictions to contribute to the text so that a comparative perspective can be drawn. Health as a concept is a generic one and the problems cross international boundaries. The book is going to press at a time when the new coalition government has announced sweeping cuts in public expenditure. Bureaucracy is being cut in the NHS and the functions of a number of organisations will be streamlined. At the time of writing, The Department of Health's Review of Arm's Length Bodies has proposed to abolish the National Patient Safety Agency (NPSA), which has, up until now, served a useful function in focusing attention on patient safety issues. Some of the NPSA functions will become part of the remit of the new NHS Commissioning Board and other functions will be supported to continue in other ways. The review also proposes that the National Health Service Litigation Authority (NHSLA) be subject to an industry review in order to identify potential opportunities for greater commercial involvement, with a view to its likely removal from the arm's length bodies sector as soon as possible. With the changes and possible fragmentation we may face, learning from other countries' experience is ever more relevant.

We convey thanks to our families and academic friends for their kind support in writing this book. Also appreciation to Katie Carpenter of Routledge for her continued support throughout the proposal stage and through to submission, and to Khanam Virjee of Routledge. Lisa Williams did an excellent job as copy editor.

John Tingle, Nottingham
Pippa Bark, London
October 2010

Table of cases

Table of statutes

Introduction

The development of a patient safety policy agenda

John Tingle

The purpose of this book is to explore the impact of legal systems on patient safety initiatives. We ask fundamental questions such as whether legal systems are used in appropriate ways to support state and local managerial systems developing patient safety procedures. What alternative approaches can and should be utilised? Chapters in this book explore the patient safety managerial and legal structures that exist in countries where there is a developed patient safety infrastructure and culture.

In the UK the Bristol Inquiry report, chaired by Professor Sir Ian Kennedy, stated well the tension that exists between English tort law and the patient safety agenda. The report states:

> 33 It is our view, therefore, that the culture and the practice of clinical negligence litigation work against the interests of patients' safety. The system is positively counter-productive, in that it provides a clear incentive not to report, or to cover up, an error or incident. And, once covered up, no one can learn from it and the next patient is exposed to the same or a similar risk.[1]

The report goes on to state;

> 35 The system of clinical negligence litigation is now ripe for review. It is over 20 years since it was last considered as part of the review carried out by a Royal commission under Lord Pearson. Much has changed in the NHS and in the practice of medicine since then. The system is now out of alignment with other policy initiatives on quality and safety: in fact it serves to undermine those policies and inhibits improvements in the safety of the care received by patients. Ultimately, we take the view that it will not be possible to achieve an environment of full, open reporting within the NHS when, outside it, there exists a litigation system the incentives of which press in the opposite direction. We believe that the way forward lies in the abolition of clinical negligence litigation, taking clinical error out of the courts and the tort system.[2]

The report made the bold proposal to abolish the clinical negligence tort based system, which was probably a step too far. In a very real sense the tort based system has its faults, as will be seen in chapters in this book, but it is also a very useful mechanism for encouraging accountability, deterrence and education. The tort system is also generally well understood and the Bolam concept of fault is familiar. The Bristol Inquiry report views above are authoritative views on the appropriateness or otherwise of the tort based system and its relationship to patient safety systems and as such require careful consideration.

The Chief Medical Officer, in *Making Amends*, also set the scene for reform when he stated:

> Legal proceedings for medical injury frequently progress in an atmosphere of confrontation, acrimony, misunderstanding and bitterness. The emphasis is on revealing as little as possible about what went wrong, defending clinical decisions that were taken and only reluctantly releasing information.[3]

These are all serious indictments against the current tort system that compensates patients for clinical negligence. Chapters in this book will test these views and explore whether the same could be said about other countries' jurisdictions and patient safety systems.

The cost of medical malpractice litigation is also an issue in the UK and there are record levels of claims. The Chief Medical Officer, in the report *Making Amends*, stated:

> Over the years, the costs of compensating injured patients through this legally based system have steadily grown. Between the 1970s and the early 1980s, allowing for inflation, the cost of settling claims increased by just over 400 per cent. Over the past decade costs have risen by over 750 per cent from £53 million in 1990 to approximately £450 million in 2001/2002.[4]

The National Health Service Litigation Authority (NHSLA) provides more recent figures:

> 2008/09 saw a significant increase in the number of claims received, compared with the same period last year. Clinical claims rose by more than 11% and non-clinical claims by over 10%. The preceding five years had seen a largely static intake of new claims and we have not been able to identify any single factor that might have precipitated the rise.[5]

A key question is how much the NHS owes in clinical negligence claims. The NHSLA states:

As at 31 March 2009, the NHSLA estimates that it has potential liabilities of £13.51 billion, of which £13.37 billion relate to clinical negligence claims (the remainder being liabilities under PES and LTPS). This figure represents the estimated value of all known claims, together with an actuarial estimate of those incurred but not yet reported (IBNR), which may settle or be withdrawn over future years.[6]

These are seriously large figures and, taking them all into account, we have a major problem of increasingly expensive medical malpractice litigation in a tort system which may not be totally fit for purpose. These issues will be further explored by contributors in this book.

What is patient safety?

Patient safety is used as a broad term. The World Health Organisation defines patient safety[7] as 'freedom for a patient from unnecessary harm or potential harm associated with healthcare'. Patient safety is a global issue which in recent years has grown in prominence in a number of countries' political and health service agendas, particularly in the UK. The World Health Organisation launched the World Alliance for Patient Safety.[8] Some of its work includes the following:

The first Global Patient Safety Challenge addresses an issue of universal relevance to patient safety – action to reduce health care-associated infections (HAI) worldwide. In industrialized countries, HAI complicate between 5–10% of admissions in acute care hospitals. In developing countries, the proportion of infected patients can exceed 25%.[9]

The focus in this book will be on how adverse incidents to patients can be avoided in main areas of NHS patient care and in the healthcare systems of some other countries. The overarching theme of the book is the exploration of civil legal compensation systems and how well they relate to state and local patient safety managerial systems.

Developed patient safety infrastructures

In this book a number of countries' patient safety infrastructures are analysed, with contributors focussing particularly on England, the USA, Canada, Australia, the Netherlands and Germany.

The UK notched up a first in patient safety with the world's first comprehensive adverse incident reporting system, the National Reporting and Learning System (NRLS).[10] In the US, there is a new federal law and regulations that establish federally certified entities called Patient Safety Organisations (PSOs). Providers who share data with a PSO to get feedback can do so under a federal umbrella of privilege and confidentiality. This is significant, especially for states that have no state-afforded protection. We have devoted two chapters to discussing the USA patient safety context.

Exploring the context

A significant number of patients are unintentionally harmed by an error in hospital, with estimates of between 4 and 16 per cent.[11] As a result the UK Government has built up a fairly large infrastructure to manage patient safety and clinical risk. Organisations such as the National Patient Safety Agency (NPSA), Care Quality Commission and National Health Service Litigation Authority, amongst others, exist to enhance patient safety and manage healthcare litigation.[12] These organisations produce a considerable amount of literature and advice in the area, along with patient safety quality tools such as root cause analysis. Key patient safety and governance organisations will be discussed, along with their key initiatives.

Answering the fundamental question

A common theme between the chapters will be attempts to answer the fundamental question of whether patient safety management activity has worked or not in the countries considered. In the UK context, can it be said that the NHS is a safer place than it was five or 10 years ago? There are views that not a lot has changed and that we do not yet have an ingrained patient safety culture. Patients are still dying of MRSA infections acquired in dirty hospitals and because of negligent healthcare. Record levels of complaints by patients are still being made. Litigation and costs in the area have reached record levels, as stated later in this collection.

In the UK we have made slow, incremental progress in developing a patient safety infrastructure. NHS Trusts are predominantly reactive in their response to patient safety incidents and parts of some organisations still operate a blame culture.[13] The National Audit Office (NAO) stated that there remains a clear need to improve evaluation and sharing of lessons and solutions by the larger number of organisations with a stake in patient safety.[14]

In 2009 the House of Commons Health Committee stated:

> We are, however, concerned that Lord Darzi's emphasis on quality and safety is an indication that, for all the policy innovations of the past decade, insufficient progress has been made in making NHS services safer. We note that the report commissioned by the Chief Medical Officer in 2006, Safety First, concluded that patient safety was attaining a significant national profile, but was 'not always given the same priority or status as other major issues such as reducing waiting times, implementing national service frameworks and achieving financial balance'. This concern is heightened by the recent cases of disastrously unsafe care that have come to light in a small number of Trusts.[15]

The Government response to the report states:

> We believe that progress has been made to embed patient safety as a priority for all NHS services, but recognise the need for sustained focus and effort. Quality and safety have been key priorities for the NHS over the past decade. Significant improvements in quality have been made.[16]

These paragraphs represent the current state of play of the patient safety agenda in the UK: a top-down driven approach exists which is having a moderate degree of success, progress is incremental and we are still a long way from having an engrained patient safety culture in the NHS. Much more needs to be done at all levels of the NHS.

NHS staff at all levels should be aware of the patient safety tools developed by organisations such as the NPSA, for example those relating to root cause analysis (RCA). Trust managers need to embrace more fully patient safety and clinical governance concepts and become less distracted by financial and other targets. Staff and managers also need to learn the lessons of errors of the past. The same errors, often very simple ones, continue to be made. This is a very evident from numerous reports of the Health Service Commissioner over the years and from the reports of the Healthcare Commission and Care Quality Commission.

Exploring the policy climate

The patient safety policy climate in a number of different countries will also be a recurrent feature in the chapters that address healthcare outside the UK. UK Government policy in this area can be seen to have been largely reactive, and there is very little outcome measurement of the success or otherwise of the patient safety, health quality reforms. There has been a lot of regulatory overkill in the area, causing many NHS staff to feel disillusioned.

The legal perspective

Patient safety initiatives encompass important legal perspectives in different countries. In the UK, which will include Scotland and Wales, in this book, medical ethics issues such as consent to treatment and clinical negligence are just some key legal, patient safety interfaces. There are many more.

In the context of the NHS, the NHS Redress Act 2006 and the Compensation Act 2006 are in many ways products of Government awareness of a potential compensation culture, and they provide in themselves a fertile area for critical discussion. The idea of a no-fault based system was rejected by the Chief Medical Officer in his review.[17] The idea of Bolam, Fault and the basic aims of a tort based system are raised by the topic of patient safety, a topic which is starting to feature in more academic writings and is discussed by chapter contributors in this book. The legal focus will largely be on tort and compensation law as it will be easier to make comparisons between countries if a common framework is chosen. The international chapters will also explore the common themes of compensation culture, no fault and better routes to redress.

Notes

1 *Final Report: Learning from Bristol: The Report of the Public Inquiry into Children's Heart Surgery at the Bristol Royal Infirmary 1984–1995*, Command Paper, CM 5207.
2 Ibid.
3 *Making Amends, A Consultation Paper Setting Out Proposals for Reforming the Approach to Clinical Negligence in the NHS*, a report by the Chief Medical Officer, London, Department of Health, June 2003.
4 Ibid.
5 *The NHSLA Report and Accounts 2009*, HC 576, London, The Stationery Office, 7 July 2009.
6 Ibid.
7 WHO, *World Alliance for Patient Safety, Forward Programme 2008–2009*, 1st edn, Geneva, WHO, 2008. Online. Available HTTP: http://www.who.int/ patientsafety/information_centre/reports/Alliance_Forward_Programme_2008. pdf (accessed 7 June 2010).
8 Project to Develop the International Classification for Patient Safety, *Report on the Results of the Web-Based Modified Delphi Survey of the International Classification for Patient Safety*, Geneva, Patient Safety Unit, WHO, 8 June 2007.
9 Ibid.
10 *National Framework for Reporting and Learning from Serious Incidents Requiring Investigation*, London, NPSA, 2010.
11 National Audit Office, *A Safer Place for Patients: Learning to Improve Patient Safety*, HC 456 Sessions 2005–2006, London, The Stationery Office, 3 November 2005.
12 *National Framework for Reporting and Learning from Serious Incidents Requiring Investigation*.
13 National Audit Office, *A Safer Place for Patients*.
14 Ibid.
15 House of Commons Health Committee, *Patient Safety*, Sixth Report of Session 2008–2009 HC 151–1, London, The Stationery Office, 3 July 2009, para. 32.
16 *The Government Response to the Health Select Committee Report, Patient Safety*, Cm 7709, London, The Stationery Office, October 2009.
17 *Making Amends*.

1 Managing quality, safety and risk

Jo Samanta and Ash Samanta

Introduction

Quality, safety and risk are key components that underpin a health service of the highest rank. The need for successful management of these elements was emphasised in *To Err Is Human*[1] and *An Organisation with a Memory*.[2] Concern about safety, quality and risk is rooted in antiquity but the challenge remains as to how to ensure that a modern healthcare system is efficient, effective and safe.[3] Despite major advancements in clinical care alongside technological innovation, the risk of iatrogenic harm to patients remains considerable.

Prior to 1999 the common law duty imposed upon healthcare providers in this jurisdiction was to exercise reasonable care and skill in the provision of services. The Health Act 1999, s18(1) stated that it was 'the duty of each [NHS provider] to put and keep in place arrangements for the purpose of monitoring and improving the quality of healthcare which it provides for individuals'. This standard was revised by s45 of the Health and Social Care (Community Health and Standards) Act 2003, which states that it is the duty of each NHS body to ensure that arrangements are in place for the purpose of monitoring and improving the quality of healthcare provided by those organisations. The Department of Health labelled these arrangements a 'framework through which NHS organisations are accountable for continuously improving the quality of their services and safeguarding high standards of care by creating an environment in which excellence in clinical care will flourish'.[4] The statutory duty of quality incorporates evaluation of organisational risk management and audit mechanisms as well as accountability.

Quality, safety and risk management of healthcare are inextricably intertwined, and in our view should be seamlessly pervasive throughout the layers of policy, provider organisations and their management, and practice resulting in good clinical care. This chapter focuses on the principal issues surrounding the management of these factors within the context of contemporary health service delivery in the UK.

Policy

The NHS constitution and legislative reform

In 2007 the Secretary of State for Health announced a wholesale review of the National Health Service. The *NHS Next Stage Review 'Our NHS, Our Future'*, led by Lord Darzi, aimed to develop a 10-year strategy for health services following engagement with patients, staff and the public.[5] The subsequent Interim Report set out a 10-year plan for the NHS to become fairer, more personalised, effective and safe. The Report puts the case for a Constitution to enshrine the values of the NHS, setting out the key rights and responsibilities of patients and staff. The NHS Next Stage Review Final Report *High Quality Care for All* (2008) advanced a conceptual strategy for health services with a clear focus on quality. The Health Act 2009 is the enabling statute that implements those aspects of the Next Stage Review that require primary legislation. Provisions include the NHS Constitution and Quality Accounts, and enables direct payments to be made in defined circumstances for healthcare services.

The sections of the Health Act 2009 that pertain to the NHS Constitution set out duties of these organisations involved with the provision, commissioning or regulation of care and those delivering NHS services under contracts or arrangements. The Constitution is subject to review by the Secretary of State for health at least every decade, following consultation with local authorities, staff and patients. The Constitution confers rights to service users, supported by redress and remedial mechanisms designed to put things right (as opposed to monetary compensation).

Strategic Health Authorities, NHS Foundation Trusts, Monitor and the Care Quality Commission have a statutory duty to have regard to the NHS Constitution when commissioning or providing services, when carrying out their functions as a regulator.[6] Part 2 of the Act describes powers in respect of failing NHS organisations. Under its auspices Foundation Trusts are designed to be accountable to local communities, as opposed to the Secretary of State. They are authorised by the National Health Service Act 2006 and are subject to regulation by Monitor, the Independent Regulator of NHS Foundation Trusts. Monitor has authority to intervene in circumstances of failure and can remove directors under its legislative powers.[7] If a Trust fails to comply the Secretary of State may make an order to dissolve the organisation or transfer its property or liabilities to another trust.[8] However, these provisions do not give Monitor or the Secretary of State power to de-authorise a Foundation Trust or return it to ordinary trust status. The Health Act 2009 also provides powers of suspension. The outbreaks of *Clostridium difficile* at Maidstone and Tunbridge Wells NHS Trust highlighted the need to ensure that quick interventions could be made and that, if necessary, authority was available to suspend chairs and members of NHS boards. To this effect, the Health Act 2009 describes enhanced powers to suspend such role holders of NHS organisations.

The Health and Social Care Act 2008 gives statutory force to the quality agenda by enhancing regulation of healthcare services. Part 1 of the Act establishes the Care Quality Commission, the body responsible for the registration, review and inspection of specific health and social care services in England. It replaces the Healthcare Commission, the Commission for Social Care Inspection and the Mental Health Act Commission.

The 2008 Act creates a system of registration for service providers, and enabling regulations will operate to identify the activities which a person will not be able to undertake unless that person is registered. The Commission has power to issue penalty notices for non-compliance and can also suspend registration.[9] It also has jurisdiction over the professional regulatory bodies, whose role is to protect patients and the public in the execution of their statutory duties.[10] The Act pertains to 12 of the regulatory bodies and operates to create an encompassing body corporate known as the Office of the Health Professions Adjudicator.[11] Its functions will be discharged by fitness to practise panels, and the standard of proof to be applied in such proceedings is that applicable to civil proceedings.[12] The Act renames the Council for Regulatory Excellence as the Council for Healthcare Regulatory Excellence and amends its constitution, functions and the way members are appointed.[13]

The Secretary of State may make regulations to require designated bodies in the United Kingdom to nominate or appoint 'responsible officers' for the regulation of doctors. Their role has been extended to cover clinical governance provisions such as the monitoring of conduct and performance of doctors. Information can be shared about concerns over the conduct and performance of healthcare workers to approve appropriate actions necessary to protect patients and the public.

National Health Service organisations have been subject to a statutory duty to ensure that arrangements are in place to monitor and improve the quality of care provided.[14] Section 139 of the Health and Social Care Act 2008 amends section 23 of the National Health Service Act 2006 to impose a duty on Primary Care Trusts to ensure arrangements are in place to secure continual improvement in the quality of healthcare provided by or for them. Since April 2010 all NHS Trusts have been required to report to the National Patient Safety Agency (NPSA) every serious patient safety incident following which a patient is injured or dies whilst receiving care.[15]

National Service Frameworks

National Service Frameworks (NSFs) are policies set by the NHS to define standards of care and reduce variations in specific healthcare services. These quality initiatives were introduced in *The New NHS, Modern, Dependable*[16] and set national healthcare standards to improve the quality of service provision and promote equitable access to healthcare. NSFs identify service models for specified care groups, alongside strategies for implementation and quality indicators against which progress within a timeframe can be assessed. They set clear quality requirements based upon best available evidence. One new framework is introduced each year as part of a rolling programme developed following input from an external reference group of service users, staff, health service managers and voluntary agencies. Topics are chosen because of their relevance to the government's agenda for health improvement, healthcare inequalities and care quality indicators as well as areas of public concern on account of perceived shortfalls between acceptable and actual practice.

The NSFs receive considerable publicity and have raised legitimate expectations. As policy documents they operate at the level of guidance, and by themselves give no new legal rights to patients. Common law shows how notoriously difficult it is to challenge resource decisions and the courts remain reluctant to intervene in matters considered to be governed by policy. This reluctance was apparent in Sir Thomas Bingham's explanation in *R v Cambridge HA, ex p B* (1995) that '[d]ifficult and agonising judgments have to be made as to how a limited budget is best allocated to the maximum advantage of the maximum number of patients. That is not a judgment which the court can make'.[17] Such judicial reluctance has since been tempered due to the need for healthcare organisations to provide reasons for decisions made.

Quality assurance

Quality assurance mechanisms such as the NSFs and nationally developed guidelines for practice rely upon local action to audit and maintain clinical standards. Davies[18] suggests that doctors might neutralise the accountability mechanisms that apply to their colleagues during clinical audits by withholding adverse comments on a colleague's performance out of concern about detrimental effects upon working relationships, or because of increased personal workloads if that colleague is suspended from duties. Whilst these effects might appear unlikely where patient safety is concerned, in pressured working environments they might interfere with a clinician's professional judgement.

Doctors are involved in the process of drafting NSFs and guidelines, through professional collegiate bodies and as individually commissioned experts, a situation that might operate to deflect standard setting onto issues that are tangential to the central issues being regulated. By way of example Davies asserts that doctors' involvement might encourage standards to be set according to process, rather than standards that require substantive clinical judgement. Opportunities are also available to ensure that audit methods are flexible and discretionary, to the extent that practitioners applying these check mechanisms are unlikely to encounter significant challenges to their working practices.

Potential safeguards have been incorporated to prevent neutralisation of audit and quality maintenance. The requirement for consultation with representatives of patients and carers operates as one form of safeguard. However, this does not necessarily guarantee that the professional voice will not dominate and lay members are known to rely heavily on expert opinion,[19] and for this reason lay involvement might give little more than the appearance of independence.

All providers of healthcare must be registered with the Care Quality Commission, and where failings in standards are identified the Commission has the power to cancel registration, impose registration conditions or levy fines on the provider, to ensure service provision meets the requisite standards. From April 2010 all providers of regulated services, including Foundation trusts, are required to comply with a full set of registration requirements in order to establish mandatory levels of quality and safety.

The Care Quality Commission has recently been criticised as being 'toothless' following publication of the Dr Foster Hospital Guide, an independent watchdog. The guide reported that 12 NHS trusts were underperforming on patient safety and infection control standards, and a further 27 hospitals were reported to have unusually high mortality rates. These findings were disputed by the Care Quality Commission, which took no action.[20]

Providers

It was not until the early 1980s that quality improvements began to take shape, with an emphasis on accountability by providers of healthcare. In October 1983 Roy Griffiths published an influential and controversial report on his 'NHS management inquiry'. A key recommendation of the report was the introduction of general management strategies and a move away from the tradition of management by consensus. At the time of the review Griffiths found few systems in place to assure the quality of care in NHS organisations. Apart from a few pilot initiatives that took place in particular organisations led by clinicians with an interest in improving quality of practice,[21] there were few, if any, hospitals that operated a systematic approach to quality improvement.[22] In fact, outside these specific initiatives many clinicians and professional organisations were sceptical about or even hostile to the concept that systematic reform and quality improvement initiatives had much to offer in healthcare.[23] The 1990s were to herald several national and local quality initiatives, accompanied by resource investment. This encouraged virtually all healthcare organisations to introduce some forms of clinical audit or quality improvement systems and structures which led to a substantial transformation of culture. It then became the norm to question established clinical practices in order to bring about improvements previously considered to be impossible.[24] A significant driver of change was the need to manage risk as a formal quality improvement activity and resources were made available to develop the necessary infrastructure and support.[25]

Managing risk

Risk is a complex concept of pervasive relevance to all healthcare organisations. Clinical risk is defined by Wilson and Tingle as 'a clinical error to be at variance from intended treatment, care, therapeutic intervention or diagnostic result: there may be an untoward outcome or not'.[26] It is a multi-faceted concept and includes risks to patients, staff and organisation. Risk management is 'a particular approach to improving the quality of care, which places special emphasis on occasions on which patients are harmed or disturbed by their treatment,[27] and is 'concerned with harnessing the information and expertise of individuals within the organisation and translating that with their help into positive action which will reduce loss of life, financial loss, loss of staff availability, loss of the availability of buildings or equipment and loss of reputation'.[28] It is a framework for safe practice based upon management by identifying potential risks to develop 'before the event' mechanisms to implement preventative action. Risk management programmes require identification of potential problems through data on incidents, near misses and organisational audits, reporting and analysis of adverse patient outcomes.

The National Health Service Litigation Authority (NHSLA)[29] is a Special Health Authority and operates to indemnify healthcare organisations as part of a risk-pooling scheme managed through a central fund. It was established in 1996 under s21 of the NHS and Community Care Act 1990 and provides cover for NHS employees in respect of clinical negligence and litigation as well as non-clinical risks. Clinical negligence claims are managed through two schemes, the Existing Liabilities Scheme for incidents that occurred prior to 1 April 1995 and the Clinical Negligence Scheme for Trusts for incidents that occurred after this time. Non-clinical incidents are operated through the Risk Pooling Scheme for Trusts. Member trusts are required to meet standards of clinical risk management set by the NHSLA and contributions are assessed according to such compliance. As of 2010 NHSLA risk management standards will also apply to Primary Care Trusts (to be replaced with commissioning bodies), the independent sector and trusts incorporating mental health and learning disability and ambulance services.

The NHSLA has a risk management function against which trusts are assessed for compliance in order to calculate annual premiums payable. NHS Trusts have economic incentives to comply with risk management systems in order to be eligible for discounted contributions. The financial incentives are considerable. Clements states that a trust might acquire up to a 30 per cent reduction by demonstrating compliance with the risk management scheme.[30] By way of example, a discount of 30 per cent for a large maternity unit might be as much as £1 million. The intention of risk management schemes is to ensure that 'organisations with memories' are able to learn from their errors and reduce reoccurrence. However, the NHSLA was designed primarily for financial reasons rather than for research or risk management purposes.

Reporting and learning from errors

Reducing the occurrence of iatrogenic harm requires a multifaceted approach due to the complex issues of causation. It is believed (within this jurisdiction and others) that a blame culture directed at the sharp end of healthcare might be misplaced. Investigation frequently reveals that a myriad of adverse underlying factors and working practices might have contributed to the resultant harm. Unsafe working environments and failings in system management provide a fertile environment for mistakes to occur. An approach towards remedying systems failure involves early reporting of incidents, learning through root cause analysis and implementing learning action plans as a means of enhancing patient safety.

The NPSA was created in April 2001 as an arm's-length body of the Department of Health. The agency was created to oversee implementation of the central recommendations of *An Organisation with a Memory*,[31] particularly by learning from adverse events and near misses. It seeks to create a change in culture to encourage reporting of incidents and near misses, with an emphasis on systems as opposed to individuals.[32]

To this extent a central achievement has been the development of a risk reporting system to facilitate the collection of data from voluntary reporting of patient safety incidents and near misses in order to systematically evaluate findings to facilitate the development of safer working systems based upon investigations of root causes. The database of the NPSA fundamentally relies upon incident reports on the nature of safety problems to ascertain clues from and indications of the causes of such problems as well as potential solutions. Whilst illuminating, such reports, being subjective recollections of incidents of relevance as perceived by the reporter, typically offer comparatively little information about causation and prevention. The next step requires clinical skill as well as in-depth knowledge of hospital environments and working practices to make effective use of the data. These processes necessarily require specialist expertise and resources, particularly to act upon findings received.

In 2004 *Seven Steps to Patient Safety* was published and aimed to provide detailed guidance for NHS organisations. These steps included, the building of a safety culture by creating an open and fair culture, to lead and support the workforce by establishing a clear focus on patient safety, and to integrate risk management activities by developing robust systems and processes to manage risks and identify potential for things to go wrong. Further requirements were to promote the reporting of adverse incidents and near miss events locally and nationally, to involve and communicate with patients and the public by listening and developing open communication pathways, to learn and share safety lessons using root cause analysis to learn how and why incidents occur, and to implement solutions to prevent harm through changes to practice, processes or systems.[33]

The NPSA has played a pivotal role in collaborating with expert multi-professional and patient groups in order to best implement World Health

Organisation (WHO) patient safety alerts as part of its Global Patient Safety Challenge. By way of example, the WHO Surgical Safety Checklist alert requires all healthcare organisations to implement a surgical safety checklist for patients undergoing surgical procedures to improve safe anaesthetic practices, ensure correct area surgery and improve communication within the surgical team. This was preceded by the Clean Hands Saves Lives alert, which gave guidance on hand hygiene and patient care in order to reduce the prevalence of Health Care Acquired Infections. Part of the remit of the NPSA has been to evaluate the effects of these patient safety alerts following a period of implementation. Other notable alerts have included crash calls and the need for a uniform system, safer use of injectable medications, and safer practice with epidural injections and infusions.[34]

For acute and general hospitals the most commonly reported incidents were patient accidents (31 per cent), followed by incidents in treatment or procedures (13 per cent), medication errors (10 per cent), incidents relating to admission and discharge, infrastructure and documentation (7 per cent), clinical assessment, care and monitoring (6 per cent), and infection control (2 per cent).[35] Between 2007 and 2009 the NPSA embarked upon a series of in-depth projects aimed at enhancing patient safety in four speciality sectors: surgery and anaesthetics; neonatal care; oncology; and intra-partum care, all of relevance for secondary care. These projects have required close cooperation with the Royal Colleges, expert clinicians and other healthcare staff, advocacy groups and patients to ensure a collaborative and multidimensional appraisal.

Technical errors represent an important category of iatrogenic harm in secondary care environments. Since medical and surgical practice is becoming ever more complex, this category may be expected to assume even greater importance. Current economic constraints together with staffing and resource limitations could lead to a potential increase in these problems unless risk management initiatives are actively developed.

Root cause analysis is the deliberate, comprehensive dissection of an error designed to expose all the relevant factors while searching for fundamental underlying causes.[36] The phrase 'root cause analysis' has been criticised as misleading due to the implication that a single root cause, or at least a small number of causative factors, can be identified.[37]

Particularly in large complex organisations, the concept of a root cause is likely to be a gross oversimplification and typically a chain of events in the context of a web of contributory factors precede the index event. Vincent suggests that root cause investigations are simply a preliminary step in the investigative process and that further deliberations are required to ascertain exactly what the incident shows about the inadequacies of the host healthcare environment. Root causes analysis tends to suggest a complex retrospective pursuance of an index event but instead should encompass a further step of prospective analysis. Without this essential step opportunities to fully learn from events are likely to be lost. On one analysis the causative

precursors of the event in question are of lesser importance than the weaknesses that remain in the system, and which could lead to a repetition of the
incident.

It remains the case that systems analysis and its concentration on
organisational factors need to be balanced with individual and team
accountability. The weighting to be applied will necessarily depend upon
the incident and contextual factors, a determination that once again calls
for expert skills and unique knowledge of the hospital environment and
working practices.

In 2001 the NPSA subsequently established the National Reporting and
Learning Service (NRLS), a database collection of reported patient safety
incidents that resulted in, or could have resulted in, patient harm. Since
April 2010 all NHS trusts in England have a mandatory duty to report all
serious patient safety incidents to the Care Quality Commission as part of
the compulsory registration process. The open access system allows reporting by patients and the public as well as healthcare staff. There is also a plat-
form for reporting via Trust risk management systems.

Following collation and analysis of reported patient safety incidents the
NRLS publishes advice for healthcare services known as 'Alerts' in order to
ensure the safety of patients. A web-based facility known as the Central
Alerting System became operational in 2008 in order to distribute critical
safety guidance to health and social care providers.[38]

Although a significant amount of data has been collected, reports have
tended to concentrate on relatively minor incidents. Perhaps this finding
should not be unexpected however since evidence presented to the House of
Commons Health Committee indicates that these types of events account for
at least 70 per cent of all events, and arguably are where most attention
should be focused. Other notable tensions are that professional groups such
as senior clinicians have been reluctant to make use of the anonymous
reporting system, and again, this factor might account for the predominance
of reporting of less significant events.

According to Vincent,[39] while reporting is unquestionably important in
order to raise awareness and highlight recurrent problems, by itself it does
not represent a meaningful patient safety activity. The NRLS was vehemently
criticised in *Safety First: A Report for Patients, Clinicians and Healthcare
Managers* for not delivering high-quality information on patterns, trends and
underlying causes of harm to patients, and for not making enough of opportunities to achieve improvements across the NHS.[40] The Report recommended the creation of the National Patient Safety Forum as a means of
facilitating the escalation and delivery of the patient safety agenda. The
Forum, which meets on a six-monthly basis, is made up of senior representatives of key organisations and minutes of these meetings are published.[41]
One year later the Report was followed by *Safety First: One Year On*,[42] in
which the NPSA reported significant progress towards making patient safety
a key priority.

The NPSA also established the Patient Safety Observatory (PSO) to access, collate and analyse patient safety incident data from a range of sources to provide a comprehensive perspective. It is apparent that local risk management systems do not always uncover even serious adverse events, and access to a variety of data sources reveals the most accurate and complete picture.[43] Assimilation and triangulation of a range of data sources, such as clinical incidents, health and safety incidents, complaints, litigation claims, inquests and case notes, are likely to represent the most accurate way of obtaining a complete picture of patient safety. A series of reports have been published by the PSO, the most recent being *Safer Care for the Acutely Ill Patient: Learning from Serious Incidents*.[44]

The NPSA's 2009 Organisation Patient Safety Incident Reports reveal that, out of around 459,500 cases of negligence in England, 5,717 patients suffered serious harm or died.[45] The data was collected by the NRLS in the form of confidential reports submitted by healthcare staff.

Training of doctors

The importance of training doctors in the management of quality, safety and risk is recognised as an issue of global relevance. The World Health Organisation has published its curriculum guide for the training of doctors,[46] and is currently being piloted to provide international guidance on how medical schools ought to teach patient safety to their undergraduate students. The WHO report acknowledges however, that some clinicians and medical educators might be resistant to the concept of raising the importance of safety as part of the curriculum. It is anticipated that there might be dislike of the importation of 'management consultancy style interference' or a 'reluctance to address knowledge that originates from outside medicine such as systems thinking and quality improvement methods'. It is anticipated that the WHO will provide feedback for the curricula for other healthcare professions based upon these initiatives and guidance.

Local accountability

Clinical governance

Clinical governance is the 'system through which NHS organisations are accountable for continuously monitoring and improving the quality of their care and services and safeguarding high standards of care and services'.[47] Its processes operate to ensure patient safety and quality provision of healthcare, and the ideology aspires to enhance robust accountability in the context of continual improvement of the delivery of healthcare.

In the health service, more than 30 public inquiries have sought to investigate catastrophic failures in patient care. The final reports indicate that five common themes can be drawn from each inquiry: isolation;

disempowerment; inadequate leadership and management; poor communication; and ineffective systems and processes.[48] A well-recognised example of a systems failure that has lead to a tragic outcome for 23 patients is where patients have received chemotherapy by the incorrect route of administration. All of these incidents have involved injection of powerful cytotoxic medication, intended for venous infusion, being inadvertently injected into the spine, thereby resulting in death or serious disability. Following one such incident Professor Brian Toft, an experienced investigator of accidents and disasters in other sectors, was invited to investigate the incident. It was reported that death or serious injury had occurred following around 40 failures of care, which had all contributed to the occurrence of the incident. Toft's investigations serve to illustrate the recognised principle that human error of itself does not usually kill patients, but human error in the context of an unsafe working environment predisposes to patients being injured or killed. Comprehensive systems weaknesses operate to greatly increase the risk of harm befalling patients.[49]

Clinical governance embodies a legal duty of care that is imposed upon healthcare provider organisations. It is an umbrella term that incorporates seven key themes: clinical audit; risk management; clinical effectiveness; education and training; public involvement; strategic capacity and capability; staff management and performance. The concept of clinical governance relates only to health and social care organisations concerned with healthcare delivery to service users. Integrated governance is the overarching framework that incorporates the contemporary NHS governance approaches,[50] and is concerned with the other business components of healthcare organisations that run in parallel with governance arrangements of companies known as corporate governance. Since 1999 NHS Trust Boards have a statutory responsibility to ensure delivery of a reasonable level of quality.

Managing complaints

Effective handling of complaints is a key element of successfully managing quality, risk and safety in healthcare organisations. Inadequate complaints management can compound the damage to doctor and patient relationships as well as the public perception of the NHS as a whole. Complaints can also be one of the first indicators of adverse patient safety incidents.[51] Following Healthcare Commission statistics in 2007,[52] which showed that over a quarter of complaints were re-referred to the Trust because of inadequate investigation and response, the NHS complaints procedure underwent a significant overhaul in 2009. Patients now have 12 months in which to lodge a complaint. The process is in two stages. The first is local resolution, which requires a written complaint to the organisational management team or medical professional. Most cases are resolved at this stage, but otherwise they can be referred to the Health Service Ombudsman, who is independent of the NHS and government. Reference to the Ombudsman is the second stage of the process.

The key changes made are removal of the 20-day response rate to facilitate in-depth investigation at the primary stage, and removal of the need for independent review by the Healthcare Commission. The focus of the new procedure is to enable healthcare providers to be more flexible in resolving patients' specific complaints. A more efficient complaints system should enhance the early clarification of what went wrong and why.

Practice

Without doubt, professional practitioners aspire to raise standards of practice. An early pioneer was Florence Nightingale, who by comparing hospital statistics on death rates was able to reveal that Crimean hospitals were 'death traps' due to unhygienic conditions.[53] Likewise, Dr Codman of Boston contributed to quality assessment through the scrutiny of his own medical practice.[54] Using a system of self-audit, Codman followed up his patients for one year, and sought to determine whether his diagnosis had been correct, whether surgery had been successful as well as the impact of surgery on each patient. Practitioners such as Nightingale and Codman, among others, laid the ground for contemporary evidence-based medicine and best practice clinical guidelines.

Clinical guidelines and law

Developing evidence-based guidelines

The National Institute for Health and Clinical Excellence (NICE) has gained a reputation for using a thorough, fair, transparent and inclusive appraisal process.[55] It is an independent organisation responsible for publishing guidance on treatment and healthcare for the benefit of professionals, patients and carers in order to inform healthcare decision-making. NICE has been variously complimented as a model for open and fair decision-making for the introduction of new technologies and pharmaceuticals to the healthcare system and publicly criticised for publishing guidance that operates to ration or restrict access to seemingly spectacular innovations in healthcare which might benefit specific groups of patients. NICE has within its remit responsibility for producing evidence-based guidelines for best practice.

Although clinical guidelines have been in existence for a considerable time, and used in practice, they attracted little attention until only recently as to whether or not they could be used in medical litigation as a measure of the standard of care. The traditional test in law is the *Bolam*[56] test, which is a measure of the standard of care against what is done (rather than what ought to be done) in medical practice. Since the inception of NICE and the development of clinical guidelines through its processes, we have suggested that these might take on a more indicative role against which the standard of care is measured in cases of alleged clinical negligence.[57] Our beliefs are based on the fact that guidelines from NICE are produced with procedural rigour and are embedded in an evidence base, they have recognition from healthcare quality regulators, and there has been a subtle doctrinal movement away from orthodox '*Bolamism*'[58] towards a more objective justification of the standard upheld on behalf of the defendant doctor.[59]

The role of guidelines in medical litigation

We undertook a questionnaire of practising solicitors and barristers in the UK to determine the extent to which clinical guidelines are perceived by lawyers as being used in medical litigation, and their potential future use.[60] Briefly, 372 subjects (practising in clinical negligence in England and Wales) were surveyed and, of the respondents, 80 per cent were familiar with clinical guidelines (particularly those from NICE and the medical Royal Colleges). Eighty-nine per cent of respondents reported that their team had used guidelines in their caseload within the preceding three years; 40 per cent believed that guidelines had influenced the decision made by the court. The majority of respondents felt there would be an increased use of guidelines by the court in the future. The principal drivers for this view were considered to be the remit of NICE, the clinical governance agenda to improve quality and heightened public awareness generally of the medical evidence base.

Our results show that a high proportion of practising lawyers within this jurisdiction have used and observed the use of guidelines in medical litigation. Our observations support the view that guidelines may act as a standard that governs legal liability. The need for the proclaimed standard by the defendant to withstand 'logical analysis' represents a doctrinal shift towards the greater potential use of extrinsic evidence as to what constitutes '*Bolitho*-justifiable' reasonable care.[61] Such a move would carry force against the well-worn criticism of the *Bolam* standard as being one that has an inherent weakness of cognitive bias in expert testimony.

A potential danger of the blanket use of guidelines in setting the standard of care is that it could encourage clinicians to practise defensively. Defensive medicine was described by Lord Scarman in *Sidaway v Bethlem Royal Hospital Governors*[62] as 'the practice of doctors advising and undertaking the treatment which they think is legally safe even though they may believe that it is not the best for their patient'.[63] However, Black states that 'litigation does not seem to be damaging the quality of care'.[64] According to Fanning, if doctors are 'defensive' to the extent that their practices comply with the *Bolam* standard, recipient patients must enjoy a more consistent quality of care.[65] Nevertheless, it is worrying that a doctor's concern for his own potential liability might influence clinical decision-making to a greater extent than the patient's welfare, and represents a tension that could be problematic.[66]

A conceptual framework for liability in law

The locus classicus of the *Bolam* standard is that a doctor does not breach the standard of care in law if her actions are in conformity with customary practice endorsed by a responsible body of medical opinion. We suggest that guidelines may be used to provide an added dimension to the evaluation of the legal standard of care.

The first stage of the model would involve the court ascertaining whether the defendant's conduct is *Bolam*-defensible. If it is, then the second stage would be to determine whether it withstands logical analysis and is *Bolitho*-justifiable. The third stage would be for the court to decide whether the proffered guidelines are admissible as evidence and, if so, whether they are valid.[67] The final stage would be the application of the guidelines to the specific facts of the case in question and it is envisaged that there would be narrow issues to address.

The proposed conceptual model is a halfway house between the traditional *Bolam* approach and one whereby guidelines are determinant of the standard of care. We believe that such an approach would provide quality assurance in terms of clinical reasoning, as well as presenting a framework for judicial decision-making.

Managing poor clinical performance

Early recognition and local resolution

The Chief Medical Officer's review of the regulation of the medical profession in *Good Doctors, Safer Patients*[68] proposes to enhance patient safety while continuing to provide high-quality clinical care by putting into place mechanisms designed to identify poor performance at an early stage and implement remedial action. At a local level this involves two main developments: GMC affiliates and recorded concerns.[69]

GMC affiliates are expected to bridge the current regulatory gap between the employer and the regulator, and performance issues will only be referred to the GMC once a certain threshold has been transcended. Affiliates, who are expected to be medical directors, will deal with poor performance by ensuring that investigations and disciplinary proceedings at local level are carried out to an expected standard. They will also assist with the development of bespoke rehabilitation, remediation and re-skilling packages. Medical directors and others in similar roles will have enhanced regulatory responsibilities, with concerns being addressed through a line management structure. A potential risk is managerial overreaction, particularly where doctors may be working in suboptimal environments. The perceived advantage of the system includes prompt local responses to patient concerns and the use of local expertise in addressing local complaints. However, lingering doubts remain about the extent to which affiliates might be influenced by loyalties to employers and commissioners, although accountability remains to the GMC.[70]

The new measure of recorded concerns is expected to allow conduct, performance or patterns of behaviour to be tracked over time and place. It will also allow further investigation if required and the GMC will review recorded concerns in order to determine whether more formal investigation is warranted. It is likely that these may also feed into the proposed revalidation process. It remains unclear what might constitute a recorded concern and the threshold should be drawn on a principled basis. Likewise, it is not certain when these concerns might escalate so that further investigation is merited. It therefore remains open whether any sanction imposed on the basis of these concerns might be in breach of a doctor's right to a fair trial and Article 6 of the European Convention on Human Rights.[71]

The role of NCAS

The consultation paper *Supporting Doctors, Protecting Patients*[72] dealt with preventing, recognising and dealing with poor clinical performance by doctors in the NHS in England and introduced the concept of clinical assessment and the advisory body known as NCAS (the National Clinical Assessment Service). NCAS provides guidance for health organisations and individual practitioners where there is cause for concern about performance. Employers have a duty to consult with NCAS at key stages of investigatory and disciplinary proceedings, and its role is to provide expert advice and support. The final decision, however, rests with the employing body concerned.

The Restriction of Practice and Exclusion from Work Directions 2003 require NHS employers to comply with the standards in *Maintaining High Professional Standards in the Modern NHS*.[73] This document introduced a new framework for the initial screening of concerns about the conduct of medical and dental employees and introduced guidance for disciplinary processes and exclusion from work. In addition to this guidance NHS employers are also subject to employment law, as well as guidance from the Advisory, Conciliation and Arbitration Service.

The key features of the framework include guidance on the investigation of concerns, separation of the investigatory from the decision-making process, and the role of remediation, with less emphasis on exclusion from the workplace wherever possible. Employers of poorly performing doctors, dentists and pharmacists are required to refer them to NCAS, a body which is part of the NPSA, particularly if the case in question involves exclusion from the workplace or a requirement for an assessment of capability, or if a capability hearing is being considered.

A report of NCAS casework[74] indicates that the number of referrals made to the organisation has increased and the organisation now receives referrals from all parts of the UK in numbers broadly in proportion to workforce size. Trends have been noticed in respect of fewer referrals for women practitioners and above average rates of referral amongst psychiatrists. There is a possible association with ethnicity and place of qualification, although these findings require careful interpretation and further research. More than half of excluded practitioners (hospital and community) eventually return to work in the same organisation, compared with only one-third of suspended contractor general practitioners. Around two-thirds of practitioners undergoing NCAS assessment were still in employment following assessment and in many cases a remediation programme had been implemented. NCAS has made a demonstrable improvement in avoiding unnecessary or unduly lengthy suspension or exclusion, as well as in implementing remediation.

Whistle blowing

'Whistle blowing', defined as the 'spontaneous reporting outside normal channels by individual members of staff',[75] is typically used by employees as a last resort to raise concerns and draw attention to unsafe practices. Several high-profile reports following public inquiries have emphasised the central role played by whistle blowing as an effective way of enhancing quality and safety as part of a risk management strategy.[76]

Potential whistleblowers may fear retaliation from their employing body as well as difficult ethical dilemmas in seeking to balance personal loyalty and the wider public interest in safe practice. Professional practice is typically underpinned by collegiate loyalty that can operate as a barrier against raising legitimate concerns. Collective reticence against whistle blowing is apparent throughout the NHS. In the aftermath of the tragic events uncovered at the Mid-Staffordshire Trust, the Secretary of State for Health referred to 'the absence of any whistleblower' despite legislative protection for whistleblowers.[77] While he did not accept that frontline healthcare staff would not be prepared on such a serious matter as patient safety he felt that perceived victimisation might operate as an inhibiting factor.

Despite potential staff reticence caused by concerns about reprisals from their governing bodies,[78] professional guidance from the professional regulatory bodies emphasises the need to make concerns known. The GMC imposes an ethical duty of disclosure on doctors to report a colleague suspected of being unfit to practice,[79] and *Raising Concerns* emphasises that, provided a doctor has given an honest account, voicing a concern will be justified even if it is later discovered to be unjustified.[80] The Nursing and Midwifery Council imposes a similar ethical duty on nurses.[81]

Although protection exists under the Public Interest Disclosure Act 1998 (PIDA) as well as NHS executive guidance,[82] evidence suggests that NHS staff remain concerned about the potential for negative repercussions. The use of confidentiality or 'gagging' clauses in NHS employment contracts was prohibited even prior to implementation of the PIDA, as proclaimed by the health secretary, who in 1997 wrote to chief executives of NHS Trusts and health authorities to make clear that such clauses contravene NHS Executive policy, and discriminate against staff's rights and responsibilities to bring unacceptable practices to light.[83] The Department of Health Circular requires every NHS Trust and health authority to have in place policies and procedures that comply with the PIDA, including staff guidance for raising concerns with the appropriate persons, the designation of senior personnel responsible for addressing concerns outside the formal managerial structure and an unambiguous assurance that those who raise concerns will be protected against discrimination.

Evidence suggests that confidentiality clauses are still used in the NHS despite provisions in the PIDA that prohibit contracts aimed at preventing legitimate disclosure of concern. The *Financial Times* reported that Peter Bousfield was granted early retirement and a financial package following the hospital's rejection of his disclosure of patient safety issues that had arisen at the Liverpool Women's NHS Trust.[84]

The independent charity Public Concern at Work (PCAW) has played a leading role in putting whistle blowing on the governance agenda and in developing legislation in the UK and abroad. The organisation has raised concerns about the role of the responsible officer under the Health and Social Care Act 2008. The responsible officer's duties include matters relating to revalidation of doctors as well as conduct and performance issues on behalf of the organisation. If these duties include reporting concerns to the regulatory bodies PCAW feels this might negatively affect the likelihood of staff raising perceived issues of public safety.

Revalidation

The introduction of revalidation represents the biggest change to medical regulation in 150 years, and implementation of this change is based on the legislative framework within which the GMC operates. The Medical Act 1983 provides the legal basis for revalidation. A section 60 Order (the Medical Profession (Miscellaneous Amendments) Order 2008) updates the legislative provisions relating to the licence to practise and revalidation. In autumn 2009, licensing was introduced for any doctor wanting to practise medicine in the UK. There is now a legal requirement for doctors to be registered and hold a licence to practise. Under the Health and Social Care Act 2008 'responsible officers' (usually medical directors) within local healthcare organisations will have specific powers for the delivery of revalidation processes at local levels, making recommendations to the GMC about individual doctors' revalidation.

The first revalidation is scheduled for 2011. Once introduced, licences will be subject to periodic renewal every five years. Revalidation covers both relicensing and recertification. If requirements for recertification of entry in the specialist register are met, then this will be sufficient for relicensing. Revalidation will be based on elements of annual appraisal and audit. Specialty specific standards will be linked to the generic standards of practice that the GMC has set for all doctors who will have to demonstrate that they continue to practise in accordance with the standards prescribed by the relevant Royal College or Faculty. Revalidation will be based upon a process of annual appraisal in the workplace organised by the employer. Outputs from a doctor's appraisal will be considered by a responsible officer, who will recommend to the GMC whether or not a doctor should be revalidated.

Conclusion

During the last decade the government has introduced a myriad of reforms to the NHS in terms of legislative changes as well as several patient-specific quality initiatives. In the main, these have focused on standards for health-care, improving safety and reducing risk to patients in the context of enhanced accountability.

Standards for healthcare delivery set the benchmark for what consumers might expect as an entitlement from the NHS. Standards are supervised by a range of organisations that have oversight responsibility. There has been an emphasis on promoting a culture of openness to encourage and facilitate opportunities to learn from adverse incidents and near misses, thereby reducing the likelihood of future occurrences of medical error. Candour as an organisational mind-set represents a unique change from the traditional position of lack of openness and defensiveness within healthcare which has been perpetuated by a blame culture. Initiatives to enhance accountability include wide-ranging changes to medical regulation strengthened by revalidation.

Proposals to maximise quality, safety and risk reduction must operate at three levels – policy, providers and practice. In order to make a real impact on patient care is the need for a seamless permeation of this ideology throughout these planes with integrated joined-up thinking to ensure practical benefit for patients.

Notes

1 L.T. Kohn, J.M. Corrigan and M. Donaldson (eds), *To Err Is Human: Building a Safer Health System*, Healthcare Services, Washington: National Academies Press, 1999.
2 Department of Health, *An Organisation with a Memory*, London: HMSO, 2000.
3 D.M. Berwick, 'The John Eisenberg Lecture: Health Services Research as a Citizen in Improvement', *Health Service Research* 40:2, 2005, pp. 317–336.
4 Department of Health, *A First Class Service*, London: Department of Health, 1988.
5 Department of Health, *Our NHS, Our Future: NHS Next Stage Review Interim Report*, London: Department of Health, October 2007. Online. Available at http://www.dh.gov.uk/prod_consum_dh/groups/dh_digitalassets/@dh/@en/documents/digitalasset/dh_079087.pdf (accessed 18 June 2010).
6 Health Act 2009, s2.
7 s52, the NHS Act 2006.
8 s54, the NHS Act 2006.
9 Care Quality Commission, 'Who Needs to Register'. Available at http://www.cqc.org.uk/guidanceforprofessionals/introductiontoregistration/whoneedstoregister.cfm (accessed 18 June 2010).

10 The Bristol Royal Infirmary Inquiry, *Learning from Bristol: The Report of the Public Inquiry into Children's Heart Surgery at the Bristol Royal Infirmary 1984–1995*, Command Paper: CM 5207, Bristol: Bristol Royal Infirmary Inquiry, 2001. Online. Available HTTP http://www.bristol-inquiry.org.uk/ (accessed 18 June 2010).
11 Health and Social Care Act 2008, s98(1).
12 Health and Social Care Act 2008, s112.
13 Health and Social Care Act 2008, s113(1).
14 s45, Health and Social Care (Community Health and Standards) Act 2003.
15 D. Campbell, 'Crackdown Will Force Hospitals to Log All Errors: Record Must Be Made Every Time a Patient Is Harmed or Dies While Receiving Treatment', *Observer*, 6 December 2009, p. 7.
16 Department of Health, *The New NHS: Modern, Dependable*, London: Department of Health, 1997. Online. Available at http://www.dh.gov.uk/en/Publications andstatistics/Publications/PublicationsPolicyAndGuidance/DH_4008869 (accessed 18 June 2010).
17 *R v Cambridge HA, ex p B* [1995] 23 BMLR 1 at 9.
18 A.C.L. Davies, 'Don't Trust Me, I'm a Doctor – Medical Regulation and the 1999 NHS Reforms', *Oxford Journal of Legal Studies* 20, 2000, p. 437.
19 J. Peay, *Tribunals on Trial: A Study of Decision-Making under the Mental Health Act 1983*, Oxford: Clarendon Press, 1989.
20 D. Rose, 'Worst Hospitals "Free to Go on Failing": NHS Regulator Is Accused of Being Toothless', *Times*, 30 November 2009, p. 3. Also reported in *Financial Times*, 30 November 2009, p. 4; *Independent*, 30 November 2009, p. 6; *Guardian*, 30 November 2009, p. 12; *Daily Telegraph*, 30 November 2009, pp. 1, 6; *Sunday Times*, 29 November 2009, p. 12; *Observer*, 29 November 2009, pp. 1, 8–10; *Sunday Telegraph*, 29 November 2009, pp. 1–2, 21; *Times*, 28 November 2009, p. 19.
21 C.D. Shaw, 'Quality assurance in the United Kingdom', *International Journal of Quality in Health Care* 5, 1993, pp. 107–118.
22 National Audit Office, *Quality of Clinical Care in National Health Service Hospitals*, London: HMSO, 1988.
23 Advisory Conciliation and Arbitration Service, *Royal Commission on the National Health Services*, London: HMSO, 1979.
24 D. Taylor, 'Quality and Professionalism in Healthcare – A Review of Current Initiatives in the NHS', *British Medical Journal* 312, 1996, pp.626–629.
25 BRI Inquiry Secretariat, *Paper on Medical and Clinical Audit in the NHS*, Bristol: Bristol Royal Infirmary Inquiry, 1999.
26 J. Wilson and J. Tingle (eds), *Clinical Risk Modification: A Route to Clinical Governance*, Oxford: Butterworth Heinemann, 1999.
27 C. Vincent, 'Introduction', in C. Vincent, ed., *Clinical Risk Management*, London: BMJ Publishing Group, 1995.
28 Department of Health, *Corporate Governance in the NHS, Code of Conduct. Code of Accountability*, London: HMSO, 1994.
29 The NHS Litigation Authority website. Online. Available at http://www.nhsla.com/home.htm (accessed 18 June 2010).
30 R. Clements, 'Healthcare Risk Management: The UK Experience – The Present and the Future', *Medico- legal Journal of Ireland*, 2003.
31 Department of Health, *An Organisation with a Memory*, London: HMSO, 2000.
32 http://www.npsa.nhs.uk/web/display?contentId=2656 (broken link, accessed 18 June 2010).
33 Adapted from National Patient Safety Agency, *Seven Steps to Patient Safety: A Guide for NHS Staff*, National Patient Safety Agency, 2004. Online. Available at http://www.nrls.npsa.nhs.uk/resources/collections/seven-steps-to-patient-safety/ (accessed 18 June 2010).

34 National Patient Safety Agency, *Alerts*, London: National Patient Safety Agency, 2009. Online. Available at http://www.nrls.npsa.nhs.uk/resources/type/alerts/ (accessed 18 June 2010).

35 National Patient Safety Agency, *National Reporting and Learning System Quarterly Data Summary,* issue 14, National Patient Safety Agency, 27 November 2009, p. 14.

36 R. Wachter, *Understanding Patient Safety*, New York: McGraw Hill, 2008, p. 160.

37 C. Vincent, 'Analysis of Clinical Incidents: A Window on the System Not a Search for Root Causes', *Quality and Safety in Health Care* 13, 2004, pp. 242–243.

38 National Health Service, Central Alerting System, London: Department of Health. Online. Available at https://www.cas.dh.gov.uk/Home.aspx (accessed 18 June 2010).

39 C. Vincent, 'Incident Reporting and Patient Safety', *British Medical Journal* 51, 2007, p. 334.

40 Department of Health, *Safety First: A Report for Patients, Clinicians and Healthcare Managers*, London: Department of Health, 2006. Online. Available at http://www.dh.gov.uk/prod_consum_dh/groups/dh_digitalassets/@dh/@en/documents/digitalasset/dh_064159.pdf (accessed 18 June 2010).

41 Department of Health, National Patient Safety Forum, London: Department of Health, 2010. Online. Available at http://www.dh.gov.uk/en/Publichealth/Patientsafety/DH_073927 (accessed 18 June 2010).

42 Department of Health. *Safety First: One Year On*, London: Department of Health, 13 December 2007. Online. Available at http://www.npsa.nhs.uk/corporate/news/safety-first-one-year-on/ (accessed 18 June 2010).

43 R.A. Hayward and T.P. Hofer, 'Estimating Hospital Deaths Due to Medical Errors: Preventability is in the Eye of the Reviewer', *Journal of the American Medical Association* 286, 2001, pp. 418–420.

44 National Patient Safety Agency, The Fifth Report from the Patient Safety Observatory. *Safer Care for the Acutely Ill Patient: Learning from Serious Incident*, London: National Patient Safety Agency, 2007.

45 National Patient Safety Agency, *Organisation Patient Safety Incident Reports*, London: National Patient Safety Agency, March 2010. Online. Available at http://www.nrls.npsa.nhs.uk/patient-safety-data/organisation-patient-safety-incident-reports/ (accessed 18 June 2010).

46 F2 Curriculum Committee of the Academy of Medical Royal Colleges, *Curriculum for the Foundation Years in Postgraduate Education and Training*, London: Academy of Royal Medical Colleges, 2004. Online. Available at http://www.who.int/patientsafety/news/curriculum.pdf (accessed 18 June 2010).

47 G. Scally and L.J. Donaldson, 'Clinical Governance and the Drive for Quality Improvement in the New NHS in England', *British Medical Journal* 317, 1998, pp. 61–65.

48 K. Walshe and J. Higgins, 'The Use and Impact of Inquiries in the NHS', *British Medical Journal* 325, 2002, pp. 895–900.

49 D.M. Berwick, 'Not Again! Preventing Errors Lies in Redesign – Not Exhortation', *British Medical Journal* 22, 2001, pp. 247–248.

50 Department of Health, *Integrated Governance Handbook,* London: HMSO, 2006. Online. Available at http://www.dh.gov.uk/en/Publicationsandstatistics/Publications/PublicationsPolicyAndGuidance/DH_4128739 (accessed 18 June 2010).

51 M. Walton, 'Patient Safety – A View from Down Under', *Quality and Safety in Health Care* 18, 2009, pp. 422–423.

52 Healthcare Commission, *Spotlight on Complaints. A Report on Second-stage Complaints about the NHS in England*, London: Healthcare Commission, 2007. Online. Available at http://www.chi.gov.uk/_db/_documents/spotlight_on_complaints.pdf (accessed 18 June 2010).

53 R.J. Maxwell, 'Quality Assessment in Health', *British Medical Journal* 288, 1984, pp. 1470–1472.
54 D. Neuhauser, 'Heroes and Martyrs of Quality and Safety: Ernest Amory Codman MD', *Quality and Safety in Health Care* 11, 2002, pp. 104–105.
55 Health Committee, *National Institute for Health and Clinical Excellence*, HC503-II (2006–07), ev. 7 (NICE) at para. 8.
56 *Bolam v Friern Hospital Management Committee* [1957] 1 WLR 582.
57 A. Samanta, J. Samanta and M. Gunn, 'Legal Considerations of Clinical Guidelines: Will NICE Make a Difference?', *Journal of the Royal Society of Medicine* 96, 2003, pp. 133–138.
58 M. Brazier and J. Miola, 'Bye-bye Bolam: A Medical Litigation Revolution', *Medical Law Review* 1, 2000, pp. 85–144.
59 A. Samanta and J. Samanta, 'Legal Standard of Care: A Shift from the Traditional *Bolam* Test', *Clinical Medicine* 3, 2003, pp. 443–446.
60 A. Samanta, M.M. Mello, C. Foster, J. Tingle and J. Samanta, 'The Role of Clinical Guidelines in Medical Negligence Litigation: A Shift from the *Bolam* Standard?', *Medical Law Review* 14, 2006, pp. 321–366.
61 *Bolitho v City and Hackney Health Authority* [1997] 4 All E R 771.
62 [1985] AC 871.
63 At 887.
64 N. Black, 'Medical Litigation and the Quality of Care', *The Lancet* 335, 1991, p. 37.
65 J.B. Fanning, 'Uneasy Lies the Neck that Wears a Stethoscope: Some Observations on Defensive Medicine', *Professional Negligence*, 2008.
66 A. Samanta, M.M. Mello, C. Foster, J. Tingle and J. Samanta, 'The Role of Clinical Guidelines in Medical Negligence Litigation: A Shift from the *Bolam* Standard?', *Medical Law Review* 14, 2006, pp. 321–366.
67 *Daubert v Merrill Dow Pharmaceuticals Inc* 509 US 579 [1993].
68 L. Donaldson, *Good Doctors, Safer Patients – A Report by the Chief Medical Officer for England*, London: Department of Health, 2006.
69 A. Samanta and J. Samanta, 'Safer Patients and Good Doctors: Medical Regulation in the 21st Century', *Clinical Risk* 13, 2007, pp. 138–142.
70 Ibid., pp. 138–139.
71 Ibid., p. 139.
72 Department of Health, *Supporting Doctors, Protecting Patients: A Consultation Paper*, London: Department of Health, 1999. Online. Available HTTP http://www.dh.gov.uk/en/Publicationsandstatistics/Publications/PublicationsPolicyAndGuidance/DH_4005688 (accessed 18 June 2010).
73 Department of Health, *Maintaining High Professional Standards in the Modern NHS: A Framework for the Initial Handling of Concerns about Doctors and Dentists in the NHS*, London: Department of Health, 2003. Online. Available HTTP http://www.dh.gov.uk/en/Publicationsandstatistics/Publications/PublicationsPolicyAndGuidance/DH_4072773 (accessed 18 June 2010).
74 NCAS Casework, *The First Eight Years*, London: NCAS, September 2009.
75 Department of Health, *An Organisation with a Memory,* London: HMSO, 2000, Section 4.9.
76 The Shipman Inquiry, *5th Report 2001*, the Shipman Inquiry. Online. Available at http://www.the-shipman-inquiry.org.uk/5r_page.asp (accessed 18 June 2010).; Department of Health, *An Inquiry into Quality and Practice within the National Health Service Arising from the Actions of Rodney Ledward 'The Ritchie Inquiry'*, London: Department of Health, 2000; The Bristol Royal Infirmary Inquiry, *Learning from Bristol: The Report of the Public Inquiry into Children's Heart Surgery at the Bristol Royal Infirmary 1984–1995*, Bristol: Bristol Royal Infirmary Inquiry, 2001. Online. Available at www.bristol-inquiry.org.uk (accessed 18 June 2010); Department of Health, *The Royal Liverpool Children's Inquiry Report*,

London: HMSO, 2001. Online. Available at http://www.rlcinquiry.org.uk/download/index.htm (accessed 18 June 2010).

77 Hansard, House of Commons, Patient Safety – Health Committee, 3 July 2009, para. 282. Online. Available at http://www.parliament.the-stationery-office.co.uk/pa/cm200809/cmselect/cmhealth/151/15113.htm (accessed 18 June 2010).

78 J. Burrows, 'Telling Tales and Saving Lives: Whistleblowing – The Role of Professional Colleagues in Protecting Patients from Dangerous Doctors', *Medical Law Review* 9:2, 2001, pp. 110–129.

79 General Medical Council, *Good Medical Practice*, London, General Medical Council, 2006, paras 43, 44, 45.

80 General Medical Council, *Raising Concerns about Patient Safety*, London, General Medical Council, 2006. Online. Available at http://www.gmc-uk.org/guidance/ethical_guidance/raising_concerns.asp (accessed 18 June 2010).

81 Nursing and Midwifery Council, *The Code, Standards of Conduct, Performance and Ethics for Nurses and Midwives*, Nursing and Midwifery Council, 2008. Online. Available at http://www.nmc-uk.org/Documents/Standards/nmc TheCodeStandardsofConductPerformanceAndEthicsForNursesAndMidwives_ LargePrintVersion.PDF (accessed 18 June 2010).

82 Department of Health, *Health Service Circular 1999/198 The Public Interest Disclosure Act 1998, Whistleblowing in the NHS*, London: Department for Health, 1999. Online. Available at http://www.dh.gov.uk/prod_consum_dh/groups/dh_digitalassets/@dh/@en/documents/digitalasset/dh_4012138.pdf (accessed 18 June 2010).

83 Secretary of State for Health, *MISC (97)65: Freedom of Speech in the NHS*, London: Department of Health, 1997. Online. Available at http://www.dh.gov.uk/en/Publicationsandstatistics/Lettersandcirculars/Miscellaneousletters/DH_4018033 (accessed 18 June 2010).

84 N. Timmins, 'NHS Accused over Illegal Gagging of Doctors' Concerns', *Financial* Times, 28 October 2009, p. 4. Also reported in *Independent*, 28 October 2009, p. 18.

2 Pre-trial clinical negligence issues

Charles Foster

Introduction

Law-makers and policy-makers are keen on the idea of patient safety. Discussion documents, protocols and even statutes are full of references to it. Some of the rhetoric is no doubt genuinely well meaning, and indicates a real ambition to learn the lessons taught by medical accidents. Some is no doubt uttered with a cynical view to politically expedient headlines. But there is a depressingly large gulf between the rhetoric and the reality. In the context of the pre-trial process, this chapter explores the rhetoric and the reality, and measures the gap between them. It asks whether the way that litigation is run concentrates the minds of defendants sufficiently or at all on the patient safety issues raised by a claim, encouraging them to avoid similar mistakes in future.

In July 1996 Lord Woolf published his famous report *Access to Justice*.[1] It focused particularly intensely on medical negligence claims because, he said, 'early in the Inquiry it became increasingly obvious that it was in the area of medical negligence that the civil justice system was failing most conspicuously to meet the needs of litigants in a number of respects'.[2] One of the reasons he gave for this was that '[t]he suspicion between the parties is more intense and the lack of co-operation frequently greater than in many other areas of litigation'.[3] That mutual suspicion was hardly likely to foster a patient safety culture. Patient safety was plainly important to Lord Woolf. Bemoaning the immense cost of clinical negligence litigation, and the fact that most of the costs came out of the public purse, he noted that the money spent on legal costs 'would be much better devoted to compensating victims or, better still, to improving standards of care so that future mistakes are avoided'.[4] He recognised that patient safety issues were often high on litigants' own agendas:

> Some patients want financial compensation, but they may also want to prevent a repetition of the mistreatment or misdiagnosis which occurred, or to get an apology or explanation for what went wrong. Sometimes, especially in cases where the physical injury was less serious, these non-monetary factors are the most important.[5]

The Civil Procedure Rules and the pre-action protocol

Access to Justice spawned the Civil Procedure Rules 1998 and also the Clinical Disputes Forum, a coalition of stakeholders established in 1997 to address Lord Woolf's concerns specifically in relation to clinical negligence litigation. The Forum's first major initiative was the Pre-Action Protocol for the Resolution of Clinical Disputes ('the Protocol'). It was published in January 1999 and came into force on 26 April 1999. It does not purport to be, and is not, a straitjacket within which litigation must be conducted. It is, instead, a code of good practice, and accordingly spells out in considerable detail the general principles which should govern the behaviour of the parties. The complaint before the District Judge is more likely to be: 'The defendant has not complied with the spirit of the protocol' than 'the defendant is in breach of clause X'. Although it is liberal in tone, it can be applied sternly, with the potential for draconian costs orders to be imposed on a party who does not pay it sufficient respect.[6]

It reiterates Lord Woolf's acknowledgement that litigating patients might want, *inter alia*, 'assurances about future action,'[7] and agreed with him that 'a climate of mistrust and lack of openness can seriously damage the patient/clinician relationship ... and reduce the resources available for treating patients. It may also cause additional work for, and lower the morale of, healthcare professionals'.[8]

Both the general and the specific aims of the Protocol should be music to the ears of the patient safety lobby. One of the two general aims is 'to maintain/restore the patient/healthcare provider relationship,'[9] and the specific aims are stated as:

- to encourage early communication of the perceived problem between patients and healthcare providers;
- to encourage patients to voice any concerns or dissatisfaction with their treatment as soon as practicable;
- to encourage healthcare providers to develop systems of early reporting and investigation for serious adverse treatment outcomes and to provide full and prompt explanations to dissatisfied patients;
- to ensure that sufficient information is disclosed by both parties to enable each to understand the other's perspective and case, and to encourage early resolution.[10]

It is explicit about the need for clinical governance, but rightly sees clinical governance structures as outside its remit: 'This protocol does not attempt to be prescriptive about a number of related clinical governance issues which will have a bearing on healthcare providers' ability to meet the standards within the protocol.'[11] It notes, though, that good clinical governance has three pillars: clinical risk management, adverse outcome reporting and a professional duty to report adverse outcomes or untoward incidents. 'Effective co-ordinated, focused clinical risk management strategies and procedures', it points out, unnecessarily, 'can help in managing risk and in the early identification and investigation of adverse outcomes';[12] and as for adverse outcome reporting, 'healthcare providers should have in place procedures for such investigations, including recording of statements of key witnesses. These procedures should also cover when and how to inform patients that an adverse outcome has occurred'.[13] It closes its section on clinical governance by noting that the General Medical Council (GMC) is preparing guidance to doctors about their duty to report adverse incidents and to co-operate with inquiries.[14] That guidance is now available. The March 2009 edition of *Good Medical Practice* summarises the position:

> If you have good reason to think that patient safety is or may be seriously compromised by inadequate premises, equipment, or other resources, policies or systems, you should put the matter right if that is possible. In all other cases you should draw the matter to the attention of your employing or contracting body. If they do not take adequate action, you should take independent advice on how to take the matter further. You must record your concerns and the steps you have taken to try to resolve them.[15]

Detailed guidance is given in the November 2006 document *Raising Concerns about Patient Safety: Guidance for Doctors*.[16]

The Protocol does not stop with these general observations about clinical governance. Rather repetitively, it continues, *inter alia*:

Healthcare providers should:

- ... develop an approach to clinical governance that ensures that clinical practice is delivered to commonly accepted standards and that this is routinely monitored through a system of clinical audit and clinical risk management (particularly adverse outcome investigation);
- set up adverse outcome reporting systems in all specialties to record and investigate unexpected serious adverse outcomes as soon as possible. Such systems can enable evidence to be gathered quickly, which makes it easier to provide an accurate explanation of what happened and to defend or settle any subsequent claims;
- use the results of adverse incidents and complaints positively as a guide to how to improve services to patients in the future.[17]

From a patient safety perspective the hearts of Lord Woolf and the Clinical Disputes Forum were plainly in the right place. But it is rather strange to read most of the material about clinical governance in the context of a pre-action protocol which is designed to ensure the smooth running of litigation. One can understand an expression of interest in clinical governance insofar as it relates to (for instance) the availability for litigation of all the relevant clinical records. But why should the wider repercussions, involving future patients, be relevant considerations? The answer presumably lies in Lord Woolf's observation that sometimes litigation is motivated by the desire to ensure that other patients will not suffer similar misfortunes. To discourage court-clogging litigation, therefore, defendants should have in place mechanisms which would reassure claimants that their own tragedies have not been ignored. Whatever the reason for the inclusion in the protocol of these clauses, it is inconceivable that any judicial disapproval of a Trust's clinical governance procedures would be met by any sanction greater than a stern mutter along the lines of: 'Should do better.' But such sanctions are often surprisingly effective. The Coroners Rules 1984 contain a provision (Rule 43) that empowers a coroner 'who believes that action should be taken to prevent the recurrence of fatalities similar to that in respect of which the inquest is being held' to 'announce at the inquest that he is reporting the matter in writing to the person or authority who may have power to take such action and he may report the matter accordingly'. This sounds like a toothless sanction, but in fact the anecdotal indications are that such reports in clinical negligence cases are taken very seriously indeed by the relevant Trust.

The protocol is the ruling instrument in clinical negligence case management. It is well within the powers of case-managing and trial judges to make observations about clinical governance failures and other patient safety issues that emerge in the course of proceedings. They seldom do so, inhibited, no doubt, by the proper caution in both *Access for Justice* and the protocol against purporting to make final decisions about clinical governance that others are far better equipped to make. Certainly it would be wrong, and against the spirit of the protocol, to increase the complexity and duration of proceedings by enlarging the scope of the judicial inquiry in clinical negligence litigation beyond that necessary to give the tribunal the information it needs to decide liability and, if appropriate, quantum. Clinical negligence cases are and should remain tort cases, concerned with compensation. Lord Woolf's main concern was to ensure that meritorious cases were compensated promptly, unmeritorious cases were recognised at an early stage and the costs incurred in investigating both were as small as possible. But there will inevitably be times when, in the course of that compensatory process, it will be clear to a judge that more widely repercussive issues, going to the safety of future patients, have arisen. What should the judge do then? Should he bite his tongue, telling himself that his only concern is with liability and quantum in the case before him? It is suggested that the plain answer is no. A judge at any stage is entitled to consider, for the purposes of sanction at least, the behaviour of parties at the pre-action stage, as judged by the benchmark of the protocol. The protocol, as we have seen, has a good deal to say about clinical governance/patient safety. It is suggested that the protocol effectively gives a judge at any stage power to make a declaration tantamount to that in Rule 43 of the Coroners Rules, and to report the matter for further consideration. At the moment that is an almost unused power. Properly used, it could be a potent weapon in the battle for patient safety.

Making Amends *and the NHS Redress Act 2006*

On 1 July 2003 the Department of Health published *Making Amends: A Consultation Paper Setting Out Proposals for Reforming the Approach to Clinical Negligence in the NHS*.[18] It reiterated many of the concerns voiced by Lord Woolf, including the fact that 'Legal proceedings for medical injury frequently progress in an atmosphere of confrontation, acrimony, misunderstanding and bitterness. The emphasis is on revealing as little as possible about what went wrong, defending decisions that were taken and only reluctantly releasing information'.[19] That, it noted, was hardly a culture likely to help the NHS learn from its mistakes. Litigation buried a good deal of wisdom which, properly applied, could help to make patients safer. This had to change: 'The NHS must ... ensure that ... bad experiences of individuals are learned from so that future NHS patients throughout the country benefit from reduced risks and safer care. The primary aim must be to reduce the number of medical errors that occur'.[20] Hence its proposals for reform, the aims of which were to ensure that

> the emphasis of the NHS is directed at preventing harm, reducing risks and enhancing safety so that the level of medical error is reduced; there is a better co-ordinated response to harm and injury resulting from health care including investigation, support, remedial care where needed and fair recompense.[21]

The law had to catch up with and reflect the changing risk management culture, it said:

> Until recently, relatively little attention had been given in any country to trying to identify the sources of risk in health care and to finding ways to reduce it in a planned and organised way. A much higher level of error has been tolerated in health care than has been acceptable in other sectors. This is now changing and the NHS is one of the first health systems in the world to give high priority to enhancing patient safety by systematically learning from what goes wrong. In the long term, learning effectively from mistakes, errors and incidents will make health care safer and will result in many fewer instances of serious harm as a complication of medical care. The relevance to medical litigation is obvious – if more of the healthcare risks that currently cause harm to patients are identified, anticipated and reduced, then the number of avoidable injuries to patients should be reduced. So too should be their severity. This must be the primary aim.[22]

This was Woolf all over again, but with more of an emphasis on patient safety for patient safety's sake, rather than because safer patients meant emptier courts and poorer lawyers.

The paper, four years after Woolf, thought that the Woolf reforms were inadequate: 'I have considered whether recent reforms and those currently in train are sufficient to improve the response to clinical negligence cases, as some commentators have argued. However, even with these reforms, the present system warrants further action.'[23] It remained complex, arbitrary, unfair, slow and expensive. But also: 'patients are dissatisfied with the lack of explanations and apologies or reassurance that action has been taken to prevent repetition', and the system 'encourages defensiveness and secrecy and stands in the way of learning and improvement in the health service'.[24] The paper was describing precisely what Woolf had seen and bemoaned. Little had changed. A new vision was needed. Any new system, the paper argued, 'should create a climate where risks of care are reduced and patient safety improves because medical errors and near misses are readily reported, successfully analysed and effective corrective action takes place and is sustained'.[25]

These were brave words. Could the Department of Health succeed where Lord Woolf had failed? It certainly had a go. The paper made nineteen recommendations for reform of the existing system of dealing with claims for medical negligence. The central proposal was the establishment of a new system for providing redress for patients harmed by seriously substandard NHS hospital care. This was the 'NHS Redress Scheme'. It would contain four main elements: an investigation of the incident and the allegedly resulting harm; the provision to the patient of an explanation and of the action proposed to prevent repetition; the development and delivery of a package of care, providing remedial treatment, therapy and arrangements for continuing care where needed; and financial compensation for pain and suffering, out of pocket expenses and care or treatment that the NHS could not provide. The details of the proposals do not matter for present purposes.[26] The upshot was that the NHS would put much of its own tortious house in order. The Scheme would not remove the right to sue in the courts, but, except for children with cerebral palsy, there would be a presumption that a claimant had first applied to the Scheme, and those accepting packages of care and compensation under the Scheme would be required to waive their right to go to court on the same case.[27] It was accepted that some cases would not fall within the Scheme's criteria, but an attempt at alternative dispute resolution would be expected, periodical payments would be strongly encouraged as a mechanism for compensating future loss, future care would not be quantified on the basis of private treatment, and judges handling clinical negligence claims would be specially trained.[28]

The potential and actual claimant's need to know the facts (often for knowledge's own sake rather than because of their importance for the compensatory process), together with the need to learn lessons from clinical errors, was behind two other key recommendations. The paper proposed the introduction of

> [a] new standard for after-event and after-complaint management by the NHS so that there is a full investigation of each case, a clear explanation is provided to victims and any necessary remedial action taken. Staff training should be undertaken to achieve a higher quality of response to complaints and incidents.[29]

Also an NHS Trust Board level individual should 'be required to take overall responsibility to ensure that the organisation rigorously investigates and learns effectively from complaints, adverse events and claims, ending the present fragmentation of these processes. Investigation of complaints and incidents should be co-ordinated under a single senior manager'.[30]

Patient groups were delighted with *Making Amends*.[31] At last it seemed as if someone in authority was taking their concerns seriously. Perhaps ambulance-chasing lawyers would starve. Perhaps the information gathered by NHS bodies in the course of litigation would be used to benefit future patients rather than to help lawyers outfox and impoverish past patients.

And for once, for a while, it seemed as if something might actually happen – as this if was one report that would not merely be commented on in the broadsheets and the law journals and then filed impotently away. For it led to a statute, the NHS Redress Act 2006, which received Royal Assent on 8 November 2006.

The Act empowered the Secretary of State to make regulations establishing 'a scheme for the purpose of enabling redress to be provided without recourse to civil proceedings in circumstances in which this section applies'.[32] Patient safety concerns were prominent. 'A scheme must provide for redress ordinarily to comprise … the giving of a report on the action which has been, or will be, taken to prevent similar cases arising',[33] and the Secretary of State was given a further power to make regulations about the handling and consideration of complaints about maladministration,[34] and these regulations 'may make provision about … the making of a report or recommendations about a complaint [and] … the action to be taken as a result of a complaint'.[35]

For cynics there were indications in the Act itself of wavering determination. One of the concerns of the would-be reformers was that the patient safety remit was divided dangerously between several different bodies. Their hopes rose when they saw the heading in the Act 'Duties of co-operation', but they waned when they read the detail. The Scheme authority, on the one hand, and the Commission for Healthcare Audit and Inspection and the National Patient Safety Agency, on the other, must co-operate with each other 'where it appears to them that it is appropriate to do so for the efficient and effective discharge of their respective functions'.[36] In other words, they did not have to co-operate with one another at all if they chose not to.

But, such quibbles aside, it seemed as if a brave new patient safety centred world might be dawning. An Act of Parliament could not be ignored, could it? The answer is that it could be and has been. The Act has been buried. No regulations establishing an NHS Redress Scheme have been made. Clinical negligence claims still proceed as they did in (depending on your perspective) the good or bad old days.

Lord Gregson put down a written question in the House of Lords, asking Her Majesty's Government 'what progress has been made in the application of the NHS Redress Act 2006'. On 18 March 2009 Lord Darzi of Denham, Parliamentary Under-Secretary, Department of Health, gave this answer:

> The NHS Redress Act 2006 is a piece of framework legislation that will need to be enacted through secondary legislation. The department has continually believed that putting in place the appropriate secondary legislation for this piece of work will require considerable stakeholder involvement to discuss the detail around the working of any scheme. This would mean that any legislation could not be implemented any earlier than at least 2010.
>
> The department considers it is currently more important to embed the general principles of wider redress across the National Health Service – those of apologies and explanations, a spirit of openness, a culture of learning from mistakes and robust investigation – rather than focussing on financial redress only for those cases.[37]

There are many problems with that answer. One of the more obvious is that one of the main mechanisms for creating the culture Lord Darzi spoke about was the NHS Redress Scheme itself, which the Government has mothballed.

If the NHS Redress Scheme ever comes into effect, pre-trial procedure will be affected in two main ways. First, far fewer claims will process through the court system, with its inherent iniquities from a patient-safety perspective. And, second, even when claims do hit the courts, the change in culture that the Scheme is likely to effect will make the courts more alert at both the pre-trial and trial stages to those patient safety considerations that were at the front of Sir Liam Donaldson's mind, and not far from the front of Lord Woolf's.

The Compensation Act 2006

By s.2 of this Act, '[a]n apology, an offer of treatment or other redress, shall not of itself amount to an admission of negligence or breach of statutory duty'. This is a serious contender for the title of the most unnecessary statutory provision of all time. No competent lawyer has ever or could ever have suggested that an apology or offer of redress has this effect. It was enacted in an attempt not to change the law (it did not), but to help to change the culture: to make defendants more conciliatory (which in clinical negligence cases at least it has not done). As we have seen, that attitude was linked in *Access to Justice*, *Making Amends* and the NHS Redress Act to wider patient safety considerations. The section is not a bad thing, just an otiose and rather pathetic thing. Pre-trial practice in clinical negligence cases remains unaltered.

Bolam, Bolitho *and pre-trial procedure*

Pre-trial preparation in any clinical negligence case in which liability is in issue is dominated by the collation of expert evidence. Where breach of duty is contested, the battle between the experts commonly ranges over the battleground delineated by the famous *Bolam* test.[38] Pre-trial procedure will include the preparation and exchange of expert reports and a meeting of experts in an attempt to iron out differences between the experts and to determine whether the defendant's conduct falls within the margins allowed by *Bolam*. If there is agreement that it does, the case should be discontinued.

Bolam (which is a principle of substantive law as well as a direction to judges as to how to consider expert evidence) says that a defendant will escape liability if what has been done would be endorsed by a responsible body of opinion in the relevant specialty. In *Bolitho v City and Hackney Health Authority*[39] the House of Lords emphasised the word 'responsible' in that formulation, saying that there would be cases where, notwithstanding support by an expert witness of the defendant's practice, a judge could conclude that the practice was so plainly unsustainable as to be irresponsible and hence negligent.[40]

The traditional *Bolam* formulation is hardly an incentive to best practice. It allows a defendant to succeed if what has been done is barely acceptable – at the outer limits of respectability. But patient safety lobbyists have no real cause for complaint against the test itself. The purpose of clinical negligence litigation is not to improve practice, but to decide whether money should be paid to claimants by defendants. En route, of course, things may be learned that, if properly processed, might improve patient safety, but that is a by-product of the existing system, not its *raison d'être*. While we have a tort-based system, that will remain the case.[41]

The real significance of the old *Bolam* test for present purposes is the adversarial angst that it generates – angst inherent (and probably inevitably inherent) in the procedural systems set up to determine whether or not the test has been satisfied. That angst contributes to the well-documented and much lamented suspicion between claimants and defendants – suspicion that inhibits lesson-learning and therefore compromises patient safety. The Civil Procedure Rules emphasise that the overriding duty of an expert is to the court: the expert is there to help the court come to the right conclusion.[42] Experts have to declare in their reports that they recognise this, and that in opining on breach of duty they have considered the range of possible opinions.[43] These declarations seem to have done little to reduce the violently partisan wrangling into which so many expert meetings degenerate.

But *Bolitho* may have added something new to the patient safety agenda. It emphasised that although there may be many ways in which medical cats are in fact skinned, there may be a way of skinning them that is so obviously better than the others that it would be negligent not to adopt it. In the emerging culture of evidence-based medicine this is increasingly the case. If definitive, evidence-based guidelines say that practice X is superior, it will be hard to argue that practice Y is defensible. In clinical negligence litigation, guidelines are increasingly coming to be the real arbiters of breach of duty. *Bolam* is bowing to them. There may come a time when it will bow out.

The clinical guidelines revolution is undoubtedly a good thing for patient safety. First, and obviously, treatment that is compliant with an international consensus on best practice is likely to be better for patients than treatment that is compliant with the whim and prejudice of an eccentric and bigoted consultant. But, second, if authoritative guidelines are the yardstick of acceptable practice, experts will increasingly be elbowed out of clinical negligence litigation. As they are, some of that mutual suspicion will haemorrhage out too, allowing some objectivity, reflection and lesson-learning to flow into the space left behind. Clinical negligence cases are too often won by the expert who shouts loudest in the expert meeting and, if it comes to that, at court. Shouting does not help patient safety lessons to be learned.

The financial and risk management functions of the NHSLA

Pre-trial behaviour is a function both of the relevant procedural rules and the way that the parties to litigation play the game.

The vast majority of clinical negligence litigation in the UK against NHS defendants other than GPs is overseen on the defendant side by the National Health Service Litigation Authority (NHSLA). The NHSLA's objective is to reduce the amount of money paid out by the NHS as damages and costs. It seeks to do this in two ways: first, by controlling the way that NHS defendants conduct litigation – reducing costs by way of early compromise, if possible, and by contesting cases if it is thought financially intelligent to do so; and, second, by way of risk management. According to the NHSLA Framework document, the NHSLA aims to 'contribute to the incentives for reducing the number of negligent or preventable incidents'.[44] The incentives are crudely financial: Trusts with a better risk management record get cheaper cover. One would have thought and hoped that the NHSLA would conduct litigation with its risk management function in mind. But the impression of many at the forensic coal face is that it does not. It litigates in a narrowly commercial way, like a motor insurer. Its ethos seems uninformed by the patient safety corollaries of litigation practice identified in *Access to Justice* and *Making Amends*. Its litigation is mainly conducted by firms of solicitors on a clinical negligence panel. Membership of the panel is crucial to those firms' livelihoods. And yet the NHSLA is not slow to drop firms with whom it is displeased. Pleasing the NHSLA therefore becomes a far higher priority in the minds of the litigators than any of the other, 'softer' considerations. And the NHSLA often seems to like to play hardball in the old-fashioned way. It is a shame. Patient safety lessons are sometimes a casualty, as Lord Woolf anticipated.

Conclusion

The pre-trial process in clinical negligence cases is adversarial. That is because, despite the best efforts of Lord Woolf and Sir Liam Donaldson, the whole process of clinical negligence litigation is adversarial. The shimmering emotional heat of much clinical negligence litigation often obscures the patient safety lessons that might be learned. More could be done by judges in clinical negligence cases to highlight patient safety issues. It is suggested that the pre-action protocol explicitly gives judges the power, analogous to the Rule 43 powers of coroners, to notify relevant bodies about such issues. If the NHS Redress Scheme envisaged by the NHS Redress Act 2006 were to be implemented, many clinical negligence cases would be taken out of the court system into an environment where patient safety lessons were much more likely to be learned. The massive proliferation in clinical guidelines, together with *Bolitho v City and Hackney Health Authority*, is having and will increasingly have the effect of reducing the adversarial nature of pre-trial and courtroom clashes between experts. That will make patient safety issues more visible.

Notes

1 H.K. Woolf, *Access to Justice*, London: Her Majesty's Stationary Office, July 1996. Online. Available HTTP http://www.dca.gov.uk/civil/final/contents.htm (accessed 18 June 2010).
2 Ibid.: chapter 15, para. 2.
3 Ibid.
4 Ibid.: chapter 2, para. 3
5 Ibid.: chapter 2, para. 18.
6 Ibid. See Clauses 1.12–1.14.
7 Ibid.: Clause 1.1.
8 Ibid.: Clause 1.2.
9 Ibid.: Clause 2.1. The other general aim is to resolve as many disputes as possible without litigation.
10 Ibid.: Clause 2.2.
11 Ibid.: Clause 2.3.
12 Ibid.: Clause 2.3(a).
13 Ibid.: Clause 2.3(b).
14 Ibid.: Clause 2.3(c).
15 General Medical Council, *Good Medical Practice: Guidance for Doctors*, London: General Medical Council, Clause 6. Online. Available HTTP http://www.gmc-uk.org/static/documents/content/GMC_GMP_0911.pdf (Accessed 18 June 2010).
16 General Medical Council, *Raising Concerns about Patient Safety – Guidance for Doctors*, London: General Medical Council, November 2006. Online. Available HTTP http://www.gmc-uk.org/guidance/ethical_guidance/raising_concerns.asp

(accessed 18 June 2010); General Medical Council, *Management for Doctors: Guidance for Doctors*, London: General Medical Council, February 2006, paras 44–45. Online. Available HTTP http://www.gmc-uk.org/guidance/ethical_guidance/management_for_doctors.asp (accessed 19 June 2010).

17 Ibid.: Clause 3.4(ii), (iii) and (iv).

18 L. Donaldson, *Making Amends: A Consultation Paper Setting Out Proposals for Reforming the Approach to Clinical Negligence in the NHS*, London: Department of Health, July 2003. Online. Available HTTP http://www.dh.gov.uk/en/Publicationsandstatistics/Publications/PublicationsPolicyAndGuidance/DH_4010641 (accessed 18 June 2010).

19 Ibid.: Executive summary, p. 7.

20 Ibid.

21 Ibid.

22 Ibid.: Executive Summary, p. 8.

23 Ibid.: Executive Summary, p. 13.

24 Ibid.

25 Ibid.

26 Ibid.: Executive Summary, pp. 16–17.

27 Ibid.: Executive Summary, p. 17.

28 Ibid.

29 Ibid.: Executive Summary, p. 18.

30 Ibid.

31 AVMA continues to advocate a State-provided system for compensating victims of medical accidents as an alternative to the courts. Court action, it notes, 'is notoriously difficult for individuals to pursue, is costly both to individuals and the State, and focuses attention mainly on individual negligence and money. It adds to the perception of "blame culture" and does little to ensure lessons are learnt to improve safety'. Action Against Medical Accidents, *A Fair Compensation Scheme*, Action Against Medical Accidents. Online. Available HTTP http://www.avma.org.uk/pages/a_fair_compensation_scheme.html (accessed 18 June 2010).

32 Donaldson, *Making Amends*, S. 1(1).

33 Ibid.: S. 3(2)(d).

34 Ibid.: S. 14(1).

35 Ibid.: S. 14(4)(h) and (i).

36 Ibid.: S. 13(1) and (2).

37 HL Deb, 18 March 2009, c49W. Online. Available HTTP http://www.theyworkforyou.com/wrans/?id=2009-03-18a.49.3 (accessed 18 June 2010).

38 In *Bolam v Friern Hospital Management Committee* [1957] 1 WLR 582.

39 [1998] AC 232.

40 *Bolitho v City and Hackney Health Authority* [1998] AC 232, per Lord Browne-Wilkinson, p. 243.

41 The test for establishing actionable breach of duty could in theory be changed: one might, for instance, say that a defendant should compensate a claimant if optimal treatment has not been provided, but the financial consequences of such a change in the law would be tectonic. It would be financially tantamount to a non-fault-based system.

42 CPR, Part 35.3.

43 Practice Direction 35: 3.2(6): 'where there is a range of opinion on the matters dealt with in the report [the report must] (a) summarise the range of opinions; and (b) give reasons for the expert's own opinion.'

44 Department of Health, *National Health Service Litigation Authority Framework Document*, Department of Health, December 2002. Online. Available HTTP http://www.nhsla.com/NR/rdonlyres/D872241A-43E3-492B-8F74-32FB0586608F/0/Frameworkdocument.pdf (accessed 18 June 2010).

3 The tort of negligence and patient safety

José Miola

Introduction

The tort of negligence is critical to the law's approach to ensuring and enhancing patient safety. This chapter considers the use of negligence in the protection of patient safety. First, it examines the tort of negligence itself by considering the function of negligence law and what constitutes the tort of negligence. Thus duty, breach and causation shall be outlined, and some elements engaged with critically. The *Bolam* test and its effects (particularly in the context of *Bolitho*) shall be analysed, as well as some issues relating to causation, such as 'loss of a chance of recovery'. The law shall be analysed in terms of its substantive content, and this analysis will include the general philosophy of the courts' decisions. In this context, then, cases such as *Chester* v. *Afshar*, which is symbolic of the courts' present attitude and perhaps an indicator of future judicial thinking, shall also be examined.

Then the chapter shall present a critical appraisal of whether the law of negligence is the best mechanism for ensuring and protecting patient safety with reference to the Woolf and Kennedy reports. The chapter shall also examine developments such as the NHS Redress Act and the Compensation Act. Drawing on case law and government reports, it shall present a synthesis of what is good and bad about the current system, identifying the reform agenda and assessing the way forward.

The function of the law of negligence

It is a common error to think that the function of the law of negligence is to punish bad behaviour (such as poor medical practice). Negligence exists instead to compensate the plaintiff for any injury suffered at the hands of the defendant. In other words, tort 'is about messes. A mess has been made, and the only question before the court is, who is to clean it up?'[1] Thus, negligence asks who it is 'just' to hold accountable.[2] The court determines who should pay to cover the losses – and the fact that the defendant medical practitioner has acted poorly helps it to make that decision. The only way in which patient safety may be protected by such a model is if we stretch matters to acknowledge that the law will compensate patients for the poor practice of medical practitioners if it causes harm, and if we ascribe to it some consequent deterrent effect. Nevertheless, it must be noted that the law of negligence does not take proactive steps to protect patients by ensuring patient safety, but is instead a retrospective remedy designed to compensate claimants for harm suffered. With that in mind, I now turn to considering the law of negligence itself.

Defining the tort of negligence

The tort of negligence is divided into three components which must result in harm. First, a duty of care must exist between the parties; the duty must be breached by the defendant; and, finally, the breach must be the legal and factual cause of the harm suffered. In order for her claim to be successful, the aggrieved party must demonstrate that *all three* of these elements are in place. It is useful to consider each in turn.

In English law, there is no legal requirement to be a 'good Samaritan' – so there is no legal duty on an in individual to help another person or persons unless there is a relationship between them that allows the law to impose a duty to act. The 'duty of care' in negligence relates to the question of whether such a relationship exists between the parties that one can be ascribed a legal 'duty to take care' of the other. In medical practice, a duty of care always exists between medical professional and patient once the former begins to treat the latter.[3]

Once a duty has been established, the claimant must demonstrate that it has been breached. This means that the defendant has not 'taken care', and that her conduct has fallen below the legally accepted standard (which is why this limb of the test is also sometimes known as the 'standard of care'). Essentially, in order to conform to the standard of care required, people must act in a 'reasonable' fashion. However, when someone has a special skill they must act as a reasonable' member of that profession. So for the doctor the standard is that of the 'reasonable doctor', and for the nurse the 'reasonable nurse'. How this test is actually carried out by the courts is the subject of the next section, but it is sufficient to say at this point that much will depend on what other professionals might do in the same circumstances.

Finally, it must be demonstrated that the breach of duty caused the harm that the claimant is seeking compensation for. Commonly referred to as the 'but for' test, it requires the claimant to prove that 'but for the breach of duty the harm would not have been suffered by the injured party'.[4] Thus, a breach of duty will only lead to liability where the harm would not have occurred in any event. For example, in one case three men presented at a hospital complaining of vomiting having drunk some tea. They were told to return home and see their GP in the morning. Unfortunately, the tea had been laced with arsenic and one of them died. A duty was owed, and it was determined that it had been breached. However, the level of arsenic in the dead man's body was so high that he would have died even if he had received reasonable care, and thus the case failed on causation.[5]

What do the elements of negligence tell us about the relationship between tort law and patient safety? The first thing to note is that the tort does not, per se, protect patient safety. Rather, as we have seen, the law seeks to compensate claimants for loss that they have suffered. For this reason, the elements of negligence are hurdles that must be overcome by claimants, and represent barriers to success. Perhaps the most pertinent to this argument is the concept of causation, which prevents a patient from claiming even if a duty of care was owed and subsequently breached – the damages are not punishment for bad behaviour, but compensation for the resulting harm. Nevertheless, as I demonstrate later, that does not mean that the law will not strive to improve standards or protect patients. Indeed, it has made great strides to this effect in the last 30 years, and in both breach of duty and causation we can see that the law has increasingly recognised and sought to protect what it sees as the 'rights' of patients.

The 'reasonable doctor' – *Bolam* and beyond

It may be said that the 'crunch point' in the law of tort is the standard of care demanded of medical professionals, and when they might be said to have fallen below it and thus breached their duty. As I mentioned above, the law demands that doctors act as a 'reasonable doctor'. But what does this mean in practice? In fact, the changing judicial method of ascertaining whether a doctor has acted as other reasonable doctors would do has provided what many consider to be a profound and fundamental shift in how medical professionals will be treated by the courts, and thus how far the law is willing to involve itself in ensuring patient safety.[6] The legal response to medical error (and therefore, by extension, patient safety) rests on its interpretation of the case of *Bolam*, and more specifically one passage from it. McNair J., while directing the jury, defined for them how they should direct themselves to determining the reasonableness of conduct:

> A doctor is not guilty of negligence if he has acted in accordance with a practice accepted as proper by a responsible body of medical men skilled in that particular art.[7]

The quotation makes clear that the reasonableness or otherwise of the doctor's conduct will be determined by whether the defendant can demonstrate that a 'responsible body of medical men skilled in that particular art' might have acted in the same way. For 40 years, the courts interpreted McNair J.'s dicta narrowly. Thus, the courts held that as long as the defendant could adduce *some* medical evidence from doctors who might have done the same as she did, it was not open to the court to find a breach of duty. This was made explicit by the House of Lords in *Maynard*, where the original judge had rejected the defence's experts because he preferred the evidence of those for the plaintiff. Lord Scarman, in finding that he was not entitled to do so, stated that the judge had 'erred in law' by preferring one set of experts to another.[8] Not unreasonably, this was seen as unduly restrictive to patients. Most obviously, the standard of care was effectively set by the medical profession, and consequently the courts could not analyse medical conduct: judges could only ask what *was* done rather than what *ought* to have been done.[9] Of course, this meant that the courts could not involve themselves in decisions made by doctors, even when they impacted on patient safety issues.

In essence, the law became a rubber stamp for accepted practice; however, that changed in 1997, when the House of Lords identified that the test in *Bolam* requires that the body of evidence be 'reasonable', and fashioned a normative role for itself. Thus in *Bolitho* Lord Browne-Wilkinson held that the duty of the court was to analyse the evidence provided and to assess reasonableness for itself. The court, rather than the medical profession itself, would judge medical conduct. Thus,

> if, in a rare case, it can be demonstrated that the professional opinion is not capable of withstanding logical analysis, the judge is entitled to hold that the body of opinion is not reasonable or responsible.[10]

The judgement is less revolutionary than it might appear, and it should be noted that the key phrases are 'rare case' and 'logical analysis'. The threshold for rejecting medical evidence is set deliberately high, and will not be used regularly. Therefore, it is virtually inconceivable that a doctor following (for example) NICE guidelines would be found to be in breach of duty. Ironically, it is the increased availability of such guidelines that allow judges the confidence to take such a proactive role,[11] although some warn of dangers inherent in making the guidelines the *de facto* standard of care.[12]

What can be seen, then, is that the court's ability to define and police the standard of care for medical professionals has undergone what appears to be a significant change. Yet, it arguably merely restores *Bolam* to the interpretation intended by McNair J.[13] Moreover, *Bolitho* cannot be said to place an unreasonable burden on medical professionals, as it only brings them into line with the law relating to other professions – including lawyers.[14] In this respect, while the law can be seen to be increasingly involved and evaluative in protecting patient safety, the rarity that is intended in the use of *Bolitho* signifies that there is little need for medical professionals to worry.

Causation: losing 'loss of a chance'

As we saw earlier, if the plaintiff manages to demonstrate that a duty of care was owed and a breach of duty has occurred, she must then prove causation. While it is not an unreasonable condition to place on claimants (particularly given that tort is based on compensation for harm suffered rather than punishment for poor performance), it is a significant hurdle to overcome.

The general rule is that it must be shown that 'but for' the defendant's breach of duty the damage would not have occurred. In medical negligence cases, it can be particularly difficult for the claimant to prove this for a variety of reasons (the aetiology of certain diseases may not be clear and patients tend to already be suffering from something before they see their doctor). However, they must satisfy the court that there was a 51 per cent chance or greater that the harm was caused by the breach of duty. If it is, the claimant will receive 100 per cent damages as causation is 'proved'. If not, she will receive nothing. One specific sub-category of causation that has been controversial, however, is the question of 'loss of a chance', where the claimant argues that the poor treatment resulted in them losing the *chance* to recover. The issues are best illustrated by the facts of a leading case on the issue, *Hotson*.[15]

The case concerned a boy who fell out of a tree and was taken to hospital. He was examined and sent home, but returned five days later still complaining of severe pain. Only then was he x-rayed, which revealed a traumatic fracture. An operation to pin the joint was performed, but the patient developed avascular necrosis, which led to a deformity of the hip and what was described by the court as a serious disability. The hospital admitted breach of duty with regard to the misdiagnosis and consequent failure to x-ray, but argued that there was no causation between the delay and the necrosis as the medical evidence showed that, even without the delay, there was a 75 per cent chance that the avascular necrosis would have developed anyway. The trial judge accepted this, but found that since the boy had lost a 25 per cent chance of recovery, he should receive 25 per cent of the damages. The case went to the House of Lords. The plaintiff argued that the 75 per cent figure meant that out of every 100 people in that situation, 25 would come out without avascular necrosis if there was no negligence. Thus it was this *chance* that the plaintiff had specified as his damage. Consequently, the plaintiff should have been awarded damages, and the correct amount was seen as being 25 per cent of the full amount. The House of Lords, however, disagreed. The 'damage' as they saw it, was the necrosis (the court failed to engage with the point that the claimants were not arguing that this was the damage). As a result, if the plaintiff could show that there was a 51 per cent chance, or more, that the necrosis was caused by the fall, then the plaintiff would receive full damages. If not, he would receive nothing at all. As the chance of avoiding necrosis without the breach was 25 per cent only, then the claim had to fail.

There are of course good arguments for the approach, exemplified by Croom-Johnson L.J. in the Court of Appeal:

If it is proved statistically that 25% of the population has a chance of recovery from a certain injury and 75% does not, it does not mean that someone who suffers that injury and who does not recover from it has lost a 25% chance. He may have lost nothing at all. What he has to do is prove that he was one of the 25% and that his loss was caused by the defendant's negligence. To be a figure in a statistic does not in itself give him a cause of action. If the plaintiff succeeds in proving that he was one of the 25% and that the defendant took away that chance, the logical result would be to award him 100% of his damages and not only a quarter.[16]

Nevertheless, the 'all or nothing' approach to causation can be criticised for being overly formalistic and inflexible, and also for being less and less fair the closer the chance comes to 50 per cent.[17] Moreover, it is the *defendant's breach of duty* that denies the claimant the opportunity to prove that she would have been one of the 25 per cent. The argument also, like the House of Lords, fails to understand the actual nature of the plaintiff's claim. The claim was not for damages due to contracting the necrosis, but for damages due to the loss of the chance to avoid developing it. So, we can say that, rather than claiming for the loss of the *chance of successful treatment*, the plaintiff was claiming for the loss of *benefit of timely treatment*. If we look at it that way, we can see that the plaintiff in *Hotson* clearly lost something, which was a fact that the House of Lords seemed to forget.

Perhaps because the House of Lords failed to engage fully with Hotson's argument, the issue remained unresolved until 2005, when their Lordships had a further opportunity to examine the issue in *Gregg* v. *Scott*.[18] The issues were similar (a cancer patient had his chances of survival cut from 42 per cent to 25 per cent due to a missed diagnosis), and this time the House of Lords confronted the issue of loss of a chance head on. In a majority judgement, it confirmed that it was not possible to claim for a loss of a chance of recovery. Essentially, the majority preferred legal certainty over what some might consider fairness:

> What these cases show is that, as Helen Reece points out in an illuminating article ('Losses of Chances in the Law' (1996) 59 *MLR* 188) the law regards the world as in principle bound by laws of causality. Everything has a determinate cause, even if we do not know what it is. The blood-starved hip joint in *Hotson*{...}had its cause and it was for the plaintiff to prove that it was an act or omission for which the defendant was responsible. The fact that proof is rendered difficult or impossible because no examination was made at the time, as in *Hotson*, or because medical science cannot provide the answer{...}makes no difference.[19]

What can therefore be seen is that the high hurdle of causation remains just that – and that loss of a chance is now definitely not a claimable head of damage. It is difficult to argue with those who consider this unfair to patients. Indeed, patients may not feel protected by the law here. Nevertheless, it should be noted that *Gregg* was a majority judgement in the House of Lords. It is thus evident that there are some amongst their Lordships who hold a different view of causation. That this is the case is demonstrated in the next section.

Chester v. *Afshar*: a new judicial attitude?

The legalistic approach taken by the court in *Gregg* is in complete contrast to another, near contemporaneous, decision of the House of Lords regarding causation in medical negligence: *Chester* v. *Afshar*.[20] *Chester* involves issues regarding risk disclosure, a sub-category of medical negligence. Essentially, before a patient's consent may be legally valid, the doctor must explain all of the risks inherent in the proposed procedure. This must be done in an adequate manner. In normal circumstances, whether this has been the case is dealt with under the law of negligence.[21] The normal rules of negligence therefore apply. Of course, a duty of care exists once a doctor has undertaken the task of treating the patient. This includes warning about risks, and consists of a requirement that the doctor disclose to the patient information about all 'material risks'. Thus, not to disclose such risks would constitute a breach of duty as the 'reasonable doctor' must disclose all material risks. Indeed, the precise definition of a material risk has been the subject of some conjecture in English courts, and it is arguable that it has not yet been settled,[22] but that is not relevant to our discussion here.

In terms of causation, the orthodox interpretation of the rule is that to satisfy it the claimant must demonstrate that, had the material risk been mentioned to her, she would not have consented to the procedure. Otherwise, the breach would have made no difference at all. *Chester* was a case about causation, since duty and breach were conceded by the defendant. However, Mrs Chester had admitted that, had she been warned of the particular risk, she might have taken some extra time to consider things, but ultimately would have consented to the procedure in any event. Normally, she would have lost on causation. However, she argued that what she had lost was a right to make an autonomous decision. What she was asking for was that the requirement of causation be, in essence, waived so that she could recover damages for the loss of self-determination. Once again, the battle lines were drawn between (what some might consider) 'fairness' or the patient's 'rights', on one side, and legal orthodoxy and formalism, on the other. This time, by three to two, 'rights' prevailed. The majority of their Lordships felt that the purpose of the law was to protect patient autonomy, and that the judgement must flow from there:

> there is no dispute that Mr Afshar owed a duty to Miss Chester to inform her of the risks that were inherent in the proposed surgery, including the risk of paralysis. The duty was owed to her so that she could make her own decision as to whether or not she should undergo the particular course of surgery which he was proposing to carry out.

That was the scope of the duty, the existence of which gave effect to her right to be informed before she consented to it. It was unaffected in its scope by the response which Miss Chester would have given had she been told of these risks.[23]

For Lord Steyn the issue was just as simple, as causation should not be allowed to stand in the way of the patient's rights: '[the] right to autonomy and dignity can and ought to be vindicated.'[24]

What can be seen in *Chester*, then, is the opposite of what was decided in *Gregg*: the rejection of legal formalism and the prioritisation of the rights of patients, even if it means modifying the law. Given that both cases were decided by majority judgements, we can only conclude that there is a significant section of England's highest court that is willing to modify legal principles in order to protect patients. Whether this is a positive development or not is something that will inspire debate, but the law relating to causation demonstrates that it is a debate that senior judges are currently engaged in, and the direction in which the law is moving.

Critiquing the tort approach/new legislation

The tort-based system is certainly controversial. Much of the criticism concerns the complaint that judges have been shown to be overly deferential to the medical profession, and that this has had a negative effect on the rights and overall safety of patients. Various arguments have been put forward to explain this, ranging from the fact that lawyers and doctors share a socio-economic space within society to an understandable desire not to limit professional freedom.[25] Indeed, it has been argued that the legal landscape has changed in the last decades – not least because of Lord Woolf – and the general direction of the law offers some support for that view, with *Bolitho* allowing the courts more involvement, and judgements such as *Chester* prioritising patients' rights even over established legal principles.[26]

However, some complaints persist. Professor Sir Ian Kennedy (an academic medical lawyer) was scathing about the cultural flaws evident in the medical profession in his report into paediatric heart surgery at Bristol Royal Infirmary.[27] These manifested themselves as 'excessive paternalism, lack of respect for patients and their rights to make decisions about their care'.[28] The notion of 'clinical freedom' encouraged a culture of autonomy that resulted in a total lack of regulation or oversight, which in turn allowed the poorly performed surgeries to continue.[29] It also dispensed with the notion that the law need not oversee medical practice because the medical profession could do that on its own. Patients – and in literal terms their safety – were failed by this system, and the law of negligence would do nothing to actively stop this.

Equally, Lord Woolf's report into civil litigation found fault with the way in which medical negligence cases frequently became 'wars' between experts rather than attempts to find the truth.[30] This problem is exacerbated by the fact that, as recent scandals have yet again highlighted, the quality of expert evidence cannot be counted on.[31] Indeed, he was particularly scathing about medical negligence, whose failings were detailed as:

(a) The disproportion between costs and damages in medical negligence is particularly excessive, especially in lower value cases.
(b) The delay in resolving claims is more often unacceptable.
(c) Unmeritorious cases are often pursued, and clear-cut claims defended, for too long.
(d) The success rate is lower than in other personal injury litigation.
(e) The suspicion between the parties is more intense and the lack of co-operation frequently greater than in many other areas of litigation.[32]

So, for a variety of reasons it is at least arguable that the tort system itself is not fit for the purpose of ensuring patient safety. First and foremost, it must be remembered that the purpose of tort is *not* to protect but to compensate. Therefore, it can only be seen as retrospective rather than proactive. More-over, the common law system that operates in England is necessarily retro-spective, and yet another failing is that judges cannot take the lead in reconsidering weak areas of law – they must wait for an appropriate case to come before them. Finally, the flaws in the medical profession and expert witnesses identified by the Kennedy and Woolf reports will not simply go away, and on that basis relying so heavily on expert 'wars' in courtrooms may be seen to be a fundamental flaw in any system.

It might be argued that a no-fault compensation system would be better, and it cannot be argued that a system which seeks partnerships between doctors and patients who have been injured, rather than conflict, would help to mitigate the worries of both Kennedy and Lord Woolf.[33] However, that is a discussion for another article, particularly as there are no plans to construct such a system in England. What has occurred instead is that two pieces of legislation have been enacted which together propose to make some modifi-cations to the tort system. The first of these is the Compensation Act 2006. This seeks to limit the amount of claims made in negligence by asking courts to take into account whether requiring the defendant to take steps to meet the standard of care required may 'prevent a desirable activity from being undertaken at all, to a particular extent or in a particular way', or 'dis-courage persons from undertaking functions in connection with a desirable activity'.[34] Moreover, it makes clear that '[a]n apology, an offer of treatment or other redress, shall not of itself amount to an admission of negligence or breach of statutory duty'.[35] This statute appears to encourage courts to find reasons to turn down claims, which is not only against the general direction that the law has been taking, but also contrary to the problems with medical negligence litigation identified by Lord Woolf.

Meanwhile, the NHS Redress Act 2006 empowers the Secretary of State to establish a tort-based scheme. The precise way in which the scheme is supposed to work is not laid out in the statute itself, but the general purpose is to speed up claims and lower their costs through trusts making offers of redress to victims of negligence. Thus section 3(2) provides that:

A scheme must provide for redress ordinarily to comprise –

(a) the making of an offer of compensation in satisfaction of any right to bring civil proceedings in respect of the liability concerned,
(b) the giving of an explanation,
(c) the giving of an apology, and
(d) the giving of a report on the action which has been, or will be, taken to prevent similar cases arising, but may specify circumstances in which one or more of those forms of redress is not required.

In addition, section 3(3) makes provision for redress to take the form of a contract to provide care or treatment. The Act is intended to apply to low-value claims, and section 3(5) makes reference to an unspecified upper limit to compensation (estimated by Jackson to be likely to be £20,000).[36] At the time of writing, the establishment of the scheme has not yet occurred, having already been postponed twice. However, evidence to the Select Committee on Health in 2009 suggests that it is being planned for 2010.[37] Given that it is an election year, such a suggestion cannot be counted on.

The philosophy of the Act is to provide faster, cheaper redress for low-value claims, but while it removes the system from the courts, the principles of tort will still apply. It shall thus be tort without the courts. If the Compensation Act addressed the unmeritorious claims identified by Lord Woolf, the NHS Redress Act deals with the clear-cut cases overly defended. Noticeably, there is nothing in the Acts that refers directly to his other four flaws in medical negligence. The signals appear to be mixed (with one Act making it harder to claim, while the other encourages settling claims), but the one thing that they have in common is that they aim to make medical negligence litigation cheaper. Patient safety, if it is thought of at all, is at best an indirect consideration.

Conclusion

The tort system is not about ensuring patient safety. Rather, it provides a method for giving compensation to patients who have suffered harm. It does not seek to prevent the harm – just to ascertain who should pay for it. Yet that is not to say that patient safety is not in the minds of judges. Rather, as the direction of case law demonstrates, the courts have looked to enforce the rights of patients more aggressively, and are deferring less to medical professional judgement. In this regard, safety is protected as one of these 'rights'. Nevertheless common law is necessarily retrospective, and patients must be injured before entering the tort system. With no-fault compensation consistently rejected, the only real reform of the tort system lies in modifications to the system itself, and therefore the retrospectivity will remain. Indeed, the two Acts do nothing to move away from tort principles and are less concerned with patient safety than with lowering costs. Ultimately, if safety is not a direct purpose of tort, it is unsurprising that it is protected only tangentially.

Notes

1 J. Coleman, 'Second Thoughts and Other First Impressions', in B. Bix (ed.), *Analyzing Law: New Essays in Legal Theory*, Oxford, Clarendon Press, 1998.
2 *Fairchild* v. *Glenhaven Funeral Services Ltd* [2003] 1 A.C. 32.
3 *Barnett* v. *Chelsea and Kensington Hospital Management Committee* [1969] 1 Q.B. 428.
4 There is also 'legal causation', which does not concern us here.
5 The facts are those of *Barnett*, in note 3.
6 Lord Woolf, 'Are the Courts Excessively Deferential to the Medical Profession' (2001) 9 *Medical Law Review* 1.
7 *Bolam* v. *Friern Hospital Management Committee* [1957] 2 All E.R. 118.
8 *Maynard* v. *West Midlands Regional Health Authority* [1985] 1 All E.R. 635.
9 K. Norrie, 'Common Practice and the Standard of Care in Medical Negligence' (1985) *Juridical Review* 145.
10 *Bolitho v City and Hackney Health Authority* [1998] A.C. 232, 243.
11 M. Brazier and J. Miola, 'Bye-Bye *Bolam*: A Medical Litigation Revolution' (2000) 8 *Medical Law Review* 85.
12 A. Samanta *et al.*, 'The Role of Clinical Guidelines in Medical Negligence Litigation: A Shift from the *Bolam* Standard' (2006) *Medical Law Review* 321.
13 Brazier and Miola, 'Bye-Bye *Bolam*'.
14 Ibid. See *Edward Wong Finance Co.* v. *Johnston, Stokes and Master* [1984] 1 A.C. 296.
15 *Hotson* v. *East Berkshire Health Authority* [1987] A.C. 750.
16 Ibid.: 769.
17 W. Scott, 'Causation in Medico-Legal Practice: A Doctor's Approach to the "Lost Opportunity" Cases' (1992) 55 *Modern Law Review* 521.
18 *Gregg* v. *Scott* [2005] 2 A.C. 176.
19 Ibid.: 196.
20 *Chester* v. *Afshar* [2005] 1 A.C. 134.
21 *Chatterton* v. *Gerson* [1981] 1 All E.R. 257.
22 J. Miola, *On the Materiality of Risk: Paper Tigers and Panaceas* (2009) 17 *Medical Law Review* 76.
23 *Chester* v. *Afshar* [2005] 1 A.C. 153.
24 Ibid.: 146.
25 S. Sheldon, 'Rethinking the *Bolam* Test', in S. Sheldon and M. Thomson (eds), *Feminist Perspectives on Health Care Law*, London, Cavendish, 1998; and Lord Woolf, 'Are The Courts Excessively Deferential to the Medical Profession?'
26 Ibid.
27 *Learning From Bristol: The Report of the Public Inquiry into Children's Heart Surgery at the Bristol Royal Infirmary 1984–1995* (Cm 5207, 2001).
28 Ibid.: 268.
29 J. Miola, *Medical Ethics and Medical Law: A Symbiotic Relationship*, Oxford, Hart, 2007.
30 *Access to Justice – Final Report*. Online. Available HTTP http://www.dca.gov.uk/civil/final/index.htm (accessed 12 January 2010).
31 M. Bishop, 'The Negligence of Medical Experts' (2004) *BMJ* 1353.

32 *Access to Justice*, chapter 15(2).
33 For analysis, see T. Douglas, 'Medical Injury Compensation: Beyond "No-Fault"' (2009) 17 *Medical Law Review* 30.
34 Compensation Act 2006 s.1(a)–(b).
35 Ibid.: s.2.
36 E. Jackson, *Medical Law: Text, Cases and Materials*, 2nd edn, Oxford, Oxford University Press, 2010, p. 162.
37 Health Select Committee, 5 March 2009. Online. Available HTTP http://www.parliament.the-stationery-office.co.uk/pa/cm200809/cmselect/cmhealth/151/9030508.htm (accessed 13 January 2010).

Bibliography

Access to Justice – Final Report. Online. Available HTTP http://www.dca.gov.uk/civil/final/index.htm (accessed 12 January 2010).
Bishop, M., 'The Negligence of Medical Experts' (2004) *BMJ* 1353.
Brazier, M. and J. Miola, 'Bye-Bye *Bolam*: A Medical Litigation Revolution' (2000) 8 *Medical Law Review* 85.
Coleman, J., 'Second Thoughts and Other First Impressions', in B. Bix (ed.), *Analyzing Law: New Essays in Legal Theory*, Oxford, Clarendon Press, 1998.
Douglas, T., 'Medical Injury Compensation: Beyond "No-Fault"' (2009) 17 *Medical Law Review* 30.
Health Select Committee, 5 March 2009. Online. Available HTTP http://www.parliament.the-stationery-office.co.uk/pa/cm200809/cmselect/cmhealth/151/9030508.htm (accessed 13 January 2010).
Jackson, E., *Medical Law: Text, Cases and Materials*, 2nd edn, Oxford, Oxford University Press, 2010.
Learning From Bristol: The Report of the Public Inquiry into Children's Heart Surgery at the Bristol Royal Infirmary 1984–1995 (Cm 5207, 2001).
Miola, J., *Medical Ethics and Medical Law: A Symbiotic Relationship*, Oxford, Hart, 2007.
Miola, J., *On the Materiality of Risk: Paper Tigers and Panaceas* (2009) 17 *Medical Law Review* 76.
Norrie, K., 'Common Practice and the Standard of Care in Medical Negligence' (1985) *Juridical Review* 145.
Samanta, A., M. Mello, C. Foster, J. Tingle and J. Samanta, 'The Role of Clinical Guidelines in Medical Negligence Litigation: A Shift from the *Bolam* Standard' (2006) *Medical Law Review* 321.
Scott, W., 'Causation in Medico-Legal Practice: A Doctor's Approach to the "Lost Opportunity" Cases' (1992) 55 *Modern Law Review* 521.
Sheldon, S., 'Rethinking the *Bolam* Test', in S. Sheldon and M. Thomson (eds), *Feminist Perspectives on Health Care Law*, London, Cavendish, 1998.
Lord Woolf, 'Are the Courts Excessively Deferential to the Medical Profession' (2001) 9 *Medical Law Review* 1.

4 Medical ethics and patient safety

Nils Hoppe

Introduction

Reflecting on medical ethics and patient safety appears, at first glance, to be an easy task. The issue appears to be straightforward because it is surely the paramount concern of all health professionals to ensure the absolute safety of the patients in their custody. A careful second look reveals, of course, that the subject of patient safety is permeated with the same tensions that influence all areas of healthcare provision: misconceptions, conflicting interests, systemic failures and complex balancing exercises. For brevity, this discussion is limited to putting questions of patient safety, adverse incidents and different levels of actors in the context of the four principles of biomedical ethics proposed by Beauchamp and Childress:[1] respect for autonomy, nonmaleficence, beneficence and justice. As these principles have been discussed in detail elsewhere, I do not intend to revisit these principles fully in this chapter. This chapter will merely identify some of the issues arising in the debate on medical ethics and patient safety and give impetus for further discussion.

This chapter will begin with an introduction of different actors which must be considered systematically when discussing the context of patient safety and medical ethics. Individuals, institutions and society have different needs for and approaches to ethical reflections and this is the actor-based differentiation I introduce. A further element is a systematic view of the kinds of adverse incidents that might occur. A categorisation of culpable and non-culpable incidents is explored by looking at harm caused through ignorance, by negligence and by harm based on wilful acts. I will then briefly discuss Beauchamp and Childress' four principles of biomedical ethics – respect for autonomy, nonmaleficence, beneficence and justice – and put these in the context of patient safety, dealing with adverse incidents and medical ethics. From this, I will distil a number of valuable conclusions in relation to which principles of biomedical ethics are particularly promising when reflecting on patient safety. I will finish with a very brief discussion of notions of honesty and error-making in the biomedical context before reaching a number of conclusions.

Actors and adverse incidents

The relationship between medical ethics and patient safety becomes particularly visible in cases of adverse incidents. The term 'adverse incident' is used here not to trivialise the sometimes drastic consequences of risks materialising and mistakes being made in the clinical context. It is simply an appropriate label as it provides a terminological umbrella for errors, accidents, wilful acts and other categories of physician–patient interaction that result in harm. Here, different relationship threads between the physician and patient are put under tremendous tension. It is important to be clear about what is meant in this discussion as the use of terminology may lead to the formation of certain kinds of understanding and thus also to responses.[2] Medical ethics provides recourse to a number of mechanisms and principles which normatively guide our deliberations.

These principles of medical ethics govern all areas of the interaction of individuals with a health system – from the first visit to a general practitioner, seeing a specialist in a hospital to subsequent ambulatory physiotherapy. It also seems clear that these principles have differing normative weight depending on which actor applies them. Three types of actors seem intuitively appropriate: (1) individuals (doctors, nurses, etc.), (2) institutions (wards, units, hospitals, etc.) and (3) society.[3]

The idea is to prevent adverse incidents and thereby increase patient safety. For the purposes of this chapter, I assume that there is a direct causal relationship between adverse incidents and the quality of patient safety. While this may sound obvious, it appears that there is a sustained lack of robust empirical information on errors influencing patient safety made in the medical setting. This in some way limits the normative value of reflections on reasons and remedies. Even if such data were widely available it is by no means clear that there would be an appropriate ethical basis for developing a sustainable culture of patient safety.[4] Using the four principles of biomedical ethics proposed by Beauchamp and Childress is offered here as an excellent starting point in a medical ethics deliberation of patient safety.

The view of physicians making errors when treating patients is often based on a fundamental misconception. It is conceivable that healthcare providers such as hospitals should be described as high reliability organisations, in that they are organisations 'that face high intrinsic hazards yet perform successfully because they treat safety systematically'.[5] This sets up a reasonable comparison with organisations such as the aviation industry, and indeed in the context of patient safety this comparison is often drawn. This means that notions of errors and mishaps are transplanted from other contexts into the medical context without due care and attention being paid to the 'unique blend of epistemological and social factors in the practice of medicine'.[6] While it is without doubt important to bear this unique blend in mind when assessing adverse incidents, it is also subject to a certain amount of criticism. The traditional approach to patient safety in the healthcare setting was based on notions of infallibility and denial,[7] and this may well have led to a culture in which claimants' legal responses to failure had to be forceful and relentless. In an increasingly litigious society, it is therefore an understandable reaction on the part of healthcare providers to encourage individuals to follow a culture of secrecy in relation to adverse incidents for fear of crippling lawsuits,[8] and many physicians do believe that 'disclosure means exposure'.[9] In the context of discussing treatment options in a case study on a complex pregnancy, Ackerman and Strong write:

> Concern to avoid lawsuits is based on the serious harm they can cause to physicians. Even if the plaintiff does not win, being sued causes emotional stress and can threaten a physician's reputation among colleagues and patients. Meetings with lawyers and court appearances result in significant time lost from practice. There are also financial costs resulting from legal fees, diminished practice time, and occasional loss of patients because of damaged reputation.[10]

These are strong persuasive arguments for not speaking about errors one makes. If I am involved in a road traffic accident, my insurance company will refuse to cover the damage if I admit fault at the scene of the accident. Why should medicine be treated differently? Where such considerations influence a physician's decision-making processes, it invariably leads to an environment incapable of producing the kind of systemic learning curves required to prevent future harm resulting from a similar adverse incident. Institutions would be put in a position where, to avoid harm in economic and reputation terms, the disclosure of adverse incidents would have to be prohibited. This in turn leads to a society in which blame has to be strongly attributed to an individual or institution in order to obtain justice and redress for such failures. It may be a convincing argument to suggest that it is *society* which has to break this deadlock by providing a system in which more value is put on learning from failures and the disclosure of such failures is encouraged.

To make matters more complex, many clinicians are also researchers and the distinction between viewing medicine as a profession and viewing medicine as a science also plays an important role when trying to understand adverse incidents in terms of medical ethics. Gorovitz and MacIntyre convincingly argue that making errors is simply part and parcel of scientific endeavour and is in fact desirable as it inevitably leads to socially useful discoveries.[11] This discussion leads to a categorisation of the kinds of adverse incidents that might conceivably occur when treating patients: (1) incidents based simply on scientific ignorance, (2) those based in one way or another on the negligence of the physician and (3) those based on wilful acts of the actor. This categorisation can be split up into two groups: culpable and non-culpable adverse incidents. Harm resulting from objective scientific ignorance can, simply put, not be the result of culpable acts. Where the actor has negligently failed to acquaint himself with the state of the art, there may be a suggestion of culpability. Harm resulting from wilful acts is without doubt produced by a culpable act and will only be defensible – ethically and legally – in restricted circumstances. As Quick put it, '[m]uch lies between the two extremes of blame-free accident and deliberate harm'.[12] It is sensible to bear these different actors in mind when discussing medical ethics in the patient safety context: individuals act and reflect differently to institutions. Institutions can be steered in different ways to alter action pathways, whereas society cannot as easily be influenced. As is clear from this discussion, the question of harm caused directly or indirectly because of honest scientific ignorance is one which is relevant at and can only be remedied at societal level. Harm as a result of negligence can be put at the door of either institutions or individuals or both, whereas harm as a result of a wilful act will in almost all circumstances be attributable to an individual.

I will now turn to discussing these actors in the context of four basic principles of bioethics: respect for autonomy, nonmaleficence, beneficence and justice.

Respect for autonomy

Both in medical ethics and in medical law, principles of autonomy represent the nucleus of almost all determinations. I will take autonomy to mean, in this context, that an individual is *prima facie* deemed capable to identify their own values, critically reflect on these values and subsequently act or decline to act based on these values, free from undue interference. The principles which underpin the requirement to obtain appropriate consent before any medical intervention are a manifestation of such autonomy.[13] Differing views of the extent of autonomy raise a number of significant questions.[14] While it appears clear that truly autonomous decisions ought to be taken independently of undue extraneous influence, the idea very much hinges on the term 'undue'. It would be naive to suggest that agents are able to take decisions fully independently of social considerations.[15] Quite where the line is between informing an agent's autonomous decision-making process and exerting undue influence is a matter for considerable debate, particularly when one assesses what can reasonably be described as the fiction of informed consent. The quality of interaction and the imbalance of power between physician and patient often mean that informed consent in the theoretical sense is practically impossible to achieve. Second, the question whether an autonomous individual, deserving of our respect, should be capable of modifying their position on the basis of reason and critical reflection inevitably leads to a further question: does this assumption mean that in cases where the individual chooses a seemingly irrational course of action no such respect is due? Current medico-legal literature and jurisprudence suggest overwhelmingly that this is not the case: quite regardless of the irrationality of the choice, it is theoretically to be respected. See, in this context, the plethora of jurisprudence triggered by Jehovah's Witnesses' refusal of life-saving blood transfusions. Any kind of value, as long as it is the agent's own value, can be said to be consistent with the principle of autonomy and thus the beneficiary of respect. Beauchamp and Childress convincingly argue that this respect must manifest in more than just attitude.[16] In reality it is often the case that those presenting for emergency medical intervention making irrational treatment decisions are overruled on the basis that their irrational behaviour suggests a momentary loss of autonomy.

Adverse incidents caused by anything other than a wilful act do little to diminish respect for a patient's autonomy. Where an individual physician goes against a patient's express wish, however, this patient's autonomy is harmed and it is likely that, at least in medical ethics terms, this should also qualify as an 'adverse' incident. Institutions which, as a matter of policy, do not inform patients of material risks certainly do harm to patients' autonomy by depriving them of an opportunity to base their decisions on appropriately detailed information. The same is true for harm where the patient is left in the dark about the iatrogenic quality of the harm – the patient is excluded from participating in the decision-making processes in relation to his further treatment. Finally, if the reason for the institutional and individual reluctance to own up to errors is because of a societal hegemony of blame attribution, it is up to society to rectify this state of affairs, which is inherently harmful to individuals' autonomy. Respect for autonomy is a principle which, in the context of patient safety, acts very much as a precursor. While it is possible that despite an adverse incident respect for autonomy was intact, where respect for autonomy is disregarded adverse incidents are more likely. In essence, this means that individuals and institutions who carefully implement strategies for ensuring respect for autonomy are more likely to avoid adverse incidents than those who do not.

Nonmaleficence

The mantra 'first do no harm', invoked in many discussions surrounding the ethical duty a physician has towards his patient, is an expression of the principle of nonmaleficence. The obligation subsumed under this principle means that an actor has a duty to not inflict harm.[17] It becomes immediately clear that this is a matter with a number of conflicting parameters. These include the distinction between acts and omissions, the fact that harm is sometimes necessary in order to prevent more serious harm, and questions of duties and negligence. The idea of not doing harm requires, *prima facie*, simply a commitment not to intentionally act in a harmful way. It is evident that it is sometimes necessary for physicians to inflict harm in order to prevent a greater harm from occurring – the notion of nonmaleficence is therefore subject to complex balancing exercises. While the injunction 'first do no harm' suggests some sort of priority over other principles of biomedical ethics, it is evident that none of the principles overrules any other.[18]

The plausible rationale behind nonmaleficence – that of not intentionally doing harm to the patient[19] – removes this principle of biomedical ethics from the majority of adverse incident discussions. Barring circumstances such as those surrounding the case of Harold Shipman[20] and other instances of intentionally caused iatrogenic harm, adverse incidents are reduced to occurrences rooted in negligence or honest ignorance. It is unhelpful to direct an accusation of contravening the principle of nonmaleficence at a hapless surgeon when it simply was not an intentional act. This distinction applies equally in cases where a surgeon acts and causes harm and in circumstances where the surgeon fails to act and harm is the result. Foster goes so far as to suggest that the principle itself is of limited use as it does not impose any positive obligation at all: '[The principle of nonmaleficence] will not complain if a doctor does no more than to stay in bed – as long as he is not in bed with a vulnerable patient.'[21] The principle of nonmaleficence therefore only reasonably finds application in cases of individuals causing wilful harm to a patient. In narrow circumstances, institutionalised policies which actively harm individual patients may fall into this category. Society, as an actor, can reasonably be excluded from this principle. Nonmaleficence as a principle of biomedical ethics in the context of patient safety is therefore only of interest in the narrow circumstances where an individual deliberately causes an adverse incident.

Beneficence

The principle of beneficence envelops the expectation that healthcare providers actively contribute to the welfare and wellbeing of those in their custody. It also includes the job of an appropriate balance between benefits and risks or costs. Some jurisdictions have enshrined a principle of beneficence in criminal law – sometimes called the Good Samaritan law – which requires individuals to positively act for the benefit of those in need or else risk punishment. This reflects a notion of general beneficence towards the world at large, which is convincingly described as overly romantic and impractical by Beauchamp and Childress.[22]

In the biomedical context, it is fair to say that we are dealing with a more specific version of beneficence: that between individuals in a special relationship. In the same way that I have a special relationship with my brother, which puts me under a moral duty to prevent harm to him, an actor engaged in the provision of health care commits to a special relationship with a patient who presents for treatment. Foster raises the issue of the subjectivity of harm in his sweeping critique of biomedical principles: who is to say whether something is in fact harm or whether there is not some kind of countervailing benefit which cancels out the perceived harm?[23] His criticism appears to be directed at more imprecise varieties of harm. In the very clearly defined context of this chapter it is evident that harm has occurred in the shape of an adverse incident. When applying the principle of beneficence in the context of patient safety, it can be summarised as the positive duty to do what is possible to prevent harm to patients. This is a duty which can be attributed to individuals, institutions and society alike. Individual health workers are under a clear duty to do what is possible to prevent harm to those put into their care. Institutions are under a duty to create an environment which underpins the provision of high quality care and prevents harm to patients. Society is under a duty to create and maintain a health system which looks after the sick and prevents harm. From this discussion and that of the other principles to this point, it is evident that the principle of beneficence is of paramount significance in the discussions surrounding patient safety.

Justice

The notion of justice is contentious at the best of times. In its incarnation as a principle of bioethics, it encompasses the challenges of fair and equal access to health resources and the allocation of these resources. It also comprises the problem of the fair distribution of risks and costs and extends to issues of social and distributive justice. It is concerned with procuring equal treatment for all (like should be treated alike) but fans out into an array of other ethical mechanisms where there is a question not of individual justice but of justice in relation to society or a group of individuals.[24] This principle can also be applied to all three categories of actors in a useful way. Individuals tasked with looking after patients should ensure fair and just access to resources and avoid discrimination. Institutions should abide by principles of fairness and justice when providing care for patients, and society should create and maintain a framework which enables the just distribution of healthcare provision to all patients. When establishing mechanisms to augment patient safety, the element of justice takes on particular meaning. Ensuring equal access to resources, including those resources which are necessary for the prevention of harm, represents an ethically defensible level of care. Where a patient is not granted such access by an individual, an institution or society on the grounds of ethically indefensible discrimination, the likelihood of adverse incidents rises.

Honesty

Honesty is not one the principles of bioethics as outlined by Beauchamp and Childress, but in the context of providing healthcare services it plays an extremely important role. The relationship between physician and patient or between hospital and patient is characterised by a level of trust which is not found in the same way in another professional relationship. In showing this kind of trust, the patient exposes himself, or, as Quick put it, 'to trust is to risk'.[25] The effect is twofold: patients want to rest assured of the best possible treatment, while the medical profession uses this trust to underpin their professional confidence. Where honesty is lacking, trust is undermined.

This works on all actor levels to a varying degree of quality: trust between individuals is more clearly defined than between individual patients and an institution. As is set out before, the apprehension in relation to looming claims for medical negligence breeds a culture of secrecy[26] and some individual physicians would rather not be honest about the mistakes they have made for fear of being litigated against.[27] This eats away at the very system on which actor interaction in medicine is based. Quick describes it as an element of professional dominance: '[t]rust is integral to both medicine and the professional dominance thesis, which remains the most widely accepted way of conceptualising the medical profession.'[28] Professional dominance, in this context, should not merely be understood as a relationship between patients and healthcare actors. It is much more than that, namely a social mechanism by which such actors are able to operate in a stressful high-stakes environment.[29] Without the trust of the patients, the actors no longer have the capacity to act with the necessary confidence.

Additionally, the cultivation of blame-based systems within a society is held responsible for the practice of defensive medicine[30] and concealment of errors.[31] Introducing systems which provide redress but do not rely on the attribution of blame, such as no-fault liability systems, has for many years been suggested as a viable alternative.[32]

In conclusion, honesty plays a vital part in sustaining the professional trust equilibrium between patient and healthcare professional and this trust is, on the one hand, essential to encourage individuals to avail themselves of health services and, on the other, necessary to underpin the self-concept of healthcare professionals. Fault-based liability systems foster a culture which erodes the quality of honesty and trust. Where errors are systematically concealed, an error which may be based on genuine scientific ignorance becomes one of negligence when institutions and individuals fail to learn lessons. The shift to a system which encourages learning from errors rather than blaming individuals is an appropriate step towards improving patient safety.[33] On the basis of this interim conclusion, we will now briefly turn to the notion of making an error in the medical context before discussing a number of overall conclusions.

Making an error

It is by no means clear that the fact that physicians make errors is as widely accepted amongst the treatment-seeking public as it is in the context of academia.[34] The general expectation of physicians is still one of infallibility, possibly because the idea of the bumbling, incompetent or simply human physician is not one that the general public wants to contemplate. To add further to this misapprehension, physicians' unwillingness to admit errors, often based on the litigious nature of contemporary society, adds to a lack of public information on this problem.[35] What we have termed a culture of blaming individuals has been identified as one of the reasons why an appropriate learning-from-errors experience is still lacking. It is naive to assume that staff do not make mistakes. It is also naive to assume that every mistake that occurs must be attributable to individuals. A shift towards not blaming individuals for every bad event which occurs seems appropriate.[36] Even in situations where the initial error may have been made by a member of staff, it is often the institution which maintains a defective system, allowing this error to occur in the first place and then go unnoticed.[37] A recent increase in awareness of this is evident in discussions of institutionalised and systemic error attribution,[38] and it appears clear that this is the direction taken by the more promising discussions in medical ethics and medical law recently.

Adverse incidents can be avoided by individuals and institutions by implementing appropriate systems based on ethical reflections. From the point of view of individual ethics, it is sometimes a sufficient starting point if healthcare actors change their perspective to that of the patient. Berlinger and Wu deploy Bonhoeffer's ethics to argue that 'the most effective way to grasp one's ethical responsibilities ... is to see it "from the perspective of those who suffer"'.[39] While this demand represents one half of a stress ratio, with the idea of professional dominance pulling the other way, it is also clear that in the medical setting we routinely demand that actors tread an almost impossible line between compassion and detachment. It is this balance, however, which permits actors to develop appropriate ethical reflections which may guide their work. Hilfiker suggests that 'if doctors and nurses and therapists and others cannot – to some extent – see the world from the victim's [sic.] point of view, they'll have a difficult time developing an ethical framework in which to work'.[40]

Conclusion

In this chapter, I have sought to demonstrate that the principle of respect for autonomy is a valuable precursor to ethical reflection on patient safety. One conclusion taken from the discussion of autonomy is that it is likely that actors who underpin their decision-making and their policies with an ethic of respect for the autonomy of their patients are likely to augment patient safety, which means that this first principle is of great value. The proscription contained in the second principle, nonmaleficence, in contrast, comes into play in situations when actors act deliberately, which limits its use in the discussion of medical ethics to what could simply be said to be common sense: do not deliberately harm your patients. Beneficence has revealed itself to be of most use in the context of patient safety. Actors who appropriately use considerations of beneficence in their activities will develop significant awareness of ethical aspects of patient safety. This may well inform their policies in a very valuable way. The final principle, justice, deals with the fair treatment of patients by the actors and this is also an important consideration in developing ethical strategies for the augmentation of patient safety. While this appears to be common sense (and while it is clear that many legal norms for ensuring equality and fairness in health care are already widely applicable), an appropriate reflection on principles of justice is necessary to produce a coherent ethical framework. The principles of respect for autonomy and justice helpfully flank the overall deliberation of patient safety in the context of the principle of beneficence. These three principles, together with an understanding of the significance of honesty and an environment where blame is less important than learning from errors, lead to a convincing reflection of patient safety and medical ethics.[41]

Notes

1 T.L. Beauchamp and J.F. Childress, *Principles of Biomedical Ethics*, Oxford, Oxford University Press, 2001.
2 O. Quick, 'Outing Medical Errors: Questions of Trust and Responsibility', *Medical Law Review* 14, 2006, pp. 22–43 at p. 25.
3 J.W. Glaser, *Three Realms of Ethics: Individual, Institutional, Societal*, Kansas City, MO, Sheed and Ward, 1994.
4 P. Singer, 'Medical Ethics. Recent Advances', *British Medical Journal* 321, 2000, pp. 282–285 at p. 283.
5 S.J. Singer, D.M. Gaba, J.J. Geppert, A.D. Sinaiko, S.K. Howard and K.C. Park, 'The Culture of Safety: Results of an Organization-wide Survey in 15 California Hospitals', *Quality and Safety in Health Care* 12, 2006, pp. 112–118 at p. 112.
6 S. Gorovitz and A. MacIntyre, 'Toward a Theory of Medical Fallibility', *The Hastings Center Report* 5:6, 1975, pp. 13–23 at p. 13.
7 J.P. Bagian, 'Patient Safety: Lessons Learned', *Pediatric Radiology* 36, 2006, pp. 287–290 at p. 287.
8 R. Mullner, 'Patient Safety and Medication Errors', *Journal of Medical Systems* 27:6, 2003, pp. 499–501 at p. 500.
9 N. Berlinger and A.W. Wu, 'Subtracting Insult from Injury: Addressing Cultural Expectations in the Disclosure of Medical Error', *Journal of Medical Ethics* 31, 2005, pp. 106–108 at p. 106.
10 T.F. Ackerman and C. Strong, *A Casebook of Medical Ethics*, New York, Oxford University Press, 1989, p. 197.
11 Gorovitz and MacIntyre, 'Toward a Theory of Medical Fallibility', pp. 14 and 19.
12 Quick, 'Outing Medical Errors', p. 24.
13 *Schloendorff* v. *New York Hospital* [1924] 105 NE 92: also see the decision in *YF* v. *Turkey* [2004] 39 EHRR 34 (at para. 43). See the much cited dictum in *Schloendorff* v. *New York Hospital* (1924) 105 NE 92: 'Every human being of adult years and sound mind has a right to determine what shall be done with his own body; and a surgeon who performs an operation without his patient's consent, commits an assault'; also see the decision in *YF* v. *Turkey* (2004) 39 EHRR 34, where, in the context of a compulsory medical examination, the European Court of Human Rights held that 'any interference with a person's physical integrity must be prescribed by law and requires the consent of that person' (at para. 43).
14 Beauchamp and Childress, *Principles of Biomedical Ethics*, pp. 57–60.
15 A. Reath, *Autonomy. Encyclopedia of Philosophy*, London, Routledge, 1998, pp. 586–592 at p. 589.
16 Beauchamp and Childress, *Principles of Biomedical Ethics*, p.63.
17 Ibid., p.113.

18 C. Foster, *Choosing Life, Choosing Death: The Tyranny of Autonomy in Medical Ethics and Law*, Oxford and Portland, OR, Hart Publishing, 2009, p. 19.
19 Beauchamp and Childress, *Principles of Biomedical Ethics*, p.115.
20 V. English. J. Gardner, G. Romano-Critchley and A. Sommerville, 'Ethics Briefings', *Journal of Medical Ethics* 27, 2001, pp. 135–136. Shipman, a general practitioner, was found guilty of murdering 15 of his patients.
21 Foster, *Choosing Life, Choosing Death*, p.18.
22 Beauchamp and Childress, *Principles of Biomedical Ethics*, p. 169.
23 Foster, *Choosing Life, Choosing Death*, p. 18.
24 Ibid.
25 Quick, 'Outing Medical Errors', p. 23.
26 Mullner, 'Patient Safety and Medication Errors', p. 500.
27 Berlinger and Wu, 'Subtracting Insult from Injury', p. 106.
28 Quick, 'Outing Medical Errors', p.23.
29 R. Dingwall, *Essays on Professions*, Aldershot, Ashgate, 2008, pp. 127–141.
30 F.A. Sloan, K. Whetten-Goldstein, S.S. Entman, E.D. Kulas and E.M. Stout, 'The Road from Medical Injury to Claims Resolution: How No-fault and Tort Differ', *Law and Contemporary Problems* 60, 1997, pp. 35–70 at p. 36.
31 Quick, 'Outing Medical Errors', p. 27.
32 Sloan *et al.*, 'The Road from Medical Injury to Claims Resolution', pp. 35–70; M.M. Mello, D.M. Studdert, A. Kachalia and T.A. Brennan, '"Health Courts" and Accountability for Patient Safety', *Milbank Quarterly* 84, 2006, pp. 459–492.
33 D. Hindle, 'What Do Health Professionals Think about Patient Safety?', *Journal of Public Health* 16, 2008, pp. 87–96 at p. 88.
34 Quick, 'Outing Medical Errors', p. 22.
35 Gorovitz and MacIntyre, 'Toward a Theory of Medical Fallibility', p. 13.
36 J. Shook, 'Reflections of a Patient Safety Officer', *Pediatric Radiology* 38, 2008, Supplement 4, pp. S690–S692 at p. S691.
37 E. Etchells, 'Patient Safety in Surgery: Error Detection and Prevention', *World Journal of Surgery* 27, 2003, pp. 936–942 at p. 937.
38 Quick, 'Outing Medical Errors', p. 23.
39 Berlinger and Wu, 'Subtracting Insult from Injury', p. 29.
40 D. Hilfiker, 'From the Victim's Point of View', *Journal of Medical Humanities* 22, 2001, pp. 255–263 at p. 255; also cited in Berlinger and Wu, 'Subtracting Insult from Injury', p. 108; S. Buetow and G. Elwyn, 'Are Patients Morally Responsible for Their Errors?', *Journal of Medical Ethics* 32, 2006, pp. 260–262.
41 Bagian, 'Patient Safety', p.287; Mullner, 'Patient Safety and Medication Errors', p. 499; Bagian, 'Patient Safety', p. 288 (in analogy to the aviation industry); J. Miola, *Medical Ethics and Medical Law: A Symbiotic Relationship*, Oxford, Hart Publishing, 2007, p. 54.

5 Psychological aspects of patient safety

Pippa Bark

When care goes wrong, patients and carers may suffer extreme distress both from the care they receive and the way it is handled. Staff are also highly affected by the unintentional harm to, or even the death of, a patient. Distress may then be compounded by the patient safety, complaints or litigation processes that follow. Those individuals involved in medical accidents may face clinical, emotional and practical consequences. In recognition of this, over the past 10 years policy documents[1] have acknowledged the human suffering experienced by patients, carers and healthcare staff when something goes wrong. There has been a national drive to improve patient safety, with improved incident reporting, openness and fair blame policies and improved processes for handling complaints and litigation. It is notable, however, that whilst patient distress is readily acknowledged, policies focus on informing the patient after an adverse event and the need to communicate with the patient and carers, and there is little focus on the emotional aspects or how to deal with them psychologically. Similarly, whilst the healthcare professional involved, sometimes referred to as the second victim, is now routinely mentioned, policy has focussed on openness, fair blame and encouraging reporting. However, there has been little written on emotional impact and this may be the key to understanding why some staff are reluctant to fully engage with the patient safety initiatives.

Unless we are aware of the experiences of all involved, it will not be possible to comprehend why policies are not fully implemented or what policies may be needed in the future. This chapter is written in three sections: the first will examine the issues and reactions of patients and carers who have experienced poor healthcare and who may then be caught up in complaints or litigation processes. There are still many who have not experienced the benefits of the policies and we need to be mindful of any gaps between policy and practice. The second section considers what happens to the staff involved in these circumstances. In particular, the psychological processes that affect how people cope by distancing or blaming will be highlighted. Finally, the third section will look at what support is in place to help those involved.

This chapter therefore discusses a neglected area in patient safety: patient, carer and staff reactions in the aftermath of medical mistakes. Research is surprisingly limited in this area, with very little on litigants' experiences or patients' involvement in root cause analysis or other patient safety initiatives. However, there has been an increased recognition in certain areas, namely the effect on staff and the importance of openness.

The experience of patients and carers

The effects of being harmed by treatment

Patients harmed, albeit unintentionally, by their medical care differ from those who suffer from other accidents; they are likely to have been unwell to start with and therefore physically and emotionally vulnerable. In addition, the trust they put in the professionals helping them has been unintentionally damaged. Although 56 per cent of those who have experienced an adverse event have no effects or a minor disability, 19 per cent suffer a temporary disability, 7 per cent permanent disability and tragically 7 per cent die.[2] After an incident the patient and their carers may be facing the ramifications of unexpected time in hospital, increased pain, worsening of their condition, additional operations and potentially a worsening prognosis. It should be remembered that this is in addition to the illness that the person was initially dealing with. This clearly has the potential to impact on quality of life, with effects on work, finance and relationships. Traumatic and life-threatening events produce reactions in any case, so since routine procedures[3] or normal childbirth[4] can result in potentially serious emotional reactions, it is not surprising that those who experience the results of a medical error suffer.

Descriptions of patient and carer reactions typically come from research on complainants[5] or litigants.[6] In an early study of 491 complainants[7] the physical effects of treatment were clear; 49 per cent reported a need for additional medical treatment, 42 per cent reported that the patient's condition had worsened as a result of treatment and 36 per cent said that unexpected side effects had been experienced. In 5 per cent of cases the patient had died. Complaints arose from serious incidents, generally a clinical problem combined with staff insensitivity and poor communication. Clinical complaints were seldom about a clinical incident alone (11 per cent); most (72 per cent) included a clinical component and dissatisfaction with personal treatment of the patient or care. All described some level of suffering as a result of the incident, with strong feelings of anger, distress, worry and depression. Over one-third (36 per cent) reported feeling humiliated. Complainants frequently described the frustration with the process itself and some felt further mistrust of the health service they were reliant on.

Since this study, government policy has striven to create a single approach to dealing with complaints. New regulations for handling NHS and adult social care complaints came into effect on 1 April 2009, giving organisations the flexibility to deal with complaints effectively under the

Local Authority Social Services and National Health Service Complaints (England) Regulations 2009.[8] These aim to encourage a culture that seeks and uses people's experiences to make services more effective, personal and safe. Over 90 health and social care organisations have tested the approach and there is a guide to help complaints professionals work with colleagues to improve listening, responding and learning from people's experiences. It is designed to be accessible to anyone working in health and social care organisations who is involved in receiving feedback and resolving concerns and complaints from patients, service users and their representatives. Additional advice sheets for complaints professionals have also been produced, covering a range of issues.

This more patient-centred approach is mirrored in the advice from the key regulating bodies, including the Medical Defence Union, the Medical Protection Society and the General Medical Council, signifying a change in attitude. One such example is the Medical Protection Society's website's[9] advice to practitioners on how to approach complaints: 'Sometimes, acknowledging that the person's feelings of frustration or anger at what happened are real and understandable, regardless of whether the complaint is justified or not, is enough to defuse the situation.'

There have been few studies on medical litigants despite the impetus to find ways to reduce medical negligence claims. In one of the few in-depth studies[10] of 277 litigants, over 70 per cent were seriously affected by incidents that gave rise to litigation, with long-term effects on work, social life and family relationships. Intense emotions were aroused and continued to be felt for a long time. The decision to take legal action was determined not only by the original injury, but also by insensitive handling and poor communication after the original incident. In addition, a protracted battle with the health service or through the courts is emotionally draining, and due to the length of time it takes support from family and friends may dwindle.[11] One of the improvements patients and carers felt could be made was an appreciation of the severity of the trauma they had suffered.[12]

Depression

The full impact of some incidents, and the attendant reactions, may only become apparent over time. For example, a surgical mishap may result in the need for further operations and time in hospital. In one case, a mismanaged pressure ulcer of a paralysed patient resulted in an additional three operations, a 14 inch scar and a further five months of bed rest in hospital. She reports that missing her son's 10th birthday because of this was one her lowest points and was one of the only times she cried in hospital.

Depression is a common response to medical injury and more typical than post-traumatic stress disorder.[13] Whether people become depressed depends, amongst other things, on the degree of injury and the level of support from family, friends and health professionals.[14] Sudden, intense and uncontrollable

events are particularly likely to lead to psychological problems,[15] with awareness under anaesthesia being one example. Anxiety, intrusive and disturbing
memories, emotional numbing and flashbacks may be experienced. As with
any stressful event these will fade with time; however, they can be deeply
unpleasant and prolonged.

Bereavement

In a study of significant mistakes made by 254 junior doctors,[16] patients had
had serious adverse outcomes in 90 per cent of cases and death had occurred
in 31 per cent. In these cases, the trauma for those left behind and the staff
involved is obviously severe.

Where the patient dies, those suddenly bereaved may struggle to come
to terms with the loss and make sense of what may have been avoidable.
Bereavement reactions, as described in the Kübler-Ross[17] stage theory of
grief, are familiar to those in the health service: denial–dissociation–isolation,
anger, bargaining, depression and acceptance. Whilst each person will experience things differently, these are seen as typical reactions for many groups
relevant to patient safety: terminally ill patients' awareness of their impend-
ing death,[18] children's reactions to parental separation,[19] and clinical staffs'
reactions to the death of an inpatient.[20] It is likely that there will be similar
patterns for family and carers dealing with a death after an adverse event.
Many people who have lost a loved one in an accident ruminate on the accident for years after seeking to work out what could have been done to prevent
it or in a struggle to find meaning. Some may blame themselves; others may
apportion blame:

> I know there wasn't a dry eye in the whole entire room when I was
> telling them about the guilt that I had felt and then [the doctor] said
> that it had nothing to do with me and it wasn't my fault.[21]

Often it may be difficult ever to ascertain whether death or disability could
be avoided, and the litigation that sometimes accompanies such cases as a
way of finding resolution and financial support may prolong grief and guilt
for the family and staff.[22]

Death in childbirth or death of a child may be particularly hard to bear as
joy and the promise of a new life end in tragedy.[23] Vincent[24] presents the
heartbreaking description of Jamie's father, who lost his son at two months
after he sustained a spinal cord injury at birth due to inadequate obstetric care:

> Mr Carter's reaction to Jamie's death was intense, violent and pro-
> longed. For a year he suffered from disturbing memories and horrific
> dreams. He became quiet and withdrawn and remote from his wife,
> feeling 'empty and hopeless'. He was tormented by disturbing images
> and memories of Jamie, of the birth, of his slow death and particularly

of his small, shrunken skull toward the end. He suffered from stress related stomach disorder. His sleep was interrupted by violent night-mares of a kind never experienced before. During the day violent images came into his head that horrified him. 'I was really angry all the time, so aggressive – I wanted to hurt people, and I'm not like that at all. I felt I had to blame someone all the time for everything.' Two years later, he is a sadder and quieter person. The anger he feels at the grave subsides.[25]

Patients' confidence and trust

One of the keystones in maintaining a relationship with the patient or carer, especially after an adverse event, is trust. The impact of an adverse event is strong since in many cases the patient is reliant on further care from, if not the same people, the same profession. They may have conflicting feelings about those involved which can be very hard to resolve, even if the staff are sympathetic and supportive. The basic essentials of confidence and trust are currently being tackled by the Department of Health in its *Confidence in Caring Project Overview*.[26] It stresses the importance of building and maintaining the relationship through:

- a calm, clean, safe environment;
- a positive, friendly culture;
- good team-working and good relationships;
- well-managed care with efficient delivery;
- personalised care for and about every patient.

There is, in many places, still a disparity between the ideals and the reality.

The reliance on care, particularly at a time of vulnerability, is likely to be part of the reason why the majority of people who have received substandard care do not complain. Whilst in hospital they are fearful of ramifications were they to voice concerns. Once home, many want to get on with their lives or cannot see what they would get out of complaining. One such example took place in a London trust.

A woman who received no post-operative checks and minimal nursing care in a teaching hospital following major abdominal surgery felt intimi-dated by nursing staff after being snapped at and then witnessing a fellow ward member being shouted at for asking for analgesia. As a result, until the next shift came on, she emptied her own urine bags and changed her own soiled sheets. Despite her resolution that she would never return to that hos-pital again, when asked to complete a patient survey form she answered in a surprisingly positive light. When asked why, she reported that she wanted the nurses to be kind to her, and since the survey was not asking about her issues the target questions about welcome, cleanliness and so on could all be rated well. She had no confidence that her fundamental concerns would be heard in a constructive way. Once home, she stated that she wanted to get on with her life. These patient experiences are particularly sobering for those staff involved in collecting patient data who genuinely believe that patients will be able to express their concerns. The *Confidence in Caring* document specifically mentions handling concerns before they become complaints, and yet the department was, I suspect, unaware of many failings.

Openness

Open Disclosure has been one of the major shifts over the last decade, with the principles ingrained in policy in Australia,[27] the USA,[28] Canada[29] and Britain.[30,31] Within the policy is an explicit statement that patients will be told as soon as possible after an event. In England and Wales, the NPSA's *Being Open Framework* (2009) has provided a set of principles describing how NHS staff need to communicate with patients, their families and carers when something goes wrong. This framework is supported by policy makers, professional bodies, and litigation and indemnity bodies. The NPSA's Chief Executive Martin Fletcher said:

> Discussing patient safety incidents promptly, fully and compassionately is the best way to support patients and staff when something does go wrong. Evidence from other countries shows that by following the principles of Being open, formal complaints and litigation claims can also be reduced.[32]

However, the extent to which individuals follow these policies may vary greatly. In a study considering cataract surgery,[33] 92 per cent of patients believed that a patient should always be told if a complication has occurred, compared to only 60 per cent of ophthalmologists, The ophthalmologists who did not believe that patients should always be told replied either that the patient should never be told or that it depended on the circumstances; 81 per cent of patients, but only 33 per cent of ophthalmologists, believed that a patient should not only be informed of a complication but also be given detailed information on possible adverse outcomes. In a more recent Australian interview study,[34] 22 out of 23 participants appreciated the opportunity to meet with staff and have the adverse event explained to them. However, they had some concerns about how Open Disclosure was being enacted: disclosure was not occurring promptly or was seen as too informal; disclosure was not being adequately followed up with tangible support or a change in practice; staff were not offering an apology; and there were not opportunities for consumers to meet with the staff originally involved in the adverse event. They found that a combination of formal Open Disclosure, a full apology and an offer of tangible support had a higher chance of a success than if one of these components was absent. Iedema and colleagues[35] concluded that staff need to become more attuned in their disclosure communication to the victims' perceptions and experience of adverse events, to offer an appropriate apology, to support victims long-term as well as short-term, and to consider using consumers' insights into adverse events for the purpose of service improvement.[36]

When staff are proactive in coming forward, acknowledging the damage and taking action, the support offered can ameliorate the harm[37] both for patients and for the staff themselves. Staff report a sense of relief in being true to themselves and in being free to offer the level of care and caring that they would normally provide. Although fears of restrictions from the trust or legal, insurance or financial bodies are seen as hampering what would be seen by some staff as a mere extension of routine good care, there has been considerable progress in encouraging openness.

It is too early to judge the extent to which policy meets reality. On recent training courses, British risk managers freely discussed reservations about full openness. They describe the norm as being that patients are told when there is a bad outcome; however, in cases of a minor negative outcome or a near miss many would regard it as inappropriate to tell the patient. They indicated that the culture of their organisations would support this selective approach. Action against Medical Accidents (AvMA), a charitable organisation set up to assist patients, still receives 5,000 cases a year.[38] The experiences of their clients appear to indicate that there is still some way to go, with carers and patients commenting that it was only with the support of the organisation that they reached a satisfactory conclusion:

> Mr B, an otherwise fit and strong gentleman of 71 years of age, underwent surgery for cancer of the oesophagus in 2002. The procedure involved the use of a nasogastric tube. It was apparent to the family after the operation that something had gone very wrong. Mr B became very seriously ill and, after suffering terribly, died five months later. The family asked the hospital for an investigation. When the hospital replied it explained that a hole had been made in Mr B's stomach when the nasogastric tube was replaced (against all guidelines) when it had come out. Although the Chief Executive expressed his and the staff's sincere condolences, there was no apology for the error itself which had brought about Mr B's death. There was no assurance given that steps would be taken to prevent similar errors in the future. There was no suggestion that Mr B's family should be entitled to compensation or should seek independent legal advice.[39]

The majority of investigative effort goes into cases where the outcome has been severe; however, despite recommendations about the benefit of involving patients and carers in patient safety initiatives[40] some staff are fearful of involving people who may be upset by an investigation and who may additionally complain or sue. As such, even in severe cases, patients and carers may not be involved and their anger and mistrust may grow over time if they are unaware of what is going on to resolve the situation.

In a tragic case where a mother and baby had died from a rare undiagnosed condition, described by Vincent and Page,[41] the first responses by staff to the deaths were seen as timely and appropriate. The widower and father of the baby was seen by senior clinicians, who expressed their sorrow and a commitment to a thorough investigation with open feedback. Although the clinicians concluded their investigation within appropriate timescales, the hospital faced potential litigation and there were considerable delays in the process of approval from a higher organisational level. There was also anxiety about sharing the report with the widower, which led to severe delay. These delays added to his grief and eventually he became extremely angry. By the time the report was released, relationships with him were strained and trust had been eroded. Soon after, he started legal proceedings. His grief was intensified and, rather than being supported by the organisation, he found himself in conflict with it.

Whilst seeking an apology is common, whether the apology is successful depends on the timing, the sincerity and who the apology is received from. In an investigation on forgiveness, John McCarthy, the journalist who was kidnapped, talked about how it was possible to forgive actions that had been done to oneself, but much harder, and sometimes impossible, to forgive those that affected our near ones. Whilst the circumstances are hugely different, as many complaints or lawsuits are delivered by carers or parents, one facet to take into account is the anger and helplessness felt by those attempting to help their charges. It may be that complaints delivered by the patient themselves are easier to resolve than those delivered by a representative.

The experience of healthcare staff

There is no doubt that patients and carers experience distress, sometimes extreme, both from a problem in the care they receive and from the way it is handled. At the same time, healthcare staff, who are by the nature of the service already in a stressful environment, also experience distress at having made an error and the attendant after-effects. Unless we are aware of what happens to all involved, it will not be possible to comprehend why policies are not fully implemented or what policies may be needed in the future. The second section then will consider what happens to the staff involved in these circumstances. In particular, the psychological processes that affect how people cope by distancing or blaming will be highlighted.

Staff distress about errors

A survey in 2007 of 3,171 physicians[42] working in internal medicine, paediatrics, family medicine and surgery examined how errors affected five work and life domains. Physicians reported increased anxiety about future errors (61 per cent), a loss of confidence (44 per cent), sleeping difficulties (42 per cent), reduced job satisfaction (42 per cent) and harm to their reputation (13 per cent) following errors. Their job-related stress increased when they had been involved in a serious error. In addition, one-third of physicians involved only in near misses also reported increased stress.

> Virtually every practitioner knows the sickening realisation of making a bad mistake. You feel singled out and exposed, seized by the instinct to see if anyone has noticed. You agonise about what to do, whether to tell anyone, what to say. Later, the event replays itself over and over in your mind. You question your competence but fear being discovered. You know you should confess, but dread the prospect of potential punishment and of the patient's anger. You may become overly attentive to the patient or family, lamenting the failure to do so earlier and, if you haven't told them, wondering if they know.[43]

The very nature of medicine means that errors will happen some of the time, and yet there is an expectation that medical staff should be so skilled and technology so advanced that bad outcomes should not happen. Training focuses on error free practice, where individuals strive for perfection, and where mistakes are seen as unacceptable and considered a failure of character. This is compounded in that role models reinforce these notions and, whilst the patient safety policy and research literature accept that good people will make mistakes, in reality this is only partially realised. One consultant commented that '[i]n the past we were treated as gods but forgiven our mistakes: today we are treated as technicians and expected to be perfect'.

Stress is high for healthcare professionals and it is known that making mistakes is a major stressor.[44] At the same time, the personal distress caused by being highly stressed makes an individual more likely to make errors, thus creating a vicious circle.[45] Where individuals perceived themselves to have made an error there were measures of decreased quality of life, increased burnout, symptoms of depression and a decline in empathy.

The extent to which a mistake impacts on staff depends on the circumstances. It will be found to be more traumatic if:

- there is a severe outcome;
- there has been close involvement with the patient;
- there is anger or distress from the patient or family;
- colleagues are critical;
- the action was a departure from the clinician's usual practice;
- the practitioner has a self-critical personality;
- there is a lack of support from family/friends/colleagues;
- the practitioner does not discuss concerns with others;
- there is a complaint or litigation.

A bad outcome resulting from making a mistake will intensify the health professional's reaction as well as the judgements of their peers. Psychiatrists dealing with patient suicide[46] will see themselves as personally responsible, with attendant feelings of blame and anxiety. They may experience irritability at home, be less able to deal with their own family, have poor sleep patterns and low moods. They themselves may become preoccupied with suicidal thoughts and have decreased self-confidence that extends beyond work.

It is not unusual for clinicians to respond to their own mistakes with anger and sometimes by projecting the blame onto someone else.[47] This could be another health professional, and at times it can be the patient. Some may blame or scold the patient or other members of the healthcare team. Some may act defensively or callously. In the long run some physicians are deeply wounded by their experience, lose their nerve, burn out or seek solace in alcohol or drugs. As Wu points out, this is likely to include some of the most reflective and sensitive colleagues. When junior doctors discussed their emotions after significant errors, they were most likely to report feelings of remorse, anger, guilt and inadequacy.[48] A few house officers reported the persistent negative psychological impact of mistakes, some after the death of a patient, leading to avoidance or unease about their specialty.

There is mixed evidence on whether openness helps physicians. Whilst some proponents have advocated that it provides relief to the staff member to be true to themselves,[49] Waterman *et al.*[50] found that physicians who were satisfied with their disclosure of a serious error to a patient were no less distressed than physicians who did not disclose. Even errors with minimal or no impact on patients had lasting impacts on physicians: physicians felt more distressed when they had disclosed a minor error or near miss to their patient than physicians who did not disclose: 'Patients who respond angrily to disclosure add coal to the fire of the physician's distress.' Clearly, disclosing errors will be highly emotive for both patients and staff in some cases. Whether the openness policy is beneficial to individual staff members may be a reflection of the quality of the disclosure,[51] the level of training in handling this situation and the level of support.

Wu[52] discusses the effect of peer responses in the aftermath. He points out that unconditional sympathy and support are rare. Reassurance from colleagues is often grudging or qualified. One way to face guilt after a serious error is through confession, restitution and absolution; however, this is discouraged by the lack of appropriate forums for discussion and risk managers and hospital lawyers. There are no institutional mechanisms to aid the grieving process. Morbidity and mortality meetings examine medical facts rather than the feelings of the patient/physician. As a result of this, it is not surprising that physicians find ways to protect themselves, some of them dysfunctional.

Despite the evolution of a systems approach and the encouragement of a fairer culture, peer disapproval and personal shame still exist. Peters *et al.*[53] suggest that identifying scapegoats serves a defensive function. A belief that risk lies with the individual nurse or doctor means that once the operator is removed, for retraining, transfer or dismissal, the risk is eradicated. The alternative of attributing the cause to organisational deficiencies such as poor communication, inadequate equipment or training offers little comfort until the weaknesses are addressed and fixed.

Staff distress about litigation and media coverage

As with the patients, litigation compounds distress. Reports of prevalence are higher than might perhaps be expected. An English study[54] found that 49 per cent of senior surgeons and 23 per cent of senior doctors in the medical specialties reported having been involved in litigation. More recently in Australia,[55] 60 per cent of GPs reported being sued.

Despite the increase in patient safety activity, the last three decades have seen few changes in reactions to being involved in litigation. In the 1980s Charles and colleagues[56] revealed that more than 95 per cent of American physicians experienced periods of distress during the lengthy process of litigation: 'This may begin...by a sense of outrage, shock, or dread about the personal and financial effects of the eventual outcome. Feelings of intense anger, frustration, inner tension, and insomnia are frequent throughout this period.' Depressive disorder, adjustment disorder and the onset or exacerbation of a physical illness occurred. In an English study[57] in the late 1990s, 79 per cent of senior doctors reported experiencing distress from being involved in litigation. The lawsuit itself affected work, but also life more generally and home relationships. Doctors reported feeling angry, guilty and ashamed. Some lost confidence. With financial implications for the health service, almost one-fifth of consultants wanted to give up medicine. This does not of course take into account those who had already done so.

It would appear that the patient safety initiatives have more to do to alleviate the distress. An Australian survey of 566 GPs in Sydney[58] showed that doctors currently involved in malpractice litigation had high rates of psychiatric problems, such as depression, and alcoholism. They also had significant impairment in work, social and family life compared to doctors who were not subject to litigation. Male doctors who had been involved in medicolegal actions in the past had significantly higher rates of alcohol use than doctors with no history of litigation. Even when the action was over, doctors had higher rates of depression and disability than doctors who had no history of litigation. One of the limitations of these findings is that we cannot infer anything about causality. We do not know whether the litigation caused the distress or whether attendant problems put the practitioner at higher risk of error and/or litigation.

In addition to the litigation, there may be negative media coverage – not everyone understands that one incident may be against a backdrop of an unblemished career or that a tragedy may have been unavoidable. And 37 per cent of claims are made when an error has not occurred.[59] The shame compounds whatever emotions the practitioner had over the original care:

We live at a time when blame and retribution are prominent in media coverage of what has gone wrong. It is important that there should be proper accountability, but we also have to ask whether the climate of blame and retribution can go too far.[60]

Human biases versus fair blame

Unsafe care can arise from human error in a weak system and from poorly performing doctors. The risks posed by the former are many times greater than those posed by the latter.[61] For a systems approach to work, there has to be a distinction between failures that arise because of weaknesses in a complex system and those that are the result of individual deficiencies.[62] Whilst there are a few poor doctors and nurses who are involved in a disproportionate number of cases, this is unlikely to account for the high number of adverse events. In addition, in cases where an inexperienced individual has been found wanting it is not unusual to find that others have made the same mistake previously. Making this distinction is made more difficult by the natural tendency to take mental shortcuts to understand one's own or others' behaviour. Parker *et al.*[63] summarise the principal biases that contribute to the natural tendency to judge or blame, inherent biases that need to be understood in any investigation if a fair blame culture is to work.

Fundamental attribution error is the tendency to explain the behaviour of others by focussing on characteristics such as personality, intelligence or status, but to use situational factors to explain our own behaviour. For example, I may consider you made an error because you were a nurse (status), but I made the error because of long hours (situation). A second bias is the belief that we 'get what we deserve'. This enables us to feel protected from chance outcomes. The more serious the outcome, the more likely we are to judge the individual as inappropriate, regardless of the professional's actions or decisions. In one experiment, anaesthesiologists changed their judgement on the appropriateness of care if they were told that the outcome was permanent rather than temporary.[64] Nurses attached more importance to the error if the outcome was severe.[65]

If there is a severe outcome, the behaviour of healthcare professionals is rated as more risky and inappropriate.[66] Judgements of responsibility (blame) are greater and judgements of appropriateness are less favourable.[67] Deviations from normal practice are deemed to be more blameworthy than either error or compliance with the protocol or guideline, irrespective of outcome.[68] This is particularly relevant for those interested in root cause analysis, who are trained to look at the secondary gain (the motivation) for deviating from practice.

Cognitive biases also lead to blame.[69] People defend themselves when a colleague is involved in an adverse outcome by distancing themselves. One strategy is to maintain an unrealistic level of optimism by thinking it could not happen to you, so that when a peer makes a mistake, others may deny personal vulnerability to the same sort of negative outcome. This is apparent when smokers, heart patients, motorcyclists and so on consider themselves at less risk than others. In terms of adverse events, this means that health professionals convince themselves the same outcome would not have occurred had they been the attendant clinician. Another strategy is the illusion of control – this is a tendency to believe that we have more control than similar others (through experience, skill or efficiency, for example) and hence could have avoided a poor outcome. These biases minimise our sense of vulnerability to negative events, but foster unsympathetic responses.

We can therefore predict that when the outcome is serious or when there has been a deviation from standard practice, colleagues are likely to reassure themselves that it could not happen to them and to engage in blame. This will have ramifications for the individual:

> When I was a house officer another resident failed to identify electrocardiac signs of the pericardial tamponade that would rush the patient to the operating theatre later. The news spread rapidly, the case was tried repeatedly before an incredulous jury of peers who returned a summary judgement of incompetence.[70]

Supporting patients, carers and healthcare staff

Organisational trust

The key to avoiding awakening shame is to foster trust at a deep organisational level.[71] Psychologists have demonstrated the benefits of trust for group cohesion and organisational effectiveness, core factors in patient safety, and teams that have a high level of trust report errors more frequently. Staff can tell the truth, and can enhance their reputation by having the confidence to admit to errors rather than providing a front of error free practice.[72] When examining what makes doctors more likely to make constructive changes in practice after a significant mistake, extensive discussions were likely to lead to a positive change, whereas perceptions that the institution responded judgementally led to defensive changes.[73] One resident expressed the desire for more discussion so that 'some of the unsaid horrors of our experiences can be discussed and dealt with'.

The NHS remains largely unsupportive of whistle-blowing, with many staff fearing the consequences of going outside official channels to highlight unsafe care.[74] Hence staff need to be able to have confidence that they are seen by management not as telling tales on colleagues but as protecting patients, that patient safety action will be seen as a result of their reporting, and that their reputation will be enhanced by honest reporting.

Management must be trusted to be open and fair about the handling of error throughout the organisation, investigate with care, integrity and sensitivity, not harm the one who reports, treat the error fairly, use the information to improve patient safety, and trust staff to provide accurate data.[75] In some trusts, boards are experienced as having a policing role rather than as being part of the patient safety process. In the endorsement of the safer patient initiatives, the House of Parliament pointed out that '[b]oards too often believe that they are discharging their responsibilities in respect of patient safety by addressing governance and regulatory processes, when they should actually be promoting tangible improvements in services'.[76] They recommended, amongst other things, that boards banish the blame culture and provide leadership to harness the enthusiasm of staff to improve safety. To borrow the words of Firth-Cozens, 'trust is fragile but essential'.[77]

If trust is present at an organisational level and staff feel confident and supported, there is a far higher chance that patients' needs will be met. Recent policy developments have aimed at increasing public trust in the drive to be more open with patients, both in terms of their own treatment and in terms of the service in general (e.g. *High Quality Care for All*, 2008; NPSA's *Being Open Framework*, 2009). If, in parallel to this, staff are trained and supported, the policies are more likely to be fully implemented. This is a significant shift over the past decade.

Removing barriers to talking to the patients

Appreciating the depth of the distress is a key factor in restoring patient confidence and many have derived comfort from the empathy or staff sadness at the experience. The NHSLA circular released in May 2009 has provided confirmation that clinicians do not need to fear the ramifications of doing so:

> It is both natural and desirable for clinicians who have provided treatment which produces an adverse result, for whatever reason, to sympathise with the patient or the patient's relatives; to express sorrow or regret at the outcome; and to apologise for shortcomings in treatment. It is most important to patients that they or their relatives receive a meaningful apology. We encourage this, and stress that apologies do not constitute an admission of liability. In addition, it is not our policy to dispute any payment, under any scheme, solely on the grounds of such an apology.[78]

One common theme from interviews with patients injured by their care is that the professionals made great efforts to deal with their medical symptoms but omitted to ask about their mental state.[79] Although *Being Open* talks about 'practical and emotional support', the advice focuses on practical issues or on providing support contacts. Vincent's recommendation to ask about crucial areas such as depression, anger or loss of trust without the fear of 'making things worse' is a useful reminder of how to resolve conflict and demonstrate caring.

Training

The communication skills for successful disclosure are specific since this is about an issue (1) which is likely to be emotive for the healthcare professional and the patient or carers and (2) where the professional may be the target of the expressed distress. Only 18 per cent of physicians in Waterman's survey had received education or training on disclosing errors to patients, while 86 per cent were somewhat or very interested in receiving it. To lessen the chance of disclosure going poorly, Waterman suggests that patient safety specialists and risk managers be present when disclosure occurs to respond to patient questions, debrief with the physician afterwards, and provide professional reaffirmation and support for the physicians.

By routinely offered training in dealing with the process, from the point of disclosing the error through to the root cause analysis and potential litigation, some of the unknown can be dealt with. The NPSA's Being Open policy is one example of providing guidance on communicating with patients, their families and carers following a patient safety incident. It offers the following:

- training workshops on *Being Open* for healthcare professionals that incorporate video and actor role-playing methods;
- an e-learning tool: *Being open*;
- training for root cause analysis;
- an e-learning tool: a guide to root cause analysis from the NPSA;
- the Incident Decision Tree.

Studies to evaluate the effects of interventions to support physicians are rare, though measures such as including patient safety in medical curricula and training, mentoring and, above all, a change in culture have been suggested to alleviate the emotional distress of physicians.

Patient and carer support

Injured patients can receive support from family, friends, colleagues, doctors or organisations. As Vincent highlights,[80] an especially important source of support will be from those who are involved in the treatment where possible. It is vital that staff do not withdraw from the patient due to guilt, anger or embarrassment. If care was substandard, the patient must be offered a referral elsewhere; however, if the incident is dealt with effectively the relationship can be maintained and trust restored.

With the relatively new literature on supporting healthcare staff, there is a risk of a belief that we already have robust systems for patient and carer support. However, despite some significant progression in dealing with incidents, there appears to be an assumption that adequate support is in place.

Without current research on this, there is the likelihood that interventions will not be as adequate as hoped.

Healthcare staff support

The marked increase in papers describing the effect of errors on healthcare staff suggests that culturally we are already becoming more accepting of the fact that healthcare staff suffer and, by implication, will need support.

On the whole, team members, other clinicians and family and friends tend to be the most common and effective source of help. Colleagues are invaluable because they know what it is like to take such responsibility and their support mitigates the sense of professional isolation that can be felt. Friends and family offer an equally vital role in bringing comfort.[81] We do know, however, that colleagues are not always nonjudgemental and that it is unwise to assume that this ad hoc approach is sufficient. In a study of staff reactions to suicides,[82] psychiatrists felt that it was important that additional access to more formal counselling or debriefing was on offer.

As with talking to patients, sensitivity to language will play a large part in how supportive an encounter is found to be. Some trusts avoid referring to 'errors'; others focus on what was done and not who did it.

Many doctors have been through litigation, whether as an expert witness or as a defendant, and could be tapped as a source of support. One Being Open policy initiative has encouraged the role of senior clinical counsellors. Senior clinical counsellors are to provide mentoring and support to their colleagues by:

- mentoring colleagues during their first discussion;
- advising on the process;
- being accessible to colleagues prior to initial and subsequent discussions;
- facilitating the initial team and debriefing meetings;
- signposting the support services for colleagues;
- mentoring colleagues to become senior clinical counsellors.

Counselling

Since it is unusual for staff to be routinely offered personal support,[83] a starting point would be to consider what talking therapy would be acceptable for healthcare staff involved in an incident. In an American and Canadian study,[84] the majority of doctors involved in serious events (80 per cent) expressed interest in counselling and few physicians (10 per cent) believed that healthcare organisations adequately supported them in coping with error-related stress. However, there were some reservations when support services were available: physicians felt that taking time off for counselling was difficult (43 per cent), expressed concerns that counselling would not be helpful (35 per cent), that confidentiality would be breached if they were sued (35 per cent) and that their counselling history would be placed in their permanent record (34 per cent). In addition, 18 per cent feared being judged negatively by their colleagues for receiving counselling.

Whilst there is no doubt that most hospitals will already have professionals with the expertise to provide support, such as counsellors, psychologists and psychiatrists, the majority are reluctant to use the services because of doubts about their value and confidentiality, and because of personal barriers such as shame, denial and reluctance to appear weak. A link with an outside contact might be useful when staff feel responsible for a serious injury or death.[85]

Peer counselling groups run by respected healthcare professionals might be one model of emotional support for physicians; however, although there is some support for them, they are not commonly used in Britain. In America,[86] peer counsellor training was set up to handle emotional stress brought on by adverse medical events, and they launched a peer support team project for Brigham and Women's Hospital which then became a hospital-wide initiative.

Self-care for healthcare staff

Whilst many of the strategies mentioned focussed on dealing with process afterwards, West *et al.*[87] also mention the importance of preventative or preparatory action. First, they recommend specific curricula on personal awareness and self-care to promote strategies for coping with the emotional impact of errors. They comment that these are needed but have been slow to develop. Second, programmes are needed to prevent, identify and treat burnout and to promote empathy and well-being for the welfare of staff and patients.

Conclusions

There have been huge strides in the last two decades in acknowledging the emotional impact of an adverse event on patients, carers and staff. Policies routinely mention the importance of supporting patients and staff and have focussed on providing frameworks (e.g. complaints, litigation, Seven Steps to Patient Safety, root cause analysis, Manchester Patient Safety Framework, Being Open) and training (e.g. Foresight Training, Patient Safety First 'How-to' guides) for bringing about a consistent patient safety approach. There is much to be proud of; however, there is still a gap between policy and practice in some areas. Open disclosure may not be as common as or of the quality intended. The emotional support of individuals can be a hit or miss approach. Fair blame in policy documents is not always experienced as such by the recipients, and blame can inappropriately overshadow systems analysis at times. Some patients feel let down. Many staff may naturally feel defensive. Studies of staff involved in litigation suggest that distress remains high, and studies of patients and carers involved in litigation are rare.

The initiatives have begun a promising journey towards patient safety and many of the frameworks have potential. In terms of the emotional reactions, there needs to be organisational trust – without this, staff will not have the confidence to be open, and patients will not receive appropriate openness and support. In-depth training for staff needs to be set up, and these training programmes need to be piloted for efficacy. There is more opportunity to explore how best to support patients and staff. Most of all, we would benefit from implementation studies to see if these initiatives are helping to support the individuals involved.

Notes

1 NPSA, 'Being Open Framework', 2009; Department of Health, *Good Doctors, Safer Patients. Proposals to strengthen the system to assure and improve the performance of doctors and to protect the safety of patients. A report by the Chief Medical Officer*, London, Department of Health, 2006; Department of Health, *High Quality Care for All*, London, Department of Health, 2008; Department of Health, *Confidence in Caring Project Overview*, London, Department of Health, 2008; Department of Health, *The NHS Constitution for England*, London, Department of Health, 2009.
2 E.N. De Vries, M.A. Ramrattan, S.M. Smorenburg, D.J. Gouma and M.A. Boermeester, 'The Incidence and Nature of In-hospital Adverse Events: A Systematic Review', *Quality and Safety in Health Care* 17, 2008, pp. 216–223.
3 D.M. Clarke, P.A. Russell, A.L. Polglase and D.P. McKenzie, 'Psychiatric Disturbance and Acute Stress Responses in Surgical Patients', *ANZ Journal of Surgery* 67, 1997, pp. 115–118.
4 J. Czarnocka and P. Slade, 'Prevalence and Predictors of Post-traumatic Stress Symptoms Following Childbirth', *British Journal of Clinical Psychology*, 39:1, March 2000, pp. 35–51.
5 P. Bark, C. Vincent, A. Jones and J. Savory, 'Clinical Complaints: A Means of Improving Quality of Care', *Quality in Health Care* 3, 1994, pp. 123–132.
6 C. Vincent, M. Young and A. Phillips, 'Why Do People Sue Doctors? A Study of Patients and Relatives Taking Action', *The Lancet* 343, 1994, pp. 1609–1613.
7 Bark *et al.*, 'Clinical Complaints'.
8 The Local Authority Social Services and National Health Service Complaints (England) Regulations (2009).
9 Medical Protection Society. Online. Available HTTP http://www.medical protection.org/.
10 Vincent *et al.*, 'Why Do People Sue Doctors?'
11 C. Vincent and L. Page, 'Aftermath of Error for Patients and Health Care Staff', in B. Hurwitz and A. Sheikh, eds, *Health Care Errors and Patient Safety*, Chichester, Wiley-Blackwell, 2009.
12 Ibid.
13 C. Vincent and A. Coulter, 'Patient Safety: What about the Patient?', *Quality and Safety in Health Care* 11, 2002, pp. 76–80.
14 Vincent and Page, 'Aftermath of Error for Patients and Health Care Staff'.
15 Ibid.
16 A.W. Wu, S. Folkman, S.J. McPhee and B. Lo, 'Do House Officers Learn from Their Mistakes?', *Quality and Safety in Health Care* 12, 2003, pp. 221–228.
17 E. Kübler-Ross, *On Death and Dying*, New York, Macmillan, 1969.
18 Ibid.
19 J. Bowlby, *Attachment and Loss*, New York, Basic Books, 1980.

20 E. Leibenluft, S.A. Green and A.A. Giese, 'Mourning and Milieu: Staff Reaction to the Death of an Inpatient', *The Psychiatric Hospital* 19, 1988, pp. 169–173.

21 R. Iedema, R. Sorensen, E. Manias, A. Tuckett, D. Piper, N. Mallock, A. Williams and C. Jorm, 'Patients' and Family Members' Experiences of Open Disclosure Following Adverse Events', *International Journal for Quality in Health Care* 20:6, 2008, pp. 421–432.

22 Vincent and Page, 'Aftermath of Error for Patients and Health Care Staff'.

23 Ibid.

24 C. Vincent, *Patient Safety*, London, Churchill Livingstone, 2006.

25 Adapted from ibid.

26 Department of Health, *Confidence in Caring Project Overview*.

27 Australian Council for Safety and Quality in Health Care, *Open Disclosure Standard: A National Standard for Open Communication in Public and Private Hospitals, Following an Adverse Event in Health Care*, Canberra, Commonwealth of Australia, 2003. Online. Available HTTP http://www.safetyandquality.org.

28 Joint Commission on Accreditation of Healthcare Organizations, *2006 Comprehensive Accreditation Manual for Hospitals: The Official Handbook*, Oakbrook Terrace, IL, Joint Commission Resources, 2005.

29 Canadian Patient Safety Institute, *Canadian Disclosure Guidelines*, Canadian Patient Safety Institute, 2008.

30 National Patient Safety Agency, in *Being Open: Communicating Patient Safety Incidents with Patients and Carers*, 2005.

31 NPSA, 'Being Open Framework', 2009. Online. Available HTTP http://www.npsa.nhs.uk.

32 NPSA, 'NHS Urged to Say Sorry When Things Go Wrong', 2009. Online. Available HTTP http://www.npsa.nhs.uk/corporate/news/nhs-urged-to-say-sorry-when-things-go-wrong/ (accessed 25 June 2010).

33 M. Hingorani and G. Vafidis, 'Patients' and Doctors' Attitudes to Amount of Information Given after Unintended Injury during Treatment: Cross Sectional, Questionnaire Survey', *British Medical Journal* 318:7184, 1999, pp. 640–641.

34 Iedema *et al.*, 'Patients'' and Family Members'' Experiences of Open Disclosure Following Adverse Events'.

35 Ibid.

36 Ibid.

37 Vincent and Page, 'Aftermath of Error for Patients and Health Care Staff'.

38 Action against Medical Accidents (AvMA), 2010. Online. Available HTTP http://www.avma.org.uk/pages/about_us.html (accessed 10 April 2010).

39 Ibid.

40 National Patient Safety Agency, *Seven Steps to Patient Safety*, NPSA, 2004.

41 Vincent and Page, 'Aftermath of Error for Patients and Health Care Staff'.

42 A.D. Waterman, J. Garbutt, E. Hazel *et al.*, 'The Emotional Impact of Medical Errors on Practicing Physicians in the United States and Canada', *Joint Commission Journal on Quality and Patient Safety* 33:8, 2007, pp. 467–476.

43 A.W. Wu, 'Medical Error: The Second Victim. The Doctor Who Makes Mistake Needs Help Too', *British Medical Journal*, 320:31, 2000, pp. 726–727.

44 J. Firth-Cozens and R. Payne, *Stress in Health Professionals*, Chichester, Wiley, 1999.

45 C.P. West, M.M. Huschka, P.J. Novotny, J.A. Sloan, J.A. Kolars, T.R. Habermann *et al.*, 'Association of Perceived Medical Errors with Resident Distress and Empathy', *Journal of the American Medical Association*, 296, 2006, pp. 1071–1078.

46 D.A. Alexander, S. Klein, N.M. Gray, I.G. Dewar and J.M. Eagles, 'Suicide by Patients: Questionnaire Study of Its Effect on Consultant Psychiatrists', *British Medical Journal* 320, 2000, pp. 1571–1574.

47 Wu, 'Medical Error'.

48 Wu *et al.*, 'Do House Officers Learn from Their Mistakes?'
49 Vincent and Page, 'Aftermath of Error for Patients and Health Care Staff'.
50 Waterman *et al.*, 'The Emotional Impact of Medical Errors on Practicing Physicians in the United States and Canada'.
51 Iedema *et al.*, 'Patients' and Family Members' Experiences of Open Disclosure Following Adverse Events'.
52 Wu, 'Medical Error'.
53 J.D. Peters, S.K. Nord and R.D. Woodson, 'Empirical Analysis of the Medical and Legal Professions' Experiences and Perceptions of Medical and Legal Practice', *JL Reform*, 1985 – HeinOnline.
54 P. Bark, C. Vincent, L. Olivieri and A. Jones, 'Impact of Litigation on Senior Clinicians: Implications for Risk Management', *Quality in Health Care* 6, 1997, pp. 7–13.
55 L. Nash, M. Daly, M. Johnson, G. Walter, M. Walton, S. Willcock, C. Coulston, E. van Ekert and C. Tennant, 'Psychological Morbidity in Australian Doctors Who Have and Have Not Experienced a Medico-legal Matter: Cross-sectional Survey', *Australia and New Zealand Journal of Psychiatry* 41:11, 2007, pp. 917–925.
56 S.C. Charles, 'Coping with a Medical Malpractice Suit', *Western Journal of Medicine* 174, 2001, pp. 55–58.
57 Bark *et al.*, 'Impact of Litigation on Senior Clinicians'.
58 Nash *et al.*, 'Psychological Morbidity in Australian Doctors'.
59 D.M. Studdert, M.M. Mello, A.A. Gawande, T.K. Gandhi, A. Kachalia, C. Yoon, A.L. Puopolo and T.A. Brennan, 'Claims, Errors, and Compensation Payments in Medical Malpractice Litigation', *New England Journal of Medicine* 354, 2006, pp. 2024–2033.
60 L.J. Donaldson, 'Lessons for the Health Field', *Journal of the Foundation for Science and Technology* 17, 2001, pp. 5–7.
61 Ibid.
62 D. Parker and R. Lawton, 'Psychological Contribution to the Understanding of Adverse Events in Health Care', *Quality and Safety in Health Care* , 12, 2003, pp. 453–457.
63 Ibid.
64 R.A. Caplan, K.L. Posner, F.W. Cheney *et al.*, 'Effect of Outcome of Physician Judgments of Appropriateness of Care', *Journal of the Americal Medical Association* 265, 1991, pp. 1957–1960.
65 C.E. Murier, 'Understanding the Nature of Errors in Nursing: Using a Model to Analyze Critical Incident Reports of Errors, Which Had Resulted in an Adverse or Potentially Adverse Event', *Journal of Advanced Nursing* 32:1, 2000, p. 202.
66 R. Lawton and D. Parker, 'Judgements of the Rule-related Behaviour of Health-care Professionals: An Experimental Study', *British Journal of Health Psychology* 7, 2002, pp. 253–265.
67 Caplan *et al.*, 'Effect of Outcome of Physician Judgments of Appropriateness of Care'.
68 Parker and Lawton, 'Psychological Contribution to the Understanding of Adverse Events in Health Care'.
69 Ibid.
70 Wu, 'Medical Error'.
71 J. Firth-Cozens, 'Organisational Trust: The Keystone to Patient Safety', *Quality and Safety in Health Care* 13, 2004, pp. 56–61.
72 Firth-Cozens, 'Organisational Trust'.
73 Wu *et al.*, 'Do House Officers Learn from Their Mistakes?'.
74 Houses of Parliament, 2009. Online. Available HTTP http://www.publications. parliament.uk/pa/cm200809/cmselect/cmhealth/.

75 Firth-Cozens, 'Organisational Trust'.
76 Houses of Parliament, 2009. Online. Available HTTP http://www.publications. parliament.uk/pa/cm200809/cmselect/cmhealth/.
77 Firth-Cozens, 'Organisational Trust'.
78 NHSLA circular, released in May 2009. Online. Available HTTP http://www. nhsla.com/NR/rdonlyres/00F14BA6-0621-4A23-B885-FA18326FF745/0/ ApologiesandExplanationsMay1st2009.pdf.
79 Vincent, *Patient Safety*.
80 Ibid.
81 Ibid.
82 Alexander *et al.*, 'Suicide by Patients'.
83 Waterman *et al.*, 'The Emotional Impact of Medical Errors on Practicing Physicians in the United States and Canada'.
84 Ibid.
85 Hirst 1996, cited in Vincent, *Patient Safety*.
86 F. van Pelt, 'Peer Support: Healthcare Professionals Supporting Each Other after Adverse Medical Events', *Quality and Safety in Health Care* 17, 2008, pp. 249–252.
87 West *et al.*, 'Association of Perceived Medical Errors with Resident Distress and Empathy'.

Blame free reporting

International developments

Johan Legemaate

Introduction

Attention concerning the safety of the care provided to patients has increased substantially in recent years, with hospitals and other health care institutions now required to have a safety management system in place. Registering and analysing incidents, where incidents are defined as 'everything unintended', represent a significant element of such systems, while the analysing of incidents can play an important role in the quality and safety of the care provided to patients. Experience with similar reporting systems in other sectors, such as the aviation sector, has been good.

It is crucially important for health care professionals to be willing to report incidents, and this willingness is now seen as part of their professional responsibilities. However, although professionals are required to report incidents, day-to-day reality can be somewhat more difficult to manage. Health care professionals may have a wide variety of reasons for not reporting incidents, including fears that the information they report could be used in action taken against the individual reporter. If that happens, the willingness to report incidents will rapidly decrease, as experience in other sectors clearly demonstrates. For this reason it is argued that health care professionals reporting incidents as part of quality assurance should enjoy a certain degree of protection so that they can be safe in the knowledge that information they report will not be used outside the context of the quality assurance system. This is often referred to as 'safe reporting'. The issue at stake here is not patient safety, but the need to protect the reporter against measures or action that could be taken in response to reporting.[1]

This prompts numerous questions of a social and legal nature, including the question of patients' basic rights. Patients are entitled to high-quality (and so also safe) care. And this means it is in patients' interests for there to be effective quality assurance systems in place, including a system for recording incidents. However, it is specifically in cases involving problems in the provision of care that patients are also entitled to information, and that right could be compromised if details of incidents recorded were not available for inspection and use by third parties, including the patient. In such cases it is both the general interest and the interests of individual patients that are at stake. This in turn brings us to the principal question posed in this article, whether it is desirable or necessary to establish statutory provisions for 'safe reporting' of incidents in the health care sector. I have sought below to answer this question in a series of stages, using an international perspective and looking at specific developments in the Netherlands.

International developments[2]

Organisations such as the Council of Europe and the World Health Organisation (WHO) have published advice on providing a legal framework for 'safe reporting' and a number of countries have already introduced legislation on safe reporting of incidents in the health care sector.

WHO and the Council of Europe

In 2005 the World Health Organisation issued guidelines specifically focusing on the health care sector and which state, for example, that '[r]eporting must be safe. Individuals who report incidents must not be punished or suffer ill-effects from reporting'.[3] The WHO guidelines are based on two starting-points:

1   The fundamental role of patient safety reporting systems is to enhance patient safety by learning from failures of the health-care system.
2   Reporting must be safe. Individuals who report incidents must not be punished or suffer other ill-effects from reporting.

These WHO guidelines were followed in 2006 by an important Council of Europe recommendation 'on the management of patient safety and prevention of adverse events in health care'.[4] The Recommendation emphasised that the primary objective of an incident reporting system is the enhancement of patient safety, by learning from adverse events and mistakes made. It stipulated:

> Reporting and collection of incident data is meaningful only if the data is analysed and evaluated and if feedback is given to the professionals involved in the incident, and to all others who could learn from the incident. Incident reporting systems are not intended to identify and punish the individual staff members involved in patient-safety incidents.

The recommendation underlined the importance of providing protection in law for reporters of incidents in such a way that no action can be taken against them 'as a sole result of such reporting'. At the same time, the recommendation stated:

> It may appear difficult to establish a patient-safety reporting system without compromising patients' rights. However, if the public is ready

to accept the presence of a confidential, anonymous, non-punitive reporting system the public must be assured that its legal and financial rights will be protected. The existence of a fair and open complaints system, a just and adequate compensation system and an efficient and reliable supervisory system will certainly make the process easier and politically more acceptable. Promoting a 'no blame' culture is not intended to diminish the effective legal protection of patients.

Box 1: Key features of the 2006 Council of Europe Recommendation

[The reporting system] should:

- be non-punitive and fair in purpose;
- be independent of other regulatory processes;
- be designed in such a way as to encourage health-care providers and health-care personnel to report safety incidents (for instance, wherever possible, reporting should be voluntary, anonymous and confidential);
- set out a system for collecting and analyzing reports of adverse events locally and, when the need arises, aggregated at a regional or national level, with the aim of improving patient safety; for this purpose, resources must be specifically allocated;
- involve both private and public sectors;
- facilitate the involvement of patients, their relatives and all other informal caregivers in all aspects of activities relating to patient safety, including reporting of patient-safety incidents.

Denmark

In Denmark, the Act on Patient Safety in the Danish Health Care System of 2004, states that information on the reporter of incidents can be made available only to those responsible for processing and analysing the information reported. No one else is allowed to know the identity of the reporter. From this it can be concluded that information reported cannot be called on for use in disciplinary or legal proceedings, and similarly that legislation on public access to information cannot be used as justification for granting access to information reported in this way. This is also the background against which we have to view Article 6 of the Danish legislation, which states that a reporter cannot be subjected to disciplinary measures (by an employer or regulator) or to measures in criminal law as a consequence of the reporting.

United States

The US Patient Safety and Quality Improvement Act (PSQIA) came into force in 2005. The Act intends to strike 'an appropriate balance between encouraging the reporting of valuable information, which will be used to save lives, and safeguarding the ability of individuals to access necessary information to seek judicial redress when appropriate':[5]

> [The PSQIA] would assure doctors and other health professionals that if they voluntarily report information to expert patient safety organiza-tions, that information will be used for health care quality improvement efforts and will be kept privileged and confidential. This protection will encourage health care professionals to report and will result in the crea-tion of valuable new information that can be used to identify best prac-tice for eliminating errors and improving patient outcomes. We believe the bill will also help reduce the number of lawsuits resulting from medical errors. Information from medical records and other existing data sources will continue to be available for injured plaintiffs to pursue their claims in court, just as that information is available today.[6]

The Patient Safety and Quality Improvement Act provides 'privilege and confidentiality protections'. These apply to information supplied by health care providers to patient safety organisations. The statutory protection pro-vided in this respect focuses on traceable information, that is, information that can be traced back to a specific institution and/or to a specific profes-sional. Essentially the statutory protection provides for the following:

- The relevant information is not permitted to be called on in civil, crimi-nal or administrative law proceedings brought against the health care institution/professional and is also not allowed to be used as evidence in any such proceedings;
- The relevant information is not permitted to be used in disciplinary or professional misconduct proceedings brought against an individual;
- The relevant information is not covered by legislation on public access to information (in other words, the Freedom of Information Act).

Australia

In Australia the federal Health Insurance Act of 1973 regulates the Com-monwealth Qualified Privilege Scheme (CQPS):

> The Commonwealth Qualified Privilege Scheme provides important safeguards for health care professionals who engage in effective quality assurance activities. This is important for all Australians – health care providers, patients, their carers and the community, as it helps to ensure the highest quality of our health care system.[7]

To improve the safety and quality of health care, it is important to review what went wrong, and to find ways to prevent the event from happening again. Medical staff are more likely to talk about the medical mistakes they made if they know that the information they disclose cannot legally be disclosed to anyone. Disclosure of medical mistakes allows the identification of environments conducive to errors, and this facilitates system redesign to create an environment in which it is impossible to make a mistake.[8]

The Australian Commonwealth Qualified Privilege Scheme (CQPS) covers a wide range of activities designed to promote quality, including 'hospital-based peer review procedures, academic studies of the incidence of or causes of adverse events and performance evaluation in individual health care professionals'. The CQPS provides two forms of protection. The first of these is the guarantee that information that can be traced back to a health care provider or a patient will be treated confidentially when provided for general quality assurance purposes. This means that in principle it is not permitted to make publicly available information that becomes known 'solely as a result of those [quality assurance] activities' and neither is such information allowed to be used in legal proceedings. The second form of protection is the assurance that committee members assessing or evaluating the quality of health care services will be protected against civil-law proceedings instigated by health care providers to whom the committee's decision relates.

Legislation in the Netherlands

No legislation on safe reporting has yet been introduced in the Dutch health care sector. In other sectors, however, statutory provision for 'safe reporting' has been made in the form of the Aviation Act (Wet luchtvaart) and the Safety Investigation Board Act (Rijkswet Onderzoeksraad voor Veiligheid), and the latter can also be applied to situations in the health care sector.[9]

The protection for reporters of incidents in the aviation sector is provided in Articles 11.25 and 11.26 of the Aviation Act, with subsection 1 of Article 11.25 stating that an unintended or inadvertent violation of a legal regulation that becomes known through being reported shall not result in the state being entitled to bring legal proceedings or in an administrative sanction being imposed by an administrative body. This protection does not apply, however, in the event of gross negligence (Article 11.25, subsection 2). Under Article 11.26 of the Act, the Public Prosecution Service must obtain authorisation from the examining judge if it wishes to use information obtained through a certified quality management system in a criminal investigation. This provision was included in the legislation at the explicit request of the Lower House of Parliament, which regarded the degree of statutory protection provided to reporters in the original Bill as too limited. Following on from Articles 11.25 and 11.26 of the Aviation Act, the Public Prosecution

Service issued the Civil Aviation (Investigation of Air Accidents and Incidents) Instructions (Aanwijzing opsporing en vervolging bij melding van voorvallen in de burgerluchtvaart),[10] which state that action by the Public Prosecution Service will in principle remain limited to cases involving alleged intent or gross negligence. The Transport, Public Works and Water Management Inspectorate and the Public Prosecution Service have agreed that reports received by the Inspectorate and meeting these criteria will be forwarded to the Public Prosecution Service. In these cases, too, it is not permitted to use information contained in the reports as evidence in criminal proceedings brought against the reporter. It is, however, possible to use such information as directional information as a way of drawing attention to other sources of information that it is permitted to use as evidence against the reporter.[11] Data from the reports can also be used without restriction as evidence in proceedings brought against someone other than the reporter.

It is also important in investigations conducted by the Safety Investigation Board that all relevant information is disclosed and that those supplying information to the Board are able to speak freely. It is against this background that we should view Article 69 of the Safety Investigation Board Act, which provides protection for people making statements in Safety Investigation Board investigations. This protection takes the form of a prohibition on using information obtained as part of a Board investigation. Under Article 69, this information cannot be used as evidence in criminal, professional misconduct or civil proceedings and neither may it serve as the basis for disciplinary measures or administrative sanctions or measures. The sources of information covered by this provision are statements made by individuals, communications recorded by technical means between people involved in operating a means of transport, medical or private information provided as part of a Board investigation and relating to people involved in the incident being investigated, opinions expressed during the process of analysing material relating to the investigation and documents compiled by the Board, including the public report issued on its findings. Information protected by Article 69 will be included in such a report only to the extent necessary for analysing the circumstances surrounding the incident or substantiating the conclusions. The report will not include names, addresses or similar details that could be used to identify people involved in an accident or incident (Article 55.3 of the Safety Investigation Board Act). Finally, Article 69.4 of the Act states that information protected under Article 69 also cannot be obtained indirectly by, for example, calling a Safety Investigation Board representative as an expert or witness in proceedings.[12]

Developments in the Netherlands

In 2007 a number of Dutch health care organisations compiled a Policy Document on Safe Reporting.[13] This Policy Document states that health care providers are permitted to make details of incidents recorded available to third parties only if required to do so by law or case law. The Policy

Document was seen as an alternative to legislation. Following the publication of the Document, the Health Care Inspectorate stated that it would never ask for or use information from health care institutions' internal incident recording systems, given the importance of assuring '100% safety' if health care professionals were to be willing to report incidents.[14] Although the Public Prosecution Service was asked to confirm its agreement with this, the Service was not prepared to do so at that moment. The Minister of Justice merely responded by saying, in December 2006:

> As soon as the plans for the reporting system to be introduced ... become more specific, the Public Prosecution Service and I will be willing ... to exchange thoughts on the opportunities for devising a policy regulation that could cover aspects such as the policy on prosecution and the policy on demanding information.[15]

In late 2008 the parties that had signed the Policy Document expressed a preference for a statutory regulation, which should be included, in their opinion, in the proposed Clients' Rights (Health Care Sector) Act (Wet cliëntenrechten zorg).[16]

This switch from self-regulation to a preference for legislation is largely attributable to case-law developments in the period from late 2007 onwards. During this period there were a number of court rulings on safe reporting that prompted doubts as to whether the Policy Document was sufficient to protect reporters of incidents. In December 2007, for example, the Zwolle-Lelystad Court ruled that, as far as protection was concerned, the interests of a surviving dependant of a patient who died because of a possible medical error outweighed those of a person reporting an incident or emergency.[17] The reason for the judge's decision in this case was that the deceased patient's medical notes had not been properly maintained. Given these circumstances the judge ruled that the surviving family members' right to information could be met only by allowing them access to information from the incident recording system. In a December 2008 case involving liability, however, the Leeuwarden Court assessed the various interests at stake differently,[18] and ultimately issued the following, somewhat categorical, statement:

> Being able to report incidents in a hospital confidentially in order to avoid their repetition and thus to further the quality of care provided is of very great importance to society. Although disclosure of the MIP (Incident Reporting Committee in Patient Care) report could be in the interests of the person seeking justice in an individual case, it is the Court's expectation that this would put the reporting system at risk, such that persons seeking justice in the future would be unable to gain access to such reports, while the quality instrument that the MIP reporting is designed to provide would also be lost. Consequently, the sole result of a decision such as that desired by [the appellant] will in

the longer term be that everyone loses out. In these circumstances the interests of [the appellant] are outweighed by the general interest.[19]

In March 2009 the Arnhem Court ordered a hospital in an interlocutory judgement in a case involving liability to submit its incident reporting to the Court.[20] In its defence the hospital raised an objection in principle to being required to produce such information and invoked the importance of 'safe reporting' to the effectiveness of the hospital's registering of incidents. The court subsequently ruled as follows:

> The court believes that, at this stage of the proceedings, the compelling importance of having an effective quality assurance system in the health care sector should outweigh the individual interests of X, however compelling these interests may be. We have taken account in this respect of the fact that there appear to be no serious gaps in X's medical notes and that all those involved have since provided witness statements on X's treatment on the specific evening. At this point it can reasonably be assumed that a fair process of justice can be assured even without [the information from the incident recording system]. If any gap in the provision of information is identified at a later stage, the possibility of reviewing this decision can be considered at that time.[21]

The approach adopted by the Arnhem Court is closer to that of the Zwolle-Lelystad Court than to the decision reached by the Leeuwarden Court. In general, the views emerging from case law have to date been anything but uniform. This only serves to increase the uncertainty about the extent to which reporters of incidents can in practice call on the protection provided. And that in turn may have an adverse impact on people's willingness to report incidents. Indeed, shortly after the Zwolle-Lelystad Court announced its decision, the Inspector General of Health stated that '[t]here are various indications to suggest that, as a result of this decision, far fewer incidents are being reported'.[22]

Exceptions to 'safe reporting'

As stated earlier, there are both individual and general interests at stake in incidents reported by health care professionals. The general interest can be viewed from various perspectives in that there is a general, public interest in ensuring that quality assurance systems are effective, while there is also a general interest in ensuring that external parties are informed and involved in investigations of serious incidents. While the first of these two aspects requires the reporter to be protected, the second specifically does not. This is why existing regulations on safe reporting may sometimes include exceptions to the need to protect the reporter.

Sometimes an exception is made for specific criminal offences. Although the Danish legislation and the Dutch Safety Investigation Board Act do not include provision for such an exception, the legislation in the United States and Australia and the Dutch Aviation Act do allow exceptions to be made in situations of this nature. The exceptions provided for in these regulations relate to evidence that the court considers to be vital and which is not able to be obtained in any other way (in the case of the United States), to information concerning 'serious offences' (in the case of Australia) and to situations involving gross negligence (in the case of the Dutch Aviation Act). If an exception is made for information to be used in criminal-law proceedings, it is very important for this exception to be worded in terms that are as restricted as possible.[23] The exception for situations involving criminal law that was included in the March 2009 draft Bill of the Clients' Rights (Health Care Sector) Act does not meet this criterion as it is worded in far wider terms than were the examples referred to above and was, therefore, very much at variance with developments elsewhere.[24]

Another exception can be found in the existing statutory requirement in the Netherlands for calamities and emergencies to be reported to the Health Care Inspectorate (Article 4a of the Care Institutions (Quality) Act [Kwaliteitswet zorginstellingen]). Although the relevant provision in the Act does not specify the nature and extent of the information to be reported, it would be hard to maintain that the identity of the reporter or relevant health care professional did not need to be reported. That is not to say, however, that the Inspectorate should not do everything it can to ensure that calamities and emergencies are reported as 'safely' as possible by adhering to the policy of asking for the identity of those involved to be made known only if required by the circumstances.[25]

An exception of a very different nature is the individual interest of the patient or the patient's family. As the cases referred to above demonstrate, patients or their families may wish to use information from a health care institution's incident reporting system in complaint or liability proceedings. Case law allows for an exception in situations where a patient's medical notes have not been properly maintained. In itself the court's approach in this respect is understandable: the patient (or the patient's family) is entitled to information one way or the other. There is no doubt that patients have a right to information on incidents with demonstrable consequences for them. The question, however, is whether it is desirable and necessary to link that right to the reporting of the incident. It would seem far more appropriate to make explicit provision in law so that – contrary to the situation currently prevailing – patients have the right to obtain information on the nature and cause of incidents, while also improving the opportunities available to patients wishing to exercise that right. In the event of problems there will then be a way for patients to demand compliance, and the incident reporting itself will remain confidential. In this way the legal position of the patient will be reinforced, while such statutory provision will also help resolve the tension, referred to above, in Recommendation (2006)7 of the Council of Europe ('It may appear difficult to establish a patient-safety reporting system without compromising patients' rights').

Regulating 'safe reporting': finding a balance

The process of regulating the safe reporting of incidents involves interests that can be at loggerheads with each other – in other words, a clash between the interest in having effective quality assurance systems in place versus the interest in being able to use information from these systems (at least sometimes) for supervisory and compliance purposes. The view that there is a need for 'a fire-wall between the systems for learning and those for accountability'[26] is widely shared, as reflected in the recommendations of the Council of Europe and the World Health Organisation. This points to a need to keep the numbers of exceptions to the protection afforded to reporters of incidents as limited as possible.[27] The more exceptions are allowed in the system, the less health care professionals will be willing to report. And that in turn, as the Leeuwarden Court – correctly, in my view – noted in 2008, will result in everyone losing out. If fewer incidents are reported, more individual claimants will be left empty-handed, while the quality of the information in incident reporting systems will also decrease. Following the experience gained in other countries, it is strongly recommended that the Netherlands establish statutory provisions for the safe reporting of incidents in the health care sector, not least because of the contradictory developments seen in Dutch case law in recent years.[28]

We are warned that systems for 'blame free reporting' can lead to the disappearance of health care professionals' individual responsibility and accountability for the quality of their actions. That is certainly not the intended result. However, it is not a case of 'either/or', but rather of 'and/and', with a balance needing to be found between 'no blame' and 'accountability'.[29] This is one of the reasons why legislation needs to make explicit provision for patients' right to information on the nature and cause of incidents, alongside the other elements referred to in Recommendation (2006)7 of the Council of Europe. Provision is needed for 'a fair and open complaints system, a just and adequate compensation system and an efficient and reliable supervisory system'. In this way we can establish a properly balanced system, with account being taken of all interests at stake (both individual and general) and all basic rights (such as the right to good health care and the right to information) being assured.

Notes

1 J. Legemaate, I. Christiaans-Dingelhoff, R.M.S. Doppegieter and R.P. de Roode, *Veilig incident melden – Context en randvoorwaarden*, Houten, Bohn Stafleu Van Loghum, 2007; J. Legemaate, 'Veilig melden van incidenten wettelijk regelen?', *Tijdschrift voor Gezondheidsrecht* 32, 2008, pp. 99–104; A.C. de Die, *De toekomst van de Wet Big – Gewaarborgde kwaliteit*, The Hague,: Sdu Uitgevers, 2008, § 50.
2 R. de Roode and J. Legemaate, *Juridische aspecten van perinatale audit*, Utrecht, KNMG/RIVM, 2008; J. Legemaate and R.P. de Roode, Veilig melden van incidenten in de gezondheidszorg: voorbeelden van (buitenlandse) wetgeving, *Tijdschrift voor Veiligheid* 8, 2009, pp. 20–34.
3 World Health Organization, *Draft Guidelines for Adverse Event Reporting and Learning Systems*, Geneva, WHO, 2005, p. 10.

4 Recommendation (2006) 7, 24 May 2006.
5 Congressional Record – House of Representatives, 27 July 2005, p. H6676.
6 Executive Office of the President, *Statement of Administration Policy: S. 544 – Patient Safety and Quality Improvement Act of 2005*, Washington, Executive Office of the President, 27 July 2005. Online. Available HTTP http://www. whitehouse.gov/omb/legislative/sap/109-1/s544sap-h.pdf (accessed 18 June 2010).
7 Information brochure of the federal Australian government. Available at http://www.health.gov.au/internet/main/publishing.nsf/Content/qps-info (accessed 11 January 2011).
8 Information brochure of the government of Western Australia. Available at http://www.safetyandquality.health.wa.gov.au/clinical_incid_man/qualified_priv.cfm (accessed 11 January 2011).
9 Dutch Safety Investigation Board's April 2008 report on heart surgery at the St Radboud University Medical Centre in Nijmegen.
10 Government Gazette, 2006, 235. Instructions applicable until 30 November 2010.
11 A provision of importance in this respect is Article 6 of the European Convention on Human Rights, which in principle prevents information that a person is required to disclose from being used against him in criminal proceedings ('right not to incriminate yourself'). Information disclosed may, however, be used as directional information. The Public Prosecution Service's Instructions refer to the European Court's 1996 ruling in *Saunders*. 17 December 1996, *Nederlandse Jurisprudentie* 1997, p. 699.
12 Cf. the statutory protection afforded to members of quality assurance committees in the Australian CQPS.
13 The Policy Document was signed by the Royal Netherlands Medical Society, the Association of Medical Specialists, the NVZ Dutch Hospitals Association, the Netherlands Federation of University Medical Centres, the V&VN association for health care professionals and the Dutch Patient and Consumer Federation.
14 J. Vesseur and G. van der Wal, 'Inspectie geeft spijkerharde garanties', *Medisch Contact* 62, 2007, pp. 184–186.
15 Policy Document on Safe Reporting, 2007, p. 12.
16 Anonymous, 'Wet clientenrechten zorg. Medisch Contact, *Medisch Contact* 63, 2008, pp. 1656–1657.
17 Zwolle-Lelystad Court, 20 December 2007, *Tijdschrift voor Gezondheidsrecht* 12, 2008.
18 Leeuwarden Court, 9 December 2008, *Nederlandse Jurisprudentie* 2009, p. 200, annotated by J. Legemaate; *Tijdschrift voor Gezondheidsrecht* 12, 2009, annotated by J.C.J. Dute; *Gezondheidszorg Jurisprudentie* 22, 2009.
19 Hubben (see note 20) seems to suggest that the Court still left some scope for allowing a patient to view the reporting of the incident. Given, however, the structuring of the Court's considerations, I would not regard that as likely.
20 Arnhem Court, 11 March 2009, *Gezondheidszorg Jurisprudentie* 78, 2009, annotated by J.H. Hubben.
21 Arnhem Court, 8 July 2009, *Tijdschrift voor Gezondheidsrecht* 32, 2009, annotated by W.R. Kastelein.
22 G. van der Wal, 'Veilig melden in de gezondheidszorg', *Tijdschrift voor Gezondheidsrecht* 32, 2008, p. 337.
23 According to Dutch Expert Group Aviation Safety (DEGAS), criminal law should be applied only in the event of intent. As expressed in the report *Liever verantwoordelijk dan vogelvrij – De rol van het strafrecht bij luchtvaartvoorvallen*, Dutch Expert Group Aviation Safety (DEGAS), May 2009.
24 See Article 11.2 of the Bill, KNMG, 19 March 2009. Online. Available HTTP http://knmg.artsennet.nl/Artikel/Reageer-op-het-wetsvoorstel-clientenrechten-zorg.htm (accessed 18 June 2010).

25 This is in line with the *modus operandi* of the Federal Review Committee pro-
    vided for in the Belgian Euthanasia Act. This committee initially assesses the
    reporting of an incident without knowing the doctor's identity. Only with good
    reason will the committee be told the identity.
26 B. Runciman, *Lessons from Australia*, in S. Emslie, K. Knox and M. Pickstone
    (eds), *Improving Patient Safety – Insights from American, Australian and British
    Healthcare*, London, Department of Health, 2002.
27 W. Mariner, *Medical Error Reporting: Professional Tensions between Confidentiality
    and Liability*, Boston: Massachusetts Health Policy Forum, 2001.
28 J. Legemaate, 'Veilig melden van incidenten wettelijk regelen?'; A. Molendijk,
    J. Legemaate and I.P. Leistikow, 'Veilig melden moet in de wet', *Medisch Contact*
    63, 2008, pp. 228–30.
29 R.W. Wachter and P.J. Pronovost, 'Balancing "No Blame" with Accountability
    in Patient Safety', *New England Journal of Medicine* 361, 2009, pp. 1401–1406.

7 Economic aspects of patient safety

Stephen Heasell

Introduction

Action to prevent adverse events from befalling patients in receipt of health services involves diverting effort and resources from alternative deployments. The broad issue addressed in this chapter is how legal systems around the world can be expected to influence the diversion of versatile but limited (scarce) resources to precautionary activity.

The US report *To Err Is Human* endorsed adopting a systemic and integrated approach, to address all aspects of patient safety.[1] In doing so, it engaged in an ongoing debate about the appropriateness of relying heavily on institutional tort law systems to ensure safety.

A systemic approach to patient safety invites systematic analysis of policy and practice. It also involves, therefore, developing awareness of interdependent decisions by various individuals and in various organisations, framed by various social institutions, including law. An economic perspective takes systemic and systematic account of interdependent cost incentives affecting the multitude of decision takers.

Decisions which imply the using up of scarce resources of any kind can be expected to reflect perceptions of beneficial and costly consequences, more systematically so if the decision making period is an extended one. Anything which appears to affect differences in cost, between adverse events and taking precautions to prevent them, generates a cost incentive which has potential to influence decisions.

Empirical evidence of costs to date has been limited, partial and often misleading as a guide for cost effective policy or practice in addressing patient safety. Headline figures purporting to represent total costs of adverse events remind us that these costs are substantial and can be painful to bear but cannot make the case for expending scarce resources on new initiatives to address them.[2]

In the spirit of systemic and systematic appraisal, making that case requires integrated analysis of benefits and disbenefits (that is, harm and costs), compared across all feasible options for addressing safety. The size and complexity of such an undertaking argues against presuming that a systemic perspective always requires an entirely centralised decision making process.

Legal systems to resolve resource rivalry

Legal systems around the world are used in determining who is liable for meeting the costs of adverse events befalling patients, if they occur. Every patient in receipt of health services stands at some risk of experiencing an adverse event. Individuals and organisations prefer to avoid being found liable for costs, as all costs reduce scope and opportunity to acquire and use scarce resources for more attractive purposes.

Attempts to prevent adverse events from happening will be made if prevention seems less costly to the decision taker than responding to adverse events if they occur while resisting liability. Effective resistance to liability shifts the burden of costs onto others, so cost shifting tends to be a competitive activity among rival users of scarce resources. The mere existence of legal liability rules does not ensure that the risks of adverse events or their overall costs are minimised.

Legal systems are among the social institutions around the world by which rivalry among individuals for the use of scarce resources is resolved; others include markets, organisational internal hierarchies and government by the state. The relationship between the various social institutions can be complex; they might be complementary or contradictory in some ways or the institutions might be alternatives to each other, at least in part.

For example, individual clinical practitioners are subject to the law but also to regulation by the institution or organisation (in the private or public sector) which employs their services. In addition, they might also be regulated by a professional association. From a perspective beyond the health services sector, these latter institutions are regarded as forms of self-regulation. If they appear to work well, then statutory or tort legal apparatus might not need to be so extensive or to be specified so precisely.

There had already been calls in print to consider more effective or less costly alternatives to institutions of traditional tort law, for maintaining patient safety, before the publication of *To Err Is Human*. The economist Patricia Danzon was prominent among those who had argued that evidence of court judgments and awards, in cases of alleged medical malpractice, showed no systematic alignment with negligence, deterrence or costs incurred by patients.[3]

Publication of *To Err Is Human* did provide a rallying point for those advocates of systemic change who rely heavily on legal rules of individual liability and on adversarial attempts to prove that particular individual practitioners or organisations were at fault. These institutions were accused of fostering a blame culture.[4] This document, however, did not identify a satisfactory alternative to court awards, as a simple signal or cost incentive to influence decisions made in response to prospects for adverse events.

Meanwhile, evidence of the alternative 'no fault' institutions evolving in New Zealand continues to indicate levels of public acceptance beyond those for malpractice law in the US. The evidence, however, does not demonstrate, beyond dispute or individual value judgment that patient safety has fared the better in New Zealand because of its distinctive institutions.[5]

Patient safety and preparedness to use up resources

Any harmful adverse event befalling a patient, through no fault of patients, is appropriately a cause for sorrow and a wish that patient safety will increase. There might also be a moral imperative against subjecting individuals who are vulnerable because of ill health to the additional risk of bearing serious harm or cost, as a result of adverse events arising from health services.

Any practical response to the risk of adverse events, however, turns on who is prepared to use up more of the versatile resources at their own command which are in demand but in shorter supply, to keep patients safe. Preparedness to do so is not limitless. Indeed, it might be severely limited, since the prospective outcomes of using up scarce resources in particular ways to increase patient safety typically seem uncertain.

That preparedness is limited can be demonstrated by individuals' consent to receive patient services, despite the possibility that adverse events will befall them as patients if they do so. Many individuals consent to pay some taxes to fund patient services received by others, despite the near certainty that adverse events will befall some patients and that some of the extra cost associated with these events will be funded by taxation.

Resources can be defined to encompass whatever is in demand (by someone) and which might be bought and sold directly for money. A full list would record some resources that are not currently bought and sold for money. The list includes access to finance or budgets to spend but also necessarily features access to services performed by individuals, including clinicians.

Patient services typically require coordination of processes involving the use of multiple resources, supplied by various individuals and organisations with a mixture of motivations. Some of those motivations will be in conflict with each other and are potentially a source of rivalry between individuals for their own preferred use of scarce resources.

Legal judgments, other aspects of a law suit and alternative means of regulating activity might all affect patient safety, if only indirectly. They might do so even if the regulatory requirements do not specify a target level of safety. The letter of the regulations alone, however, would have little effect unless the difference between complying and not doing so is regarded as sufficiently important. That judgment is likely to be affected by perceived benefits and costs.

Many kinds of resources are often measured and evaluated according to a scale denominated in monetary terms but seldom in a way which is comprehensive and which commands a consensus. For example, the amount of hospital resources used up in attempts to improve patient safety, as measured by the monetary expenditures on them, or by budget allocations, is not the same as the costs to everyone of achieving improvements in patient safety. Cost per unit of resources used, even in a worthy cause, is not the same as cost per unit number of desirable outcomes obtained.

Any effective attempt to prevent potentially unsafe practice would use up scarce resources, so denying their use to expand the overall quantum, range and quality of health services. It is quite possible that continuing to increase the amount of resources expended on attempts at prevention would eventually result in a reduced quantum of safe patient services. It is almost certain that, before that point had been reached, some would be arguing that the drive for safety was restricting fulfilment of overall aspirations for effective patient services.

Regulations would be redundant if they prescribed levels of activity or achievement inferior to what would happen anyway. They would also be redundant if compliance imposed prohibitively high costs. Any costs of redundant regulatory activity and responses to it would be truly wasteful of scarce resources; they would thereby reduce the scope for undertaking safe and effective patient services.

Activities associated with the mere existence of any social institution use up or transform some scarce resources, just as other activities do. For example, legal costs necessarily extend beyond payment of court awards and lawyers' fees. Health service costs necessarily include those incurred in maintaining organisational governance, as well as those directly for delivering patient services.

Accurately costing the patient safety impact of implementing a particular legal system would identify the value of the next best use of the resources used to implement that system. The most highly valued alternative might be a different way to uphold patient safety, perhaps one that does not rely so much on the legal system but relies on other social institutions instead.

An accurate comparison between the value placed on the impact of a particular legal system and its cost would indicate whether or not the legal system uses up resources in the most valuable way possible. No such accounting appraisal has ever been widely accepted, largely because explicitly attributing particular values to consequences (of adverse events) tends to be controversial. Any decision taken (about patient safety), however, does indicate an implicit lower bound on the value attributed to the consequences, since those decisions will impose some costs.

The senses of priorities of patients, individuals who supply patient services, organisations from which patient services are obtained, governments and individuals who supply government services, and taxpayers who are currently neither patients nor suppliers of patient services or government services, do not automatically coincide. Priorities differ between these different constituencies and also between individuals within any one constituency. Some individuals will move between constituencies over time.

Some commonality of interests exists between these individuals. That makes some attempt to reach agreement or compromise seem worthwhile, in order to avoid worse personal outcomes. Agreements, however, are often vulnerable to opportunistic pursuit of divergent individual priorities.

Law, social institutions and prices

Some decisions which emerge from a social institution, such as judgments that emerge from a legal system, can resemble a price to be paid for the use of worldly resources in a particular way. The price might be payable by one individual or one organisation for a use that affects others.

Price might be denominated directly according to a monetary scale, as for a fine and the award of costs or compensation by order of the courts. Decisions by governments might include offering specific financial payments as subsidies to support individuals or organisations. Decisions within organisations might include allocation of divisional budget limits.

Price might instead be denominated in alternative, non-monetary ways; such as by a curb on freedoms of action, including a custodial sentence in some cases. Governments might vary criteria of eligibility to tender for government contracts, while organisations might vary conditions of employment. These non-monetary prices might be measured or evaluated according to a scale denominated in monetary terms, perhaps especially if the non-monetary price clearly has financial consequences for someone.

Prices set according to one social institution might be influenced by powers exerted by others. For example, working hours set for individuals working within the organisations which constitute the UK National Health Service (NHS) are subject to broader powers of UK and EU governmental regulation. The consequences of excessive working hours might lead to the additional risk of adverse events and a claim of negligence in tort law.

Some organisations have sought derogation from the requirements of the European Union Working Time Directive of 2009, on the grounds that too speedy a transition to comply with upper limits on working hours of clinical practitioners would compromise the total amount of care that could be provided and increase the risk of adverse events befalling patients.[6]

Offers to buy or to sell (quantities of) anything at a market price create incentives or signals which might affect the demand for or the supply of marketed commodities by others. Some resources that are in demand are not available at a market price, however, even if they conceivably could be.

In some cases, market price is deliberately suppressed, as extensively it is for patients of the NHS and for health services in the private or public sector elsewhere around the world. In other cases, it might prove impossible for buyer and seller to agree a market price. Failure to agree a price can happen for various technical or social reasons, even if both buyer and seller would secure a net gain if exchange did take place. In any such case of market failure, which might include patient safety as a commodity in itself, incentives to improve patient safety can only be non-market ones or else might be derived by creating conditions in which effective market price incentives emerge.

There might be good reason, in some cases, for suppressing the possibility of transactions at a market price, but doing so would not eliminate the costs of engaging in activities (or changes) which use up scarce resources. Someone, perhaps more than one person, will bear those costs and hence will experience a reduced scope for using resources in alternative ways as they wish.

Clarity and certainty about the price to be paid for deploying resources to provide safe patient services could increase the cost effectiveness of decision making, unless the process of making prices clear is itself very costly. Clarity and certainty about price would at least speed the process of calculating costs and revenues, even if the decision taken remained controversial.

Legal institutions and multiple cost trade-offs

Legal judgments, other aspects of a law suit and alternative means of regulation might affect decisions to prevent risk of adverse events befalling patients (ex ante), instead of waiting to respond to them if they occur (ex post). Costs are incurred whichever option is chosen, and costs of any kind inhibit the scope to use scarce resources for preferred purposes.[7]

Suppose that costs of precaution and costs of response to error are both subject consistently to (the law of) diminishing returns, on increases in the physical activity which achieves prevention or effects a response. If so, then costs would accelerate upwards, as increased preventative activity took place within the same specified period of time, while response costs could fall if prevention was increasingly effective as a result.

Conversely, response costs would accelerate upwards if effective preventative activity were reduced. The combined prevention and response costs would then be minimised at some mixture involving only partial prevention and possibly only partial compliance with any relevant regulations imposed. Posner and others have argued that court judgments of tort negligence under English Law resemble an attempt to minimise the combined costs of accident and precaution (prevention). If so, then those legal judgments reflect principles of economic efficiency.[8]

Called in evidence to support such a counterintuitive proposition, a US court decision by Judge Learned Hand in 1947 embraced the main factors used in English Law to frame discussion of the legal standard of care in negligence. The 'Hand Test' determined a defendant's culpability by balancing the burden of adequate precaution against the likelihood of an accident, multiplied by the gravity of such an event. By the Hand Test, liability is imposed if it can be demonstrated that taking (greater) precautions to avoid an accident would have been the least cost solution.[9] The Hand Test strongly resembles the notion of a trade-off between the conflicting sets of costs, as specified with more technical precision by Calabresi.[10]

Suppose the combined precaution and response costs of adverse events increase, for some reason, beyond the full control of decision takers. If so, then the increase might be tolerated or else some attempt might be made to moderate it, by cost reduction or by redistribution to different categories of cost, including those borne by different people. The term 'cost shifting' is used to denote action to reduce the burden of costs borne by one decision taker, in ways which cause those of others to increase.

Individual decision takers are likely to find that cost reduction and cost redistribution are both subject to the law of diminishing returns, as outlined above. If so, then individual decision taking is likely to result in attempts to minimise total costs by undertaking some cost shifting activity, instead of cost reduction alone. Total costs associated with adverse events, borne by someone or other, are likely to be higher as a result.

Suppose all decision takers in those circumstances similarly compromise, deliberately or unwittingly, on minimising the overall cost of addressing the possibility of unsafe practice. If so, then the likelihood is that most decision takers would bear some of the extra costs to be incurred and that most patients would bear some extra risk of experiencing adverse events.

Risk and cost could be reduced for a majority of decision takers, including a majority of patients, if everyone could be persuaded to moderate attempts to shift costs onto others. The costs of achieving and maintaining agreement to do so, however, might prove prohibitive.

Success would depend on maintaining mutual trust in each other to comply. The temptation to strive to be among the minority of decision takers (which might include some patients) who can benefit from cost shifting, alternatively known as a type of rent-seeking behaviour, might outweigh the inclination to seek a more cooperative overall outcome.

Legal institutions and cost shifting

Aspects of a law suit and alternative means of regulation might all affect the scope for cost shifting by individuals or on behalf of organisations, instead of cost reduction (or cost toleration), when deciding how to address the possibility of adverse events befalling a patient.

If disproving negligence or upholding peer-approved clinical practitioner standards ceased to be effective legal defences against the imposition of liability for adverse events, then these defences could no longer be used to shift costs of accidentally injurious practice onto other clinical practitioners; or onto patients, employers or taxpayers.

Similarly, if organisational budget allocation decisions or upholding peer-approved patient service standards ceased to be effective legal defences against the imposition of liability, then they could no longer be used to shift the costs onto other organisations; or onto patients, individual practitioners or taxpayers. Such a change would also diminish the cost shifting potential of organisational peer-approved guidelines, complaints procedures or risk management arrangements more generally.

Attempts to cost shift might occur even with full knowledge by the decision taker of the consequences for others of doing so. They are more likely to occur in the absence of full knowledge, especially if any advantage in applying overall cost reducing strategies is also not well known. If causing those unknown consequences could be priced, either in the open market or by regulatory means, in accordance with how much they affect others, then more overall cost reducing decisions might be taken. Disseminating detailed consequences of cost shifting more widely might support such a change in decision taking. Disseminating is also an activity which would be costly for at least someone, however, and would not of itself provide a cost incentive to prompt a reduction in cost shifting attempts.

Legal institutions and regulatory capture

Putting a legal case for or against a finding of liability for adverse events befalling a patient is a formalised version of lobbying activity, directed at a particular set of regulators. Lobbying might be directed at the letter of the regulation, its interpretation or at the authoritative judgments handed down in respect of it. Activity directed towards each of these targets might generate distinctive benefits but without doubt would be distinctively costly. Almost by definition, such activity would also constitute an attempt at cost shifting.

Lobbying for a change in the letter of a regulation is typically a longer-term investment of costly resources than is lobbying for a particular judgment in a particular case. Much of any benefit from either activity, however, might be experienced by people or organisations beyond the instigator.

At least some of the information used to frame and implement regulations depends on data supplied by those being regulated. Regulators are often unable to verify those data with certainty. For example, evidence of what happened to produce a particular adverse event befalling a patient would include descriptions provided by clinical practitioners directly involved in the episode. Evidence of compliance with peer-approved clinical standards would include description or opinion provided by clinical peers.

Costly lobbying activity, therefore, could yield regulatory capture; that is, a judgment could be affected by data that disproportionately favour a case against being found liable. Changes in the regulatory process which reduced reliance on data supplied by those being regulated, therefore, might affect findings of liability and hence patient safety. Alternative sources of costly data on which to base judgments, however, would then have to be found and used.

Legal institutions and predictable outcomes

Legal judgments that are consistent with precedent or with established statute lend a degree of predictability for all parties in respect of liability for adverse events which befall a patient. Greater predictability tends to make the process of decision making simpler and less costly, whatever the cost attributable to the outcomes of the decision.

Predictability tends to reduce data processing costs, including the cost of errors in processing and also to reduce the scope for disagreement about consequences of particular decision options. Individual value judgments, however, will always affect interpretation and evaluation. If greater simplicity means that more individuals have confidence in their own calculations of decision consequences, rather than deferring to calculations made by others, then they might also have more confidence in continuing to assert their own divergent evaluation of decision options.

Strict and all-encompassing liability rules tend to be expressed more clearly than is a mosaic of mixed liability ones, although the consequences of any set of rules in particular cases are less predictable. Fixed and inflexible caps on maximum court awards remove one source of unpredictability. Inflexible prices, however, also bar one means for inducing systems to adapt constructively in response to changing circumstances or priorities.

The limits of evidence to hand add uncertain data interpretation to other uncertainties about the outcomes of decisions involving the use of scarce resources, especially those about new initiatives with little precedent. Even imperfect evidence, however, might serve to reduce the scope for dispute about benefits and disbenefits (including costs) of particular decisions.

Legal institutions, patient safety and insurance products

Legal systems might affect the viability of insurance products as a means to manage risky patient services. It has been suggested that what is often described as a malpractice crisis in the US is more appropriately regarded as an insurance market crisis. It is observed that periods of pressure for tort law reform, as distinct sometimes from health service reform, tend to coincide with unusually large increases in the costs of liability insurance and reductions in its availability, especially for physicians.[11]

Insurance products ('policies') provide financial support to those for whom an adverse event would otherwise prove more costly. These products thrive commercially, only if pooling the risk of some adverse consequence faced by many individuals makes insurance cover attractive to buy and to sell at an agreed price ('premium').

Policies thrive commercially only if the chances that a particular individual will claim seem small but not negligible, such that claimants will always be in the minority of policyholders. Commercial success also requires that the consequences of the possible adverse event seem substantial but are not open-ended. Beyond those parameters, either the buyer or the seller would regard agreeing a price, even for partial cover, prohibitively costly unless it was subsidised in some way by another party.

Some health service organisations, such as NHS Trusts in the UK, assume liability for consequences of adverse events befalling patients that are caused by clinicians or others while working for the organisation. These arrangements have characteristics of subsidised but regulated insurance cover, from the perspective of those covered by the scheme. The Clinical Negligence Scheme for Trusts (CNST) is one such device used in the UK in recent years to extend these principles of internally regulated insurance cover to embrace large numbers of constituent organisations within the complex NHS institution as a whole.

Insurance policies to cover the consequences of adverse events befalling a patient could differ from policies to cover consequences of regulations, a law suit or court awards. If a small but substantial minority of individuals or organisations face an increased or more predictable risk of being found liable in law, then that might motivate increased demand for and supply of insurance cover at an agreed price (premium).

If that increased risk of incurring legal costs of a law suit clearly applies to most of the interested parties, then suppliers of insurance cover might not find it commercially attractive to accommodate the increased demand for policies. Similar comments apply to increased costs or predictability of regulations which do not involve the courts. Predictability in cases beyond the courts, including pre-judgment settlements, would tend to be the greater, however, for regulators and the regulated than for other parties that are affected but are more remote from the relevant information.

The greater the extent to which individuals or organisations are insured against consequences of adverse events befalling patients, the less powerful is the cost incentive for the insured to prevent these events from occurring. Lower sensitivity to the costs to be borne might result in greater prevalence of adverse events and hence higher total costs. Lower sensitivity of the insured to those costs also reduces the commercial incentive to supply insurance cover at an affordable premium (a problem known to economists as moral hazard).

Partial insurance cover leaves some prominent cost to be borne by the policyholder if the adverse event occurs. Partial insurance is less costly to buy than comprehensive cover would be. It might also maintain cost incentives to prevent adverse events sufficiently to moderate the burden of costs for the majority of people.

The more predictable the law or other forms of regulation which affect patient safety, the smaller is the scope for individuals or organisations to misrepresent the risk of them incurring costs on being found liable. There is some cost incentive for those seeking to buy insurance to under-report such a risk, in the hope of securing cover at lower premiums (prices). Prospects for overall supply of cover, however, are diminished by these misrepresentations. Adverse selection of what terms to agree with each policyholder then makes it more difficult for supply of cover to remain commercially viable: payouts prove to be higher than the revenue generated by the low premiums set according to the misrepresented risk.

It is comparatively rare in many cultures for a patient to purchase insurance cover against the prospective costs of a possible law suit. It is common, however, for welfare payments by the state and any availability of legal aid for supporting the bringing of a suit to be taken into account when the size of any legal award of compensation or costs to patients is considered. Indeed, rules of acceptance of welfare payments can disqualify some patients from seeking redress under tort law, as under the New Zealand 'no fault' system.[12]

The availability of welfare payments in these circumstances, in effect, is a type of partial insurance cover. Payments benefit not only the patient but also anyone explicitly found liable for any costs of adverse events befalling patients. The provision of welfare payments, alongside the possibility of legal compensation or awards, can be understood as a way of representing the beneficial effects to taxpayers in general from the bringing of a costly law suit by particular individuals.

A law suit, especially any legal judgment, generates valuable public information about where the extent of liability lies and the costs of being held legally liable when adverse events occur. Inhibition of information flow is one of the possible disadvantages of early settlement, if cases do not reach court because of prohibitive legal costs, or for other reasons. Full disclosure of adverse events is held to be an advantage of 'no fault' schemes over traditional tort institutions. Full disclosure would include who bears what costs associated with any such adverse events.

Legal institutions and systemic perspective on patient safety

A systemic perspective, as advocated in *To Err Is Human*, lends itself to an appreciation of interdependence, both in decision making and in its consequences. Designing a fully specified systemic initiative would be a more complex and costly undertaking than designing ones which each focus independently on only part of that system. If interdependence within the system is pervasive and much more substantial than within any part of it, then a systemic or holistic initiative might prove cost effective and justify any extra initial cost.

It might be possible to reduce that cost, by designing a systemic initiative without fully specifying its consequences or how they occur. The success of it would depend upon a complex set of decisions, taken by many individuals according to circumstances unforeseen by anyone but driven by their mutually compatible motivation without tightly constraining rules.

Among such initiatives would be those which involve stimulating a new market between constitutionally independent buyers and sellers, instead of instigating an entirely bureaucratic rule-orientated one. Each buyer and each seller would be free to seek their own advantage. The new market might be accompanied by some bureaucratic elements, not only for sustaining the continued existence of that market but also to influence the motivation of buyers and sellers, and hence the consequences of their decisions or actions.

The design of an initiative to obtain a centrally prescribed target increase in patient safety would be different from one to obtain an improved combination of patient safety prospects and other outcomes without specifying any precise target. Means of securing compliance with achieving the target would be integral to the former type of initiative, while means of securing compliance with any rules of practice would be a feature of the latter type.

Different mixtures of centralisation and decentralisation of systemic decision taking for health service investment, quality and safety are exemplified by patterns of arrangements established over many years in different territories. In broadly descending order of centralisation, we have systems in the UK (dominated largely by the NHS); New Zealand (including cooperative no-fault arrangements) and the US (heavily dependent on traditional tort law). Australia, on balance, lies towards the US end of the spectrum and Canada exhibits a more complex mixture.[13] It is possible that a different blend of institutional types is cost effective for patient services in the distinctive conditions prevailing across each territory, especially if distinctive cultural norms are included in the list of conditions.

Relying heavily on centralised decision taking about which initiatives would produce the best outcomes for patient safety would also require extensive centralised powers to acquire and process data effectively. Decision taking by many individuals requires less data acquisition and processing by any one individual or sub-group of people. It relies instead on some means by which decision making by that many individuals results in successful overall outcomes.

It might be in the interests of good, systemic decision making for some individual contributors to the system to pursue simple, observable targets which are inflexible and only indirectly connected with fundamental outcomes. The risk of perverse outcomes if they do so rigidly, as unanticipated circumstances unfold, however, is heightened if the causal link between targets and fundamental outcomes is obscure. Opportunities for constructive improvisation might be lost. For example, target waiting times might be pursued to the exclusion of a longer and more productive consultation with a patient who exhibits unanticipated complications.

Division of individual responsibility within or between organisations and other social institutions might well be efficient at simplifying decision making by each individual. It could, nevertheless, result in decisions about cost and about effectiveness (of responding to the risk of adverse events) becoming detached from each other. Both types of decision could also become detached from those about whether the effectiveness of any particular response would be sufficient to outweigh the costs of using up scarce resources which might instead be used effectively in alternative ways.[14]

The most practically effective decision making process might well be one that employs a holistic perspective which retains an opportunity to take account of all systemic determinants of patient safety. The effectiveness of such a process would be greater, however, if it also retained an opportunity to take into account detailed determinants of the system whose potential impact is known to be substantial and highly valued. Tractability is likely to be greater for any determinant whose interdependence with others and with the whole is known to be limited.

Multiple initiatives, decided and implemented separately, might be duplicates or might be incompatible with each other. If so, they would not result, overall, in a worthwhile use of scarce resources. The targets set by or for individual decision makers must be compatible, when pursued simultaneously, with the overall outcomes sought from the system. Some cost effective means of integrating these various decision making processes, by various individuals and in various organisations, would be required to ensure that a worthwhile overall outcome emerges.

Conclusion

Taking active measures to prevent adverse events from befalling patients diverts scarce resources from other uses, including the provision of risky but often highly effective patient services. Some of the riskier health services might be among the usually more effective ones. A consensual balance between adverse events and precaution cannot be assured, either by individual decision taking alone or by centrally prescribed rules of policy and practice alone, in the presence of divergent priorities for discretionary use of resources. A centralised design of systemic cost incentives which also retain discretion for local initiative and improvisation, as new circumstances arise, may be the holy grail of patient safety initiatives. Tort law and market price, among other non-centralised social institutions, offer opportunities within an integrated system to simplify what could otherwise become a more complex, costly bureaucracy of regulation for patient safety. All individual decision takers can stay alert to systemic and interdependent cost incentives for preventing and tolerating adverse events that befall patients in receipt of health services. That precaution would be a low cost, first step towards agreeing a balance between effective risky and safe patient services.

Notes

1 L.T. Kohn, J.M. Corrigan and M.S. Donaldson (eds), *To Err Is Human: Building a Safer Health System*, Committee on Quality of Health Care in America, Institute of Medicine, Washington, DC, National Academy Press, 2000.
2 M.M. Mello, D.M. Studdert, E.J. Thomas, C.C. Yoon and T.A. Brennan, 'Who Pays for Medical Errors? An Analysis of Adverse Event Costs, the Medical Liability System, and Incentives for Patient Safety Improvement', *Journal of Empirical Legal Studies* 4:4, 2007, p. 857.
3 P.M. Danzon, *Medical Malpractice: Theory, Evidence, and Public Policy*, Cambridge, MA, Harvard University Press, 1985.
4 House of Commons, *Patient Safety, HC 151-I Health Committee Sixth Report of Session 2008–09 – Volume I*, London, Her Majesties Stationery Office, 2009, ch. 6.
5 M. Bismarck and R. Paterson, 'No-fault Compensation in New Zealand: Harmonizing Injury Compensation, Provider Accountability, and Patient Safety', *Health Affairs* 25:1, 2006, pp. 278–283.

6 House of Commons, *Patient Safety*, ch. 10.
7 G. Calabresi, *The Costs of Accidents: A Legal and Economic Analysis*, New Haven, CT, Yale University Press, 1970.
8 R.A. Posner, *Tort Law: Cases and Economic Analysis*, Boston, Little, Brown & Co, 1982.
9 United States v. Carroll Towing Co., 159 F.2d. 169, 173 (2d. Cir. 1947).
10 Calabresi, *The Costs of Accidents*.
11 W.M. Sage, 'The Forgotten Third: Liability Insurance and the Medical Malpractice Crisis', *Health Affairs* 23:4, 2004, pp. 10–21.
12 Bismarck and Paterson, 'No-fault Compensation in New Zealand'.
13 J.M. Gilmour, *Patient Safety, Medical Error and Tort Law: An International Comparison, Final Report*, Health Policy Research Program, Health Canada HPRP Project Number 6795-15-203/5760003
14 Mello *et al.*, 'Who Pays for Medical Errors?'

References

Bismarck, M. and Paterson, R. (2006) 'No-fault Compensation in New Zealand: Harmonizing Injury Compensation, Provider Accountability, and Patient Safety', *Health Affairs* 25:1, pp. 278–283.

Calabresi, G. (1970) *The Costs of Accidents: A Legal and Economic Analysis*, New Haven, CT, Yale University Press

Danzon, P.M. (1985) *Medical Malpractice: Theory, Evidence, and Public Policy*, Cambridge, MA, Harvard University Press.

Gilmour, J.M. (2006) *Patient Safety, Medical Error and Tort Law: An International Comparison, Final Report*, Health Policy Research Program, Health Canada HPRP Project Number 6795-15-203/5760003.

House of Commons (2009) *Patient Safety, HC 151-I Health Committee Sixth Report of Session 2008–09 – Volume I*, London, The Stationery Office.

Kohn, L.T., Corrigan, J.M. and Donaldson, M.S. (eds) (2000) *To Err Is Human: Building a Safer Health System*, Committee on Quality of Health Care in America, Institute of Medicine, Washington, DC, National Academy Press.

Mello, M.M., Studdert, D.M., Thomas, E.J., Yoon, C.C. and Brennan, T.A. (2007) 'Who Pays for Medical Errors? An Analysis of Adverse Event Costs, the Medical Liability System, and Incentives for Patient Safety Improvement', *Journal of Empirical Legal Studies* 4:4, pp. 835–860.

Posner, R.A. (1982) *Tort Law: Cases and Economic Analysis*, Boston: Little, Brown & Co.

Sage, W.M. (2004) 'The Forgotten Third: Liability Insurance and the Medical Malpractice Crisis', *Health Affairs* 23:4, pp. 10–21.

United States v. Carroll Towing Co., 159 F.2d. 169, 173 (2d. Cir. 1947).

8 Patient safety in secondary care

Ash Samanta and Jo Samanta

Introduction

More than thirty years ago Ivan Illich cautioned the public about medically induced harm. His monograph *Medical Nemesis* subjected western medicine to a considered attack on the basis of detailed statistical evidence of surgical side-effects and medicine induced illness.[1]

Clinical care provided in hospitals remains fraught with risk for patients, as revealed by media headlines and published reports. The failings of the Mid-Staffordshire NHS Foundation Trust[2] and the Maidstone and Tunbridge Wells Trust[3] provide objective evidence that much must be done to make the hospital experience a safer one for patients. The risk of unanticipated harm in secondary care is significant and evidence presented to the House of Commons Health Committee demonstrates that about 10 per cent of patients admitted to hospital are likely to suffer iatrogenic harm as an outcome of their stay.[4] Furthermore, prevalence rates might be even higher since documentary proof is likely to underestimate the true incidence of adverse events.[5] What is clear is that the emotional and financial harm experienced in the aftermath of a patient safety incident can be enormous, with repercussions for the victim and her family, other patients, practitioners, organisations and the wider public interest.[6]

Complex secondary care environments provide fertile ground for the occurrence of errors. Adverse safety incidents will occur and eliminating all human error is difficult, if not impossible. Data collected by the National Patient Safety Agency (NPSA)[7] as well as global evidence obtained by the World Health Organisation[8] show that iatrogenic harm in secondary care typically includes errors and delay in diagnosis, drug and treatment errors, technical faults with equipment, and hospital acquired infections. Incident rates vary between specialities but overarching themes are apparent.

The need for enhanced patient safety in hospital environments has been recognised for some time within this jurisdiction (and others). For the United Kingdom the landmark report commissioned in 2000 by Sir Liam Donaldson, *An Organisation with a Memory*, was to substantially raise the profile of the patient safety agenda.[9] This was soon followed by *Building a*

Safer NHS for Patients: Implementing an Organisation with a Memory, which detailed the Department of Health's patient safety strategy.[10] Several progress reports came next, such as *Safety First*[11] and *A Safer Place for Patients*,[12] all of which emphasised the central importance of a safe environment to avoid harm to patients in secondary care settings. These reports showed that accidental errors and system failures were often repeated, even in the same hospital. Around half these events could have been avoided if timely recognition and intervention had occurred.

This chapter considers the principle themes of patient safety in the context of contemporary secondary care environments and focuses on issues that could lead to (avoidable) harm. The emphasis is predominantly on transgressions caused by systems failures rather than individual culpability. Recent and proposed changes in law and policy are evaluated as possible ways forward.

Creating a safer secondary care environment

A safety culture

Greater emphasis is now given to organisational cultures in order to implement effective and sustained patient safety policies within hospitals,[13] although action is invariably required at the level of individual practitioner as a means of ensuring positive change.

Changing an organisation's culture is notoriously difficult, but is not impossible.[14] McCarthy and Blumenthal's in-depth review of six hospitals that sought to implement proactive changes to their organisations' safety culture discovered that top-down and bottom-up approaches could be effective.[15] A top-down approach, change being driven by policy initiatives and dictats from government down to senior officials through to frontline staff, was shown to have a considerable positive effect. Of the organisations reviewed, the Sentara Norfolk General Hospital successfully introduced a comprehensive change strategy to facilitate organisational change. Compared with bottom-up strategies, this type of approach, whilst effective, required greater investment of time and resources, particularly in respect of senior managerial commitment.

An exemplar of a successful bottom-up approach to implementing positive cultural change in a secondary care health environment is one developed by the Kaiser Permanente institution, based upon integrated managed care within organisations. The initiative aimed to enhance teamwork and communication skills, particularly in high risk specialities such as surgery and obstetrics, principally by enhancing pre-operative care discussions on patient transfer. Outcomes demonstrated that successful implementation of change resulted in an improved safety culture, more effective teamwork and reduced staff turnover. Pre-operative briefings were considered to be an effective mechanism for changing the way people perceived and practised teamwork, which ultimately led to positive cultural change. A bottom-up approach is an effective and efficient method of implementing change in secondary care, particularly when supported by physician involvement and strong managerial leadership.

The Safer Patients Initiative

Patient safety is an international agenda. The World Health Organisation's *World Alliance for Patient Safety*[16] sought to prioritise the urgent need to reduce the incidence of medical error and iatrogenic harm to patients across the world. In the United Kingdom the Health Foundation, an independent charity, launched the Safer Patients Initiative in 2004 to ascertain practical ways of making the acute sector a safer one for patients.[17] The first phase of the initiative ran from 2004 and included four hospitals; the second commenced in 2006 with twenty hospitals. Selected hospitals worked in collaboration with the Health Foundation, a charity with the aim of improving the quality of healthcare, and the Institute of Healthcare Improvement, a United States based organisation that focused on global healthcare improvement. The Safer Patients Initiative highlighted those clinical areas recognised as having an accepted evidence base in this jurisdiction and included: the better management of patients in intensive care; infection control; prophylactic antibiotic therapy for surgical patients; as well as medicine safety. Key personnel were trained in quality and safety, as well as senior officials such as chief executives and executive teams in order to ensure that the initiative became a strategic priority for the Trust concerned.[18]

The Safer Patient Initiative was a top-down systems based approach to focus executive attention on the need to ensure that safety was a central and overriding priority to be filtered down to promote cultural change amongst frontline care givers. The sites involved in the ongoing first phase were Luton and Dunstable Hospital NHS Trust; Conwy and Denbighshire NHS Trust; South Eastern Health and Social Care Trust; and NHS Tayside. The second phase operated a paired approach to implement safety improvements that had been learnt from phase one.

Several positive outcomes occurred following this initiative. These included reductions in the number of crash calls following use of an effective early warning system that encouraged staff to monitor patients and implement remedial action; a substantial reduction in the prevalence of *Clostridium difficile* infections; enhanced surgical care due to better communication amongst the surgical team; and reduced central line infections in critical care units. The need for quality assurance was identified as a central aspect of clinical and nurse training, as well as the need to engage patient involvement to develop effective local solutions. Strong leadership, clear lines of accountability and the need to prioritise patient safety were shown to be key components in achieving enhanced patient safety and improved outcomes.

Further invaluable lessons and insights gained from the initiative included the need for the acute sector to implement better and more effective systems to monitor the effectiveness of safety improvements. It is apparent that whilst positive attention has focused on the development of robust standards and guidelines, insufficient attention has been given to introducing practical, sustained and reliable change. An adequate infrastructure and a collective team based approach to patient safety are central components, as well as the recognition of the impact of change on the wider system of community care. The Safer Patients Initiative received a commendation from the House of Commons Health Committee in its Patient Safety Report,[19] and the Health Foundation has recently published a research report, *Safety and Risk Management in Hospitals*.[20]

Collective approaches

Traditional approaches to reduce iatrogenic harm caused by error tend to be accompanied by legal and regulatory sanctions. Contemporary initiatives in secondary care are inclined to rely on collective approaches and incentives to achieve the same ends. Although regulatory sanctions and civil, and possibly criminal, liability remain real possibilities following actionable patient harm, current initiatives emphasise the need to learn from patient safety incidents as a way to eliminate or reduce the likelihood of recurrence. This shift in thinking is in recognition of the fact that whilst legal and disciplinary sanctions are popularly perceived as deterring further events, causal analysis demonstrates that fear of legal or regulatory penalties does not, by itself, positively influence behaviour or reduce unintentional patient harm. This finding seems particularly pertinent for healthcare environments, where the overriding motivation of staff is to help patients.

Current approaches to patient safety tend to concentrate efforts on systems of work within organisations. An example of a collective financial incentive designed to promote patient safety is the Clinical Negligence Scheme for Trusts (CNST), which operates a risk-pooling indemnity scheme operated by the NHS Litigation Authority (NHSLA). The NHSLA provides indemnity for NHS organisations against clinical negligence actions. Membership is voluntary, although at present all Trusts in England belong to the scheme. Each Trust contributes a predetermined sum to a collective pool, from which claims are settled, and each Trust's contribution is assessed according to actuarial calculations based upon exposure to clinical risk. Discounts on membership contributions provide a positive incentive to meet NHSLA standards and are given to those Trusts that operate robust risk management schemes and have a non-adverse claims record. Trusts are assessed against NHSLA standards in the following areas: governance; competent and capable workforce; safe environment; clinical care; learning from experience. Discounts are awarded on their premiums of 10, 20 and 30 per cent, respectively, depending upon whether they comply with Level 1, 2 or 3 of the standards. Level 1 pertains to documentation and having appropriate policies in place; Level 2 requires evidence of implementation; and

Level 3, actual performance by way of monitoring and improvement. As an example of a top-down approach, this incentive would be expected to offer an effective way of promoting a safety conscious environment, particularly considering the financial constraints on NHS organisations. The most recent NHSLA Annual Report indicates that the majority of Acute Trusts operate at Level 1 (46 per cent) or Level 2 (46 per cent).[21] Only 6 per cent operate at Level 3, even though the CNST has been in existence since 1995. In its role as assessor of risk management programmes, the NHSLA has assumed a duty for developing and setting standards for NHS Trusts. The need for such a role is readily apparent. However, the extent to which this duty ought to be separate from a body which has a vested interest in litigation avoidance through settling claims is perhaps questionable.

Crew resource management is a team building approach which has proven to be an effective means of enhancing safety within the aviation industry. A variant of this scheme was used by the University Hospitals of Coventry and Warwickshire NHS Trust with the aim of improving adverse incident reporting by staff. An external review had identified that the Trust did not learn from errors as staff felt that they would be blamed for reported mistakes. Staff training was used to encourage incident reporting through a team based approach to safety. The scheme resulted in an increase in the number of incidents reported, from fifty per month to an average of 700 per month (including minor incidents such as slips, trips and falls) between 2002 and 2005. As a consequence, there were improvements for the Trust in respect of external performance review ratings.[22]

The clinical governance initiative has been implemented across all NHS organisations. It combines structures and arrangements to monitor and manage clinical performance to facilitate continued improvements in the quality of patient care. Recent strategies that seek to address the patient safety agenda, such as integrated governance and risk management, are designed to operate at an organisational level rather than targeting individual practitioners under the traditional culture of blame. Despite its success, the concept of governance could in some instances be criticised for its structural approach to quality and its tendency to focus on procedures and processes rather than improved patient services.

The patient's role

The overwhelming majority of patient safety initiatives have sought to target those delivering care, unsafe systems of work and healthcare environments. Systems theories show that most adverse incidents are attributable to a confluence of factors that include errors of patients as recipients of care. Despite this knowledge, patient involvement in safety initiatives remains relatively low profile, although organisations (such as the NPSA) are now actively promoting patient involvement in some campaigns. Patient focused initiatives tend to concentrate on education and the need to seek clarification

where there is concern about care. It is vital that patients consider themselves a central part of the healthcare team and that their contributions are
valued. This is imperative since the effectiveness of campaigns is likely to be
limited due to patient reticence about challenging staff on safety issues, as
was found with the NPSA 'Cleanyourhands' initiative.[23]

In the United States public access to reliable performance data of healthcare organisations and individual clinicians is reported to have had a positive
effect on patient safety. Armed with comparative information, patients
ought to be able to make informed decisions about healthcare providers
which could positively drive clinical and organisational standards.[24] In the
Bristol Inquiry, failure to disclose shortcomings in clinical performance and
patient safety was stridently criticised, particularly since professional colleagues at the Bristol Royal Infirmary had been aware of the poor clinical
outcomes of surgeons operating on paediatric cardiac patients. Since this
information was not in the public domain, parents had been denied the
opportunity to make informed choices about healthcare provision. The
Agency for Healthcare Research and Quality has recommended that patients
choose hospitals and doctors that are high volume providers of care.[25] The
extent to which these recommendations are truly transferable to the United
Kingdom experience is perhaps doubtful. At present, reliable performance
data are not freely available for all specialities, although moves are underway
to improve this situation and are led by the independent organisation
Doctor Foster, an initiative to make information about hospitals and
consultants freely available to the public.[26]

Patient-held records are a useful and reliable strategy to enhance effective
self-management of obstetric care,[27] and for patients with cancer.[28] Outside
these specialities patient-held records are relatively rare, even though evidence shows that such practice can promote patient participation and
engagement with self-care and enhance shared care. It can also improve the
accuracy of clinical records.[29] What is clear, however, is that patient involvement programmes will only be effective in organisations which value and
recognise consumer input.

Clinical transitions within and from secondary care

Lord Darzi's final report, *High Quality Care for All*,[30] responds to the 10
Strategic Health Authority healthcare plans by introducing a planned policy
programme for the NHS with an overriding focus on quality enhancement.
The Report emphasises the need to improve patient care by provision of
a high quality seamless service between secondary and primary care sectors
to integrate more accessible and convenient care for all, particularly those
suffering chronic or life-threatening conditions.

A key aspect of a patient's experience of hospital care is that of 'transitions' describing the necessary changes that confront the patient during
the hospital stay. Change can be on account of physical location (such as

admission to, and discharge from, hospital) or can arise from the need to ensure continuity of care (such as hand-over from day to night staff). Further transitions occur on transfers to and from theatre as well as between wards. Increasing specialisation of health services has led to more transitions during hospital care. Whilst necessary, and typically unavoidable, such transitions represent considerable 'pinch-points' for exposing the patient to heightened risk of harm if they are not managed and performed adequately. Most of the risk is caused by inadequate provision and communication of vital information on transfer of care, such as between community based services and secondary care.

Drug errors are the most likely category of error on admission to hospital. According to a systematic review by Tam *et al.*, typical errors include: omission (46 per cent); dosage (25 per cent); mistakes in frequency (17 per cent); and errors of commission (11 per cent).[31] Forster suggests that high rates of error are caused by clinicians' tendency to prioritise new acute clinical complaints over management of underlying chronic conditions.[32] A possible medium-term solution would be implementation of comprehensive electronic health records and more closely integrated IT systems, particularly between primary and secondary care.

Empirical work shows that intra-hospital transfers pose a further and considerable patient safety risk, most notably on transfer from intensive therapy units to regular wards. Patient transfers that take place at night reportedly result in an increased risk of death in the order of 33–70 per cent (after adjusting for other factors associated with death).[33] Goldfrad *et al.* contend that the underlying cause of this finding is because transfers at night tend to be driven by resource constraints rather than patient need. Decisions to transfer during the night tend to be premature, in response to the need to admit another critically ill patient as an emergency and in the context of acute bed shortages. In these circumstances, the receiving wards might not have sufficient capacity to offer the high staff to patient ratio that the patient's condition might require. Intra-hospital transfers are also characterised by drug errors,[34] as well as technical failures in equipment, which occurred in 33–45 per cent of intra-hospital transfers.[35] Typical incidents included loss of power in cardiac monitors, intravenous pumps and portable ventilators, inadvertent disconnection of equipment, hypothermia and prolonged delays.

Avoidance of technical problems is difficult, although a robust and regular monitoring and recording system with appropriate back-up supplies could ameliorate risk of harm. Premature discharge from intensive care settings needs to be avoided, and clinical teams need to communicate effectively about medication regimes, outstanding test results and the clinical stability of the patient at the time of transfer.

Discharge from hospital represents a further period of heightened risk, particularly for the elderly and those with complex care needs. Evidence suggests that one out of five patients is likely to experience an adverse event during the month following discharge.[36] For one-third of medical patients, suffering an adverse event on discharge leads to readmission, admission to an accident and emergency department or even death. Post-discharge events were most commonly attributable to drug errors, nosocomial infection, errors of diagnosis, procedural complications or errors in therapeutic management.[37] For surgical patients a similar picture emerges, although post-operative wound infections were present in up to 10 per cent of patients.[38]

Forster believes that most post-discharge adverse events would have been avoided or considerably reduced if robust safety mechanisms had been introduced. These include patient education to enhance involvement with therapeutic care plans, drug induced side-effects and better communication between secondary and community care. A positive initiative from the United States has been the inclusion of dedicated 'transition coaches' as part of the care team for patients ready to be discharged from secondary care environments. Transition coaches are specialist nurses charged with facilitating the patient's discharge to ensure that the patient is fully aware of planned follow-up treatment regimes, changes to medication and the need to report side-effects and adverse events, as part of a seamless transition to community care.[39] The need for successful management of the discharge process is vital and is expected to assume ever greater significance with the trend to move care into the community.

Never Events

In *High Quality Care for All* Lord Darzi introduced the concept of 'Never Events', which are recognised as serious and largely preventable patient safety events that should not occur if available preventative measures are implemented.[40] The concept derives from the United States, where some private insurers and government-funded schemes have developed policies of refusing to pay providers for costs that arise following such incidents. In this jurisdiction it is not yet clear whether Never Events will be linked to financial penalties, which would mean that primary care trusts could refuse to meet the costs of remedial action following the occurrence of such an events.

Financial penalties might operate as a double-edged sword. The threat of financial penalties could positively enhance risk management and governance strategies. More pessimistically, penalties could detrimentally impact upon patient safety, particularly if secondary care providers suppress the reporting of such events in order protect their own self-interest. A further practical concern about attaching financial penalties is the difficulty of separating the costs associated with a Never Event from those that relate to the care of the patient's index condition,[41] a complex causation element that typically accompanies clinical negligence litigation actions.

The core list of Never Events includes: wrong-site surgery; retained instruments following surgery; wrong-route chemotherapy; non-detected misplaced feeding tubes; suicide of in-patents by non-collapsible bed rails; escape by prisoners from medium or high secure mental health hospitals; in-hospital maternal death from post-partum haemorrhage after elective caesarean section; and erroneous intravenous administration of concentrated potassium chloride.

Effects of the European Working Time Directive

Most secondary care providers offer placements as part of a rotation for specialist medical training. Implementation of the European Working Time Directive (EWTD) under the Working Time Regulations, and its potential to negatively impact upon patient safety as well as the training of junior doctors in the NHS, has been of some concern to the medical profession and public.[42] The main effect of the health and safety legislation is that workers are entitled to an eleven-hour break in each twenty-four-hour cycle and that junior doctors must work for no more than an average of forty-eight hours per week. Although the original European Directive became part of health and safety law in 1993, junior doctors were initially excluded from these requirements, but this has been phased in and is now fully in force.

Substantial clinical experience is an essential and central aspect of medical training programmes. Evidence from educational psychologists indicates that around 10,000 hours of practice are needed to acquire specialist levels of expertise such as those required in clinical specialities.[43] Surgical training and the development of necessary expertise is considered to be at particular risk because of the need to develop skills in cognition and dexterity. Although role play and simulation provide an ever-increasing part of medical training, hands-on clinical experience remains the cornerstone of achieving competence. Prior to the change in law it was not uncommon to hear reports of junior doctors working in excess of seventy-two hours per week, and the effects of fatigue and sleep deprivation on human cognitive and motor performance, as well as error, are well recognised.[44] The EWTD is expected to represent a positive and necessary change to the previous 'unlimited' working hours of junior doctors in training. However, there is a genuine concern as to whether doctors who are training will get adequate 'hands-on' practical experience. Medical Education England is set to review the impact of the EWTD on medical education.[45]

The case of *Nettleship v. Weston* is authority that lack of experience will not operate to reduce the standard of care expected from a trainee.[46] More specifically in the context of the hospital environment, the Court of Appeal in *Wilsher v. Essex Area Health Authority*[47] held that the standard of care to be expected was determined by the post held by the defendant, rather than the defendant's personal expertise or rank. In effect, this means that a patient can expect a certain level of care from a healthcare professional according to the role being performed. Since almost all the safety benefits of the EWTD potentially arise out of an entitlement to adequate rest periods, one way forward might be to retain the rules on rest periods whilst allowing more than forty-eight hours to be worked per week.[48]

It has always been somewhat confounding that junior doctors were required to work excessive hours in order to provide medical cover for wards and operating theatres (particularly out of hours), as well as to gain clinical expertise. Trusts may find it challenging to provide sufficient out of hours cover unless adequate and sustainable staffing solutions are developed. A potential effect of the health and safety legislation designed to protect patient safety is that it could have a negative impact. One solution would be to use locum doctors to provide the necessary cover. As yet there is no mechanism to regulate or monitor the number of hours worked per week by locum doctors, and it is questionable whether this method of circumventing the effects of legislation could be condoned. The clinical cover provided by a fatigued locum doctor can hardly be considered adequate. Another solution is to extend the scope of practice of healthcare professionals such as nurses, who have already received training to take on aspects of patient care that would otherwise have been provided by junior doctors. It remains to be tested in court whether in the event of litigation the standard of care expected of the enhanced non-medical practitioner would be the same as that of a doctor.

More positively, Reid has found that some of these challenges have been successfully addressed by many Trusts by using a mixture of shifts and on-call from home rotas for surgical trainees, Furthermore, where implementation has been successful, patient length of stay, access to speciality care training and trainee satisfaction have all improved.[49]

Innovative therapy

There is rising demand for less invasive surgical interventions and most innovative surgical techniques are carried out in secondary care settings. New operative techniques can be undertaken without full regulatory oversight, unlike clinical drug trials that fall within the auspices of the research governance framework.[50] It is inevitable that when novel techniques are introduced surgeons will necessarily embark on a learning curve in order to gain proficiency and experience. This poses complex ethical and legal issues for patient safety and care.[51]

According to law, clinical interventions may be classified as established treatment, innovative therapy or research.[52] Although this categorisation is convenient and intellectually attractive, it obscures the reality that no clear line of demarcation exists particularly between innovation and research. Tinkering at the edges of established practice might be subject to professional discretion; clinical research is governed by a stringent regulatory framework, however therapeutic innovation remains within an intermediate and nebulous area with regard to regulation and even safe practice.

Use of innovative therapy raises important patient safety issues in the context of the expected standard of care. The test used in law to determine the standard of care expected from clinicians is governed by the *Bolam* principle[53] in that the standard of care is that which is endorsed by a responsible body of professional opinion. However, an innovative procedure is likely to be at the frontier of medical knowledge and there might be no other expert(s) who could constitute a responsible body sufficient to assert an authoritative opinion. Nevertheless, in *Simms v. Simms*[54] it was established that deviation from approved practice will not necessarily amount to negligent care since it would be against the public interest to impede medical progress in the unavoidable absence of *Bolam* endorsement. Within this jurisdiction the National Institute for Health and Clinical Excellence is responsible for the assessment of the efficacy of innovative therapy.

The Declaration of Helsinki requires patients to be informed of all risks and benefits inherent in innovative procedures,[55] a requirement that is difficult to satisfy. As a result, innovation could represent a category of risk to patient safety that is unique to secondary (and tertiary) healthcare environments. This could not only result in harm to patients and organisational reputational damage but also precipitate civil litigation or possibly a challenge under articles 3 and 8 of the European Convention of Human Rights. Secondary care organisations need to be alert to the unique challenges to patient safety posed by innovative practices which need to be subsumed within clinical governance.

Healthcare associated infections

During the last decade healthcare associated infections (HCAI) (previously known as hospital acquired infection) such as meticillin-resistant *Staphylococcus aureus* (MRSA) and *Clostridium difficile* have assumed international importance for the patient safety agenda. The prevalence of HCAIs is estimated as 7.6 per cent of adult patients in acute hospitals in the United Kingdom and Northern Ireland,[56] a figure that imposes an economic burden of at least £1.6 billion.[57] Harmful effects range from death to an extension in the length of the patient's hospital stay.

HCAI can be classified into three categories: autoinfection due to the patient's own microbial flora and commensals; cross-infection from other patients or staff; and cross-infection from environmental sources, typically caused through inadequate decontamination of equipment. In reality infection tends to be caused by several interrelated factors superimposed upon a patient who may have considerably weakened defence mechanisms.

Preventative measures can reduce the risk of disease. Risks of autoinfection can be reduced by prophylactic measures such as skin and mucosal disinfection and pre-operative antimicrobial use. Planned operative procedures can be preceded by prophylactic antibiotic administered within an hour of surgery to ensure sufficient blood levels to prevent organisms present at the site of incision causing infection. Strategies to prevent cross-infection by staff and patients aim to interfere with the route transmission of organisms.

Infection is typically caused by the failure by staff to decontaminate their hands before and after contact with patients, and for this reason cleansing with alcoholic and other antiseptic lotions is to be advised.[58] Infection transmitted by the environment is best controlled by effective decontamination of equipment prior to use on other patients.

These approaches can operate to reduce the incidence of HCAIs in hospital. However, HCAIs are caused by a multitude of causative agents, all of which operate to make the patient more susceptible to infection. A survey undertaken by the National Audit Office found that English hospital infection control teams considered that approximately 15 per cent of HCAIs could be prevented.[59] Clinical governance arrangements to ensure clear lines of accountability and responsibility facilitate preventative strategies within hospitals. Practice based upon current best evidence as well as robust quality control mechanisms are required to detect and correct unacceptable practice in secondary care settings, where the entire organisation needs to be involved.[60]

In 2005 the Healthcare Commission reported evidence of poor standards of hygiene in a substantial number of hospitals in England. In the following year the Department of Health published its first Hygiene Code and set a target for the NHS to reduce rates of MRSA infection by 50 per cent. In 2007 the Healthcare Commission conducted unannounced inspections at 120 NHS trusts to monitor compliance with the Hygiene Code and rates of HCAIs in order to ensure that infection control is a priority.

Since the Care Quality Commission assumed its responsibility for health and social care regulation part of its remit has been to monitor HCAIs, and the Commission is empowered to take remedial action wherever patients are at risk. From 1 April 2009 all NHS Trusts must be registered with the Care Quality Commission, which requires compliance with regulations that pertain to HCAIs.[61] To assess ongoing compliance the Commission has developed a system whereby hospitals submit their assessments against core standards that are evaluated as part of each organisation's annual health check.

The Department of Health has published a revised code of practice for HCAIs under the Health and Social Care Act 2008, known as the *Code of Practice for the NHS on the Prevention and Control of Healthcare Associated Infections and Related Guidance (the Hygiene Code).*[62] The revised Code sets out 10 criteria against which NHS hospitals (as well as NHS Blood and Transplant) are judged on compliance. The Care Quality Commission uses these 10 criteria in unannounced inspections to assess compliance with government regulation regarding HCAIs.

In circumstances where a hospital is failing to comply with the regulation the Commission is empowered to take enforcement action. Conditions may be imposed on registration, for example to improve decontamination procedures or stop using a particular facility. A trust that fails to comply with its conditions of registration commits an offence. Other enforcement action that can be taken includes the issue of a warning notice, the imposition, variation or removal of conditions, prosecution, imposing a financial penalty or cancellation of registration.[63]

The House of Commons Third Report states that the Department of Health has achieved significant reductions in *Clostridium difficile* and MRSA infections and has successfully improved the cleanliness of hospitals. Statistically significant reductions in other HCAIs were not achieved in other preventable HCAIs. The Public Accounts Committee recommended a range of initiatives, including monitoring of the impact of patient movement within hospitals and following discharge into the community, as well as recording the finding of HCAIs on death certificates.[64]

Operational challenges

Electronic patient records

Errors in secondary care environments may be precipitated by failure to transfer relevant clinical information between locations where care is provided, typically due to non-availability of paper based medical records. The introduction of electronic medical records seems to offer an unrivalled solution to the perpetual problem of missing notes. For maximal effectiveness, factors such as user efficiency, ease of use and speed of data input are likely to be essential components of an electronic based system. Experience from the United States indicates that unanticipated inherent risk can accompany use of electronic records. This has included errors caused by shortcuts used by frontline staff, such as the 'cut and paste' facility. Since cut and paste commands can be used to copy one day's entry as a template for the next, these practices are often found in healthcare environments and result in erroneous or inaccurate entries.[65] The introduction of electronic medical records without adequate training could lead to new types of unanticipated patient harm due to incorrect entries in clinical records.[66]

The introduction of Electronic Patient Records has proved controversial in this jurisdiction (the UK), as seen from the House of Commons Health Committee Report published in 2007.[67] Typical arguments against the use of electronic records revolve around consent, confidentiality, the potential for hackers to obtain sensitive personal data and cost. Concerns about patient confidentiality are addressed by safeguards that control access to patient health records by the use of Smartcards based on chip and pin technology.[68] The organisation NHS Connecting for Health has been created to support the patient safety agenda by developing informatics systems to improve storage and accessibility of patient information.[69]

Clinical Dashboards

Healthcare computerisation and increased use of information technology ought to play a key role in the delivery of safe patient care. Implementation requires incremental change and effective training for all users. Electronic technology is expected to offer advancements in patient safety by improving communication and making essential information more readily available to inform decision-making. Innovations such as automated decision and pre-scribing support systems, assistance with calculations and identification assistance using bar-codes are expected to promote opportunities to enhance care as well as reducing the likelihood of human error.[70] It is apparent, however, that electronic systems are not a panacea. In the area of prescrip-tion and dispensing, computerisation tends to reduce the occurrence of certain types of error but increase the likelihood of others.[71]

The concept of the Clinical Dashboard was announced in Lord Darzi's Next Stage Review and the Health Informatics Review as a toolset to provide frontline clinical staff with the relevant information required to inform clinical decisions to enhance the quality of patient care.[72] A 'Clinical Dashboard' allows easy access to data in an accessible format to enhance the quality of decision-making. The initiative was piloted by 24 dashboards across all of the strategic health authorities in England, which developed the necessary technical infrastructure for implementation and subsequent organ-isation into a 'toolkit' in readiness for national uptake.

Medicines safety

Drug errors are a large and important group of patient safety incident and between July 2005 and July 2006 more than 40,000 drug errors were reported by NHS Trusts in England.[73] Medication groups such as anticoagu-lants, corticosteroids and hypoglycaemic agents significantly increased the likelihood of adverse events. In the hospital environment the safety and accuracy of prescription decisions is enhanced by condition or medication specific guidelines, supported on evidence based principles, expert opinion and the literature.[74] Accurate dispensing, administration and monitoring are foundational aspects of safe care.

Following discharge from secondary care, adverse events tend to be related to newly prescribed medication or changes to dosage or frequency of adminis-tration. Patients who recall being informed of the nature of possible side-effects are significantly less likely to experience adverse events.[75] For this reason, patient education programmes, particularly for those taking medica-tion from the high risk categories, ought to be a priority. At the Bradford Teaching Hospitals a safety risk was identified in that nursing staff were fre-quently interrupted and distracted during medicine administration rounds. To address this concern two schemes were introduced: first, nurses were given coloured aprons to wear when giving medicines in order to provide a visual cue for others; and, second, responsibility was clearly designated to a named nurse on each shift. Neither approach was particularly effective.

Whilst some were aware that nurses involved with the medicine round ought not to be distracted, others did not fully appreciate the reasoning behind the rule. Many suspected that the initiative was designed to enhance productivity rather than safety, a factor which significantly reduced its potential to enhance patient safety. A more effective intervention proved to be a combined approach of visual cue plus a short sharp explanation being delivered by the nurse to any person who caused distraction. This approach was found to be more effective, particularly for a ward where interruptions were predominantly caused by non-nursing staff.[76]

Surgical care practitioners

The NHS has been subject to continual and incremental change in order to meet overriding policy objectives that include the changing healthcare needs of society. Government targets and the introduction of the NHS Constitution alongside implementation of the EWTD have meant that ways have had to be found to increase the number of staff able to provide safe surgical services and support. The development of new roles that transcend traditional boundaries between the clinical and non-clinical is one potential way of meeting this need and has been driven by politicians and non-medical healthcare professionals seeking to extend their roles.

Introducing new roles and extending the scope of more traditional ones was also promoted by reports such as the *Scope of Professional Practice*,[77] *Making a Difference*,[78] *The NHS Plan*[79] and *A Health Service of Talents: Developing the NHS Work Force*,[80] all of which emphasised the benefits to be gained by proactive development of non-medical staff. A good example is the Surgical Care Practitioner (SCP), a grade of non-medical staff introduced to perform surgical procedures as well as provide non-operative clinical care.

An SCP is a 'non-medical practitioner, working in clinical practice as a member of the extended surgical team, who performs surgical intervention, pre-operative and post-operative care under the direction and supervision of a consultant surgeon'.[81] The SCPs currently in practice hold a primary healthcare qualification, for example in nursing or as an operating department practitioner.

Whilst the potential benefits can readily been seen, patient safety issues are a central factor in the development of such new roles, particularly in circumstances where such roles do not readily fall under any overarching regulatory framework or training and educational system.

To address these concerns the National Association of Assistants in Surgical Practice was created in 2001 with the specific aim of developing a national standard for the education and training of SCPs in collaboration with the Royal College of Surgeons of England. The organisation also established professional standards for practitioners irrespective of their original professional status. Furthermore, SCPs are subject to liability under the civil and criminal law, as well as being accountable as an employee and team member.

The role of the SCP was initially piloted under the banner of 'surgical assistant', a title subsequently felt to be unacceptable since it demeaned the status of the well-qualified and experienced professionals performing in the role. The position entailed assisting the surgeon with pre-operative, operative and post-operative care. Overlaps were apparent with the responsibilities of the Advanced Scrub Practitioner (ASP) and the Perioperative Surgical Practitioner (PSP), although neither the ASP nor the PSP performed surgery. The surgical assistant attracted significant criticism from surgeons, who felt strongly about patient safety and called for urgent explicit national standards for their education and training.

Foundation Trust status

The emergence of Foundation Trusts is part of the government's drive to decentralise public services and create a patient-led NHS.[82] As of March 2010 there were 129 NHS Foundation Trusts.[83] These bodies have specific freedoms and responsibilities, and increased levels of autonomy and local accountability through the provisions of the Health and Social Care (Community Health and Standards) Act 2003.

NHS Foundation Trusts operate independently of the Strategic Health Authorities and are assessed by Monitor, an independent regulator which reports directly to Parliament. The remit of Monitor is to grant authority for Trusts to become Foundation Trusts according to the principle of 'earnt autonomy' on the grounds that only well-governed and financially sound organisations achieve this status. Following approval, Monitor ensures that these bodies continue to meet the terms of their licence to operate. Foundation Trusts are registered by the Care Quality Commission for essential standards of safety and quality. Failure to meet the standards may lead to the removal of status or the imposition of conditions on the registration. Whilst Monitor has no explicit role in the management of patient safety, its remit to ensure clinical quality and governance ought to operate as an effective safeguard. However, this has been brought into doubt by the recent tragedies at the Mid-Staffordshire Trust due to apparent shortcomings in Monitor's assessment process in granting authorisation. The Healthcare Commission inquiry reported that the pursuit of Foundation status was one of the factors which had distracted the Trust from its patient safety responsibilities.

Foundation Trusts enjoy unprecedented levels of financial discretion and are able to prioritise spending in accordance with local need and priorities. The Department of Health proclaims that this economic independence will facilitate the development of solutions to challenges such as chronic staff shortages. It remains to be seen whether actions will be brought against such bodies, where the root cause of patient harm is inadequate staffing. It is possible that the court's traditional reluctance to pass judgement on NHS bodies because of public policy and the providers' lack of direct control over finances might dissipate. The court might also be minded to take a more interventionist stand in terms of prioritising the use of resources if patient safety is compromised.

Liability for secondary care organisations

Tort

The approach of the law to medical error largely focuses on individual responsibility since tort liability typically requires that a person can be blamed in order to succeed in a case. Yet such incidents seldom involve moral culpability of those charged. According to Brennan, '[a]ny effort to prevent injury due to medical care is complicated by the dead weight of a litigation system that induces secrecy and silence'.[84] It is apparent that whilst a proportion of medical accidents in secondary care are accompanied by moral culpability the vast majority are not and instead represent a complex interplay between human and systems error. Whilst efforts are made to find an answer individual attention may be diverted from wider considerations of systems failures and root cause analysis, all of which should be addressed to avoid a repeat occurrence of the same tragedy. Approaches to effectively minimise the potential for human error within organisations that provide secondary care might be more effective in terms of enhancing patient safety, rather than imposing criminal or civil liability.

Systems approaches, however, should not necessarily be seen as a panacea. A systems approach might risk dilution of the concept of individual professional responsibility and reduce accountability.

The majority of actions for compensation of patients who have suffered harm are brought under negligence, which requires the court to find that the defendant owed the claimant a duty of care, that this duty was breached and that this breach caused the harm as a matter of law. It is therefore apparent that under tort liability not all losses will be adequately compensated by legal redress and, in particular, that it will fail to compensate for injuries where no fault can be found. In the context of tort liability, fault does not necessarily imply or equate with any moral culpability and instead represents a loss adjustment exercise made necessary by the defendant's failure to provide sufficient care that would have been reasonably expected in the circumstances. This type of legal interpretation fails to recognise the ubiquitous public perception of fault and moral culpability, and that a finding of negligence is a punitive one. A clear example is seen in the finding that a senior clinician has been successfully sued in negligence on account of a momentary lapse in an otherwise unblemished career. The description of the doctor as being negligent seems hardly befitting.

The tort liability system of clinical negligence can be compared with the concept of strict liability, where the duty to compensate for loss arises by virtue of the finding that loss has been caused irrespective of any notion of fault. Several erudite analysts have provided detailed analyses of why the tort based approach to compensation of victims does not easily lend itself to hospital environments.

Ultimately, mechanisms for change must emanate from those who are able to make a difference and effect necessary amendments to make the secondary healthcare system safer. To date, no manager or chief executive has been named as a defendant for tort liability even where root cause analysis points to a managerial or strategic decision. The extent to which such measures would perpetuate the blame culture, with little positive effect, and whether this would in fact promote necessary changes in culture, is arguable. In addition, hospital administrators are not answerable to a regulatory body, whereas medical practitioners who are sued in negligence might also be subject to a sanction from the regulator.

Despite the existence of vicarious liability and Crown Immunity the reputation of the doctor concerned is likely to be coloured with obloquy. Furthermore, even where a claim for compensation is met by the Trust (or more frequently the CNST) the Trust may well have a contractual claim against the doctor as an employee. The corollary to such an event might be disastrous for the individual concerned, and whilst in the circumstances blame might be apportioned, it is often organisational failures that are the root cause of patient adverse events.

Vicarious liability

Claims against hospitals or employees are most often brought under the doctrine of vicarious liability, a form of joint and several liability where the hospital as employer assumes liability for the torts of its employees. Despite such liability of the employer, an action may still be brought against the employee who retains personal liability for his negligence. Vicarious liability hinges upon the master–servant relationship. The requirement to find an individual at fault lies at the heart of the traditional tort based system and helps to perpetuate the blame culture. In circumstances where the wrong arises due to deficiencies in care pathways and delivery systems identification of a named individual may be impossible, for example where patients have been harmed through HCAIs such as MRSA.

NHS Trusts have a direct, non-delegable primary duty to provide a safe and reasonable standard of care to patients. Direct liability may extend to failure to provide competent staff or a safe working environment. Although it does not require an individual to be identified, proof of causation is still necessary. Root cause evaluations often demonstrate that the wrong done to a patient has been caused by an individual operating in an unsafe system of working practice.

An action of primary liability can be brought against an institution or a provider of NHS care in respect of organisational failure. Several successful cases have been brought, such as *Bull v. Devon*,[85] where the system in place for summoning doctors to provide emergency obstetric care was inadequate, and in *Robertson v. Nottingham Health Authority*.[86]

The more recent decision of *Farraj v. King's Healthcare NHS Trust (KCH)*[87] provides that the non-delegable duty of care owed by a hospital to its patients can be discharged by delegating performance of a task to a competent independent contractor. This decision is of considerable importance to patient safety and secondary care due to the outsourcing of many specialities such as laboratory services and radiology reports.

Corporate manslaughter

The Corporate Manslaughter and Corporate Homicide Act 2007 came into force in April 2008 and is of relevance for NHS organisations. Prior to implementation of the Act a corporate body could be prosecuted under the common law offence of gross negligence manslaughter provided that the company was in gross breach of a duty of care owed to the victim. In order to convict an organisation a 'directing mind', in the guise of a senior individual who could be deemed to embody the organisation in his actions and decisions, had to be guilty of the offence.

Under section 1(1) the offence of corporate manslaughter (corporate homicide in Scotland) depends upon a finding of gross negligence in the way in which the activities of the organisation are run. Rather than liability being contingent on the guilt of one or more individuals, liability is founded on proof of gross negligence in the manner in which the organisation is run. The offence is committed in circumstances where an organisation, such as an NHS Trust, owes a duty to take reasonable care for a person's safety but the way in which the organisation's activities have been managed or organised amounts to a gross breach of that duty and causes the person's death. By section 4(c) 'senior management' refers to those with significant decision-making roles in managing the whole or a substantial part of the organisation. The Act creates a new homicide offence that can be committed only by organisations and not persons.

The Act has wide implications for patient safety in secondary care.[88] It ought to heighten awareness at boardroom level and promote a stronger patient safety culture within all hospitals. The actions of senior managers are likely to be scrutinised more closely, and in the event of litigation will form a major part of the prosecution's case.

Section 8(3) of the Act allows the jury to consider the attitudes, policies, systems or accepted practices within the organisation, which would include an analysis of the safety culture of the Trust under scrutiny. Trusts will have to show that they have a positive and transparent culture for patient safety, with effective lines of communication. In theory, the Act could apply to all situations that have lead to the death of a patient, including, for example, outbreaks of hospital infections, inadequate staffing and cutbacks in services.

In *R v. Southampton University Hospitals NHS Trust*[89] the court showed that it was not averse to imposing corporate liability on a hospital. The case concerned a thirty-one-year-old man who was admitted to the Southampton General Hospital for a routine operation, and subsequently developed fatal staphylococcal toxic shock syndrome, which two senior house officers had failed to detect. The doctors were convicted of gross negligence manslaughter and the Trust was prosecuted under health and safety legislation (the Corporate Manslaughter and Corporate Homicide Act 2007 was not in force at that time). The Trust pleaded guilty to an amended charge of failing to adequately manage and supervise the doctors in this case, and was convicted and fined £100,000 (subsequently reduced to £40,000 on appeal).[90]

Recognising systems failure and moving in the direction of system culpability rather than apportioning individual blame may be one long-term outcome, although the Act does not specifically provide for the protection of the individual. Relatives of those who have died in hospital may demand that the death is investigated in order to determine whether a new corporate offence might have been committed, and coroners may be more likely to pass on cases to the police. Following the Department of Health's recent memorandum of understanding,[91] Trusts are encouraged to liaise more closely with the police and the Health and Safety Executive following unexpected deaths or serious untoward harm in the NHS. It is hoped that this will lead to more robust systems to enhance patient safety within the secondary environment.

Conclusion

A myriad of government initiatives, as well as independent charitable and world health campaigns, are focused on the need to enhance patient safety in secondary care environments. Progress has been intermittent and hospital healthcare remains a risk to patients. In the drive to improve patient safety, a plethora of organisations are apparent with the shared goal of delivering the patient safety agenda. Whilst this escalation of interest is undoubtedly to be welcomed for raising the profile of this agenda, it might operate as a double-edged sword. If several organisations and initiatives perform, and perhaps duplicate, the very same functions, this could lead to wasting of time and resources, with no real change occurring. Despite the emergence and development of promising government initiatives it seems inevitable that the new coalition government will introduce radical change of direction and pace. The Department of Health report *Liberating the NHS*, the report of the arms-length bodies review published in response to the White Paper *Equity and Excellence: Liberating the NHS*[92] supports the decision to review the health sector's arm's-length bodies to ensure their cost-effectiveness and fitness for purpose. The proposals include the abolition of the NPSA on the basis that quality and safety initiatives are dispersed across several organisations. If the White Paper becomes law the quality improvement functions of the NPSA will be consolidated with the mainstream activities of the new NHS Commissioning Board to maximise the potential leverage that commissioning ought to provide to enhance quality and safety. This uncertainty, together with an environment of scarce resources means that the involvement of charitable and patient organisations such as Action Against Medical Accidents (AvMA) is to be welcomed. Enhancements to patient safety initiatives in secondary care are becoming apparent, but the challenge remains of how best to facilitate and enhance positive change. In the wake of inevitable fiscal restraint there is a real risk that quality and patient safety will suffer unless these issues are prioritised.

Notes

1 I. Illich, *Limits to Medicine: Medical Nemesis, the Expropriation of Health*, London, Marion Boyars Publishers, Ltd, 1999.

2 R. Smith, 'NHS Targets "May Have Led to 1,200 Deaths" in Mid-Staffordshire', *The Telegraph*, 17 March 2009. Online. Available at http://www.telegraph.co.uk/health/healthnews/5008442/NHS-targets-may-have-led-to-1200-deaths-in-Mid-Staffordshire.html (accessed 30 December 2009).

3 BBC News, 'Hospital Bug Deaths "Scandalous"', 11 October 2007. Online. Available at http://news.bbc.co.uk/1/hi/health/7037657.stm (accessed 30 December 2009).

4 House of Commons Health Committee Patient Safety, Sixth Report of Session 2008–09, HC 151-1, 3 July 2009, London, The Stationery Office. Online. Available at http://www.parliament.the-stationery-office.co.uk/pa/cm200809/cmselect/cmhealth/151/151i.pdf.

5 P. Michel, J.I. Quenon, A.M. de Sarasqeta *et al.*, 'Comparison of Three Methods for Estimating Rates of Adverse Events among Hospital Patients in Acute Care Hospitals', *British Medical Journal* 328, 2004, pp. 199.

6 C. Vincent and L. Page, 'Aftermath of Error for Patients and Health Care Staff', in B. Hurwitz and A. Sheikh (eds), *Health Care Errors and Patient Safety*, Oxford, Wiley-Blackwell, 2009, pp. 179–192.

7 S. Scobie and R. Thomson, *Building a Memory: Preventing Harm, Reducing Risks and Improving Patient Safety*, London, National Patient Safety Agency, 2005. Online. Available at http://www.nrls.npsa.nhs.uk/resources/?entryid45=59797&q=0%c2%acbuilding+a+memory%c2%ac.

8 World Health Organisation, *International Patient Safety Event Classification*, Geneva, WHO, 2006.

9 Department of Health Expert Group, *An Organisation with a Memory*, London, Department of Health, 2000.

10 Department of Health, *Building a Safer NHS for Patients – Implementing an Organisation with a Memory*, London, Department of Health, London, 2001. Online. Available at http://www.dh.gov.uk/prod_consum_dh/groups/dh_digitalassets/documents/digitalasset/dh_098565.pdf.

11 Department of Health, *Safety First: A Report for Patients, Clinicians and Healthcare Managers*, London, Department of Health, 2006.

12 National Audit Office, *A Safer Place for Patients: Learning to Improve Patient Safety*, London, National Audit Office, 2005. Online. Available at http://www.nao.org.uk/publications/0506/a_safer_place_for_patients.aspx?alreadysearchfor=yes.

13 L.L. Leape and D.M. Berwick, 'Safe Health Care: Are We Up to It?', *British Medical Journal* 320, 2000, pp. 725–726.

14 R. Boaden and B. Burnes, 'Health Care Safety and Organisational Change', in B. Hurwitz and A. Sheikh (eds). *Health Care Errors and Patient Safety*, Oxford, Wiley-Blackwell, 2009, pp. 56–74.

15 D. McCarthy and D. Blumenthal, 'Stories from the Sharp End: Case Studies in Safety Improvement', *Milbank Quarterly* 84:1, 2006, pp. 165–200.

16 World Health Organisation, *World Alliance for Patient Safety: Forward Programme*, Switzerland, 2005. Online. Available at http://www.who.int/patientsafety/en/brochure_final.pdf.

17 The Health Foundation. Online. Available at http://www.health.org.uk/current_work/demonstration_projects/safer_patients_1.html#chapter5.

18 Online. Available at http://www.health.org.uk/current_work/demonstration_projects/safer_patients_1.html#chapter5.

19 See http://www.health.org.uk/current_work/demonstration_projects/safer_patients_1.html#chapter5.

20 M. Dückers, M. Faber, J. Cruijsberg, R. Grol, L. Schoonhoven and M. Wensing, *Safety and Risk Management in Hospitals*. Online. Available at http://www.health. org.uk/publications/research_reports/safety_and_risk.html.

21 The National Health Service Litigation Authority, *Report and Accounts 2009*, HC 576, July 2009, at p. 21.

22 http://www.saferhealthcare.org.uk/IHI/Topics/ManagingChange/SafetyStories/ 8268_humanfactorsapproachatUniversityhospitalsCoventry.htm.

23 National patient Safety Agency, *Achieving our Aims: Evaluating the Results of the Pilot Cleanyourhands Campaign*, London, National Patient Safety Agency, 2004.

24 The Leapfrog Group website: http://www.leapfroggroup.org/.

25 C. Vincent and A. Coulter, 'Patient safety: What about the Patient?', *Quality and Safety in Health Care* 11, 2002, pp. 76–80.

26 http://www.drfosterhealth.co.uk/features/.

27 D. Elbourne, M. Richardson, I. Chalmers, I. Waterhouse and E. Holt, 'The Newbury Maternity Care Study: A Randomised Controlled Trial to Assess a Policy of Women Holding Their Own Obstetric Records', *British Journal of Obstetrics and Gynaecology* 94:7, 1987, pp. 612–619.

28 M. Drury, P. Yudkin, J. Harcourt *et al.*, 'Patients with Cancer Holding Their Own Records: A Randomised Controlled Trial', *British Journal of General Practice* 504:51, 2000, pp. 105–110.

29 C. Pyper, J. Amery, M. Watson, B. Thomas and C. Crook, *ERDIP Online Patient Access Project*, Oxford, Bury Knowle Health Centre, 2001.

30 A. Darzi, *High Quality Care for All: NHS Next Stage Review Final Report*, 2008. Online. Available at http://www.dh.gov.uk/en/publication-sandstatistics/ publications/publicationspolicyandguidance/DH_085825.

31 V.C. Tam, S.R. Knowles, P.L. Cornish, N. Fine, R. Marchesano and E.E. Etchells, 'Frequency, Type and Clinical Importance of Medication History Errors at Admission to Hospital: A Systematic Review', *Canadian Medical Association Journal* 173:5, 2005, pp. 510–515.

32 A. Forster, 'Clinical Transitions: Implications for Patient Safety', in B. Hurwitz and A. Sheikh, *Health Care Errors and Patient Safety*, Oxford, Wiley-Blackwell, 2009, pp. 129–149.

33 C. Goldfrad and K. Rowan, 'Consequences of Discharges from Intensive Care Units at Night', *Lancet* 355: 9210, 2000, pp. 1138–1142.

34 Forster, 'Clinical Transitions'.

35 M.A. Lovell, M.Y. Mudalier and P.L. Kleinberg, 'Intrahospital Transport of Critically Ill Patients: Complications and Difficulties', *Anaesthesia and Intensive Care* 29:4, 2001, pp. 400–405.

36 A.J. Forster, H.D. Clark, A. Menard *et al.*, 'Adverse Events Affecting Medical Patients Following Discharge from Hospital', Canadian Medical Association Journal 170:3, 2004, pp. 317–323.

37 A.J. Forster, H.J. Murff, J.F. Peterson, T.K. Gandhi and D.W. Bates, 'The Incidence and Severity of Adverse Events Affecting Patients after Discharge from the Hospital', Annals of Internal Medicine 138:3, 2003, pp. 161–167.

38 M. Delgado-Rodriguez, A. Gomez-Ortega, M. Sillero-Areas and J. Llorca, 'Epidemiology of Surgical Site Infection Diagnosed after Hospital Discharge: A Prospective Study', *Infection Control and Hospital Epidemiology* 22:1, 2001, pp. 24–30.

39 E.A. Coleman, C. Parry, S. Chalmers and S. Min, 'The Care Transitions Intervention: Results of a Randomized Controlled Trial', *Archives of Internal Medicine* 166:5, 2006, pp. 565–571.

40 Available at http://www.nrls.npsa.nhs.uk/resources/collections/never-events/.

41 http://www.publications.parliament.uk/pa/cm200809/cmselect/cmhealth/151/ 15112.htm#a36.

42 T. Richards, 'Running Out of Time', *BMJ* 338, 2009, p. b1507.
43 K.A. Ericsson, N. Charness, P. Feltovich *et al.* (eds), *The Cambridge Handbook of Expertise and Expert Performance*, New York, Cambridge University Press, 2006.
44 D. Dawson and K. Reid, 'Fatigue, Alcohol and Performance Impairment', *Nature* 388, 1997, p. 235.
45 http://www.mmc.nhs.uk/news_events/latest_news/ewtd_-_a_guide_to_the_implicat.aspx.
46 *Nettleship v. Weston* [1971] 3 All ER 581.
47 *Wilsher v. Essex Area Health Authority* [1986] 3 All ER 801 (CA).
48 S.W. Lockley, L.K. Barger, N.T. Ayas, J.M. Rothschild, C.A. Czeisler and C.P. Landrigan, 'Harvard. Work Hours, Health and Safety Group. Effects of Health Care Provider Work Hours and Sleep Deprivation on Safety and Performance', *Joint Commission Journal on Quality and Patient Safety* 33, 2007 (11 supplement), pp. 7–18.
49 W. Reid, 'Wendy Reid Replies to Roy Pounder', *British Medical Journal* 339, 2009, p. b4488.
50 The Bristol Inquiry, *Learning from Bristol: The Report of the Public Inquiry into Children's Heart Surgery at the Bristol Royal Infirmary* 1984–1995, CM 5207. Online. Available at http://www.bristol-inquiry.org.uk/.
51 P. Healey and J. Samanta, 'When Does the "Learning Curve" of Innovative Interventions Become Questionable Practice?', *European Journal of Vascular Surgery* 36, 2008, pp. 253–257.
52 D. Price, 'Remodelling the Regulation of Postmodern Innovation in Medicine', *International Journal of Law in Context* 2, 2005, pp. 121–141.
53 *Bolam v. Friern Hospital Management Committee* [1957] 1 WLR 583.
54 *Simms v. Simms* [2003] 1 All ER 669.
55 World Medical Association, *Declaration of Helsinki: Ethical Principles for Medical Research Involving Human Subjects*, 2008. Online Available at http://www.wma.net/en/30publications/10policies/b3/index.html.
56 Hospital Infection Society, Infection Control Nurses Association, *The Third Prevalence Survey of Healthcare Associated Infections in Acute Hospitals in England 2006*, Report for Department of Health (England), June 2007. Online. Available at www.dh.gov.uk/.
57 B. Cookson, 'Hospital-Acquired Infection', in M. Powers, N. Harris and A. Barton (eds), *Clinical Negligence*, Haywards Heath, Tottel, 2008.
58 E.L. Teare, S. Stone and B. Cookson on behalf of the HandHygiene Liaison Group, 'HandHygiene' (Editorial), *British Medical Journal*, 323, 2001, pp. 411–412.
59 National Audit Office, *The Management and Control of Hospital Acquired Infection in Acute NHS Trusts in England*, London, The Stationery Office, 2000. Online. Available at http://www.nao.org.uk/publications/nao_reports/9900230.pdf.
60 Department of Health, *Detailed Guide to Governance Including Risk Management and Assurance: Statement on Internal Control and Other Statutory Governance Assurance and Audit Details*. Online. Available HTTP http://www.dh.gov.uk/Policy AndGuidance/OrganisationPolicy/Governance/fs/en.
61 Details on the registration process can be found at http://www.cqc.org.uk/guidanceforprofessionals/registration.cfm.
62 http://www.dh.gov.uk/prod_consum_dh/groups/dh_digitalassets/documents/digitalasset/dh_110435.pdf. This version will come into force on 1 April 2010.
63 http://www.cqc.org.uk/guidanceforprofessionals/healthcare/allhealthcarestaff/managingrisk/healthcare-associatedinfec/hcaiinspectionprogramme.cfm.
64 House of Commons Public Accounts Committee, *Reducing Healthcare Associated Infection in Hospitals in England: Fifty-second Report of Session 2008-09: Report, Together with Formal Minutes, Oral and Written Evidence*, 10 November 2009.

Online. Available at http://www.publications.parliament.uk/pa/cm200809/cmselect/cmpubacc/812/812.pdf.

65 R.E. Hirschtick, 'A Piece of My Mind. Copy-and-Paste', *Journal of the American Medical Association* 295, 2006, pp. 2335–2336.

66 R. Wachter, *Understanding Patient Safety*, New York, McGraw Hill, 2008.

67 Online. Available at http://www.publications.parliament.uk/pa/cm200607/cmselect/cmhealth/422/422.pdf.

68 http://www.nhscarerecords.nhs.uk/security.

69 http://www.connectingforhealth.nhs.uk/.

70 Department of Health, '*Coding for Success: Simple Technology for Safer Patient Care*, London, Department of Health, 2007. Online Available HTTP http://www.dh.gov.uk/prod_consum_dh/groups/dh_digitalassets/@dh/@en/documents/digitalasset/dh_066098.pdf.

71 R.L. Howard and A.J. Avery, 'Medicines Management', in B. Hurwitz and A. Sheikh, *Health Care Errors and Patient Safety*, Oxford, Wiley-Blackwell, 2009, pp. 150–165.

72 http://www.connectingforhealth.nhs.uk/systemsandservices/clindash/overview.

73 S. Boseley, '40,000 Drug Errors Logged in a Year', *Guardian*, 11 August 2006.

74 National Institute for Health and Clinical Excellence, *Reviewing and Grading the Evidence*, London, National Institute for Health and Clinical Excellence, 2006.

75 A.J. Forster, H.J. Murff, J.F. Peterson, T.K. Ghandi and D.W. Bates, 'Adverse Drug Events Occurring Following Hospital Discharge', *Journal of Internal Medicine* 20:4, 2005, pp. 317–323.

76 http://www.saferhealthcare.org.uk/IHI/Topics/ManagingChange/SafetyStories/DontDistractMe.htm.

77 Nursing and Midwifery Council, *The Code: Standards of Conduct, Performance and Ethics for Nurses and Midwives*, 2008. Online. Available at http://www.nmc-uk.org/aDisplayDocument.aspx?DocumentID=5982.

78 Department of Health, 'Making a Difference Strengthening the Nursing, Midwifery and Health Visiting Contribution to Health and Healthcare', 1999. Online. Available at http://www.dh.gov.uk/prod_consum_dh/groups/dh_digitalassets/@dh/@en/documents/digitalasset/dh_4074704.pdf.

79 Department of Health, *The NHS Plan. A Plan for Investment, a Plan for Reform*, 2000. Online. Available at http://www.dh.gov.uk/prod_consum_dh/groups/dh_digitalassets/@dh/@en/documents/digitalasset/dh_4055783.pdf.

80 Department of Health, *A Health Service of All the Talents: Developing the NHS Workforce – Consultation Document on the Review of Workforce Planning*, 2000. Online. Available at http://www.dh.gov.uk/prod_consum_dh/groups/dh_digitalassets/@dh/@en/documents/digitalasset/dh_4080258.pdf.

81 L. de Cossart, 'Surgical Care Practitioners: New Members of the Surgical Team', in M. Powers, N. Harris and A. Barton (eds), *Clinical Negligence*, 2008, Haywards Heath, Tottel.

82 Department of Health. Online. Available at http://www.dh.gov.uk/en/Healthcare/Secondarycare/NHSfoundationtrust/index.htm.

83 http://www.monitor-nhsft.gov.uk/.

84 T.A. Brennan, 'The Institute of Medicine Report on Medical Errors – Could It Do Harm?', *New England Journal of Medicine* 342, 2000, pp. 1123–1125.

85 *Bull v. Devon Area Health Authority* [1993] 4 Med LR 117.

86 *Robertson v. Nottingham Health Authority* [1997] 8 Med LR 1.

87 *Farraj v. King's Healthcare NHS Trust (KCH)* [2009] EWCA Civ 1203.

88 J. Samanta and A. Samanta, 'The Corporate Manslaughter Act 2007 – A Catalyst for Patient Safety?', *Health Care Risk Report* 13, 2007, pp. 19–21.

89 Unreported, 11 April 2006 Crown Court, Winchester.

90 *R. v. Southampton University Hospital NHS Trust* [2006] EWCA Crim 2971.

91 'Memorandum of Understanding: Investigating Patient Safety Incidents Involving Unexpected Death or Serious Untoward Harm', February 2006. Online. Available at http://www.dh.gov.uk/.
92 Published 26 July 2010. Online. Available at: http://www.dh.gov.uk/en/Publicationsandstatistics/Publications/PublicationsPolicyAndGuidance/DH_117691.

9   Patient safety in mental health care

Eva Sundin, James Houston and Jamie Murphy

Introduction

Mental disorders are common, with over 10 per cent of all adult people worldwide suffering from at least one diagnosable illness at some point in their lives.[1] However, as was shown by a European Union survey, not all people with mental health problems receive treatment and care from mental health services: 'The treatment gap (the percentage of individuals who require mental health care, but do not receive it) is high for most mental disorders in Europe'.[2] In fact, the treatment gap for severe disorders such as schizophrenia and non-affective psychosis was 17.8 per cent in studies from Western Europe, and for diagnoses such as generalized anxiety disorder and major depression the treatment gap was even larger (62.3 per cent and 45.4 per cent, respectively). While every effort should be made to reduce this treatment gap, it is of paramount importance that those individuals who do receive treatment remain safe while doing so. This chapter will focus on the safety and quality of care for people who receive mental health treatment from the National Health Service (NHS) in England and Wales.

What distinguishes patient safety in mental health care from patient safety in general health care?

Patients receiving health care are often psychologically vulnerable, even when the diagnosis is clear and the treatment plan is unquestionable. However, all patients are not necessarily vulnerable in the same way. Frequent psychological problems in people with severe mental disorders include high levels of suspicion, fear and/or mistrust of others. Also, patients with severe mental health issues are often disorganised; they may miss appointments, lose prescriptions and medication, and forget instructions. Those who are service users may make demands on health service staff that may seem unreasonable or inappropriate. Therefore, service users in mental health treatment are at risk of many of the patient safety issues that exist in any health care setting (e.g. receiving the wrong dose or wrong medicine, faulty medical equipment or errors in diagnosis). In addition, there are unique risk factors in the mental health setting either because they are more common among service users with a mental disorder or because they are uncommon in other health care settings (e.g. use of restraint and seclusion, management of violent and aggressive behaviours, sexual abuse, and suicide and deliberate self-harm).

This means that mental health service users as a group are extremely vulnerable, and they often need help from carers and staff to handle risk issues. This was confirmed by one of the first surveys of patient safety events in mental health, produced by the National Patient Safety Agency,[3] the body responsible for collecting reports on patient safety incidents in England and Wales. The report showed that the adverse events most commonly reported from mental health services were accidents, absconding/elopement, aggression and self-harm. These patient safety issues combine into a unique pattern of risk factors in mental health care settings, which is associated with the patient population and the treatment setting. Because of the unique patterns of risk factors in mental health care settings, this chapter sets out to explore the following issues:

1   How are the generally recommended policies and procedures to ensure patient safety in NHS services in England and Wales implemented in mental health care? This section will illustrate good practice, with examples of recent reports on how mental health care services implement patient safety policies. The section will also examine to what extent mental health staff in England and Wales report patient safety risk events.

2   What do we know about patient safety experienced by patients who receive mental health treatment? Listening to patient experiences can provide important information about the quality of care, and this understanding can contribute to enhancing patient safety and reducing harm. Patients are a valuable source of information about a health care system's communication and they are the only source of information about whether they are treated with respect and dignity This section summarises and discusses reports on how patients in mental health care settings experience patient safety and quality of care.

Patient safety practices in mental health care services

The seven steps to patient safety framework in mental health care

Many initiatives around the world have demonstrated that patient safety can be improved. Up until now, the only initiative that has been translated to a whole healthcare system is the NHS *'Seven steps to patient safety'* framework, which acts as guidance for all health care units in NHS:

Step 1: Build a safety culture: create a culture that is open and fair

Staff members who are actively involved in developing principles and procedures around safety and in making incident reports are more likely to respond in a systematic and fair way.

Good practice example:

> When the 100-bed Rochford Hospital in South Essex was rebuilt, the aim was to create a new mental health facility where risks of patients harming themselves or others were minimised. Because promoting safety was considered as important as facilitating treatment and care, decisions on details such as anti-ligature door handles and sensor taps and non-breakable mirrors were made after careful consideration.

Step 2: Lead and support your staff: establish a clear and strong focus on patient safety throughout an organisation

A safer culture depends on a strong sense of purpose and leadership, along with the organisation's ability to listen to all members of the healthcare team.

Good practice example:

> Sussex Partnership Foundation NHS Trust has developed a *Report and Learn Bulletin*. The bulletin publishes reports of important issues such as safety risks and incidents to be shared and discussed throughout the Trust. The bulletin also advertises training linked to reported incidents. For example, following an incident where essential safety information about a patient was not passed on from one team to another, training that targeted inter-agency working and communication was made known.

Step 3: Integrate your risk management activity: develop systems and processes to manage risks and identify and assess things that could go wrong

Patient safety is a key component of risk management, and should be integrated with staff safety, complaints, litigation and claims handling, and financial and environmental risk.

Good practice example:

> In response to the *National Confidential Inquiry into Suicide and Homicide by People with Mental Illness*, North Wales NHS Trust created a 'positive risk management' framework which requires collaboration between agencies, service users and carers. This framework aimed at helping staff members balance service users' right to freedom and self-determination with the reduction of risk to the service users, their families and the public.

*Step 4: Promote reporting: ensure staff can easily report incidents locally
and nationally*

There are three types of incidents that should be reported:

- incidents that have occurred;
- incidents that have been prevented (near misses);
- incidents that might happen.

Good practice example:

> Historically, the practice on a ward in Cornwall Partnership NHS
> Trust was not in line with the Trust's policy on incident reporting.
> There was confusion as to when an incident report should be submitted.
> To solve this issue, the ward manager organised a health and safety away
> day with the aim of addressing the culture on the ward regarding
> reporting; identifying incident reporting training needs; and educating
> staff in preventing slips, trips and falls. Following the away day, staff
> reported having identified new and critical risk factors; for example,
> reports had highlighted frequent incidents relating to the flooring
> and thus there was a rationale for new specialised flooring throughout
> the ward.

*Step 5: Involve and communicate with patients and the public: develop
ways to communicate openly with and listen to patients*

Good practice example:

> Following a patient suicide in the Norfolk and Waveney Mental Health
> NHS Foundation Trust, a root cause analysis showed that the family
> and carers of the deceased were not always provided with adequate
> information regarding possible triggers and warning signs in relation to
> suicidal ideation and behaviour.

A booklet, *Information and Guidance for Those Who Are Involved with Suicidal
People*, was developed and incorporated into the ongoing suicide prevention
work within the Trust. This development was shared within the Trust. The
booklet also gained approval from the local coroner, and meetings were held
for service users and their families, mental health practitioners and members
of voluntary organisations.

*Step 6: Learn and share safety lessons: encourage staff to use root cause
analysis to learn how and why incidents happen*

Good practice example:

North Staffordshire Combined Healthcare is a large mental health/ learning disabilities Trust, with over 6,000 staff who work in a wide geographical area. Previously, over 1,000 incident reports per month were submitted on paper. An electronic system was developed by the health care teams and IT experts. The new reporting system means that patient safety incidents are reported quickly and solutions to improve the healthcare environment can be found.

Step 7: Implement solutions to prevent harm: embed lessons through changes to practice, processes or systems

Good practice example:

To handle the problem of patients who go missing, Riley Ward, Meadowbrook Unit, Greater Manchester West Mental Health Foundation NHS Trust, have introduced *protected time*. During *protected time* the nurses give all their time to patients on the ward, engaging them in therapeutic activities. The *protected time* takes place on a regular basis and visitors are encouraged not to come to the ward during these times.

Mental health staff's reports of patient safety events

Each year, approximately one million people in England and Wales are referred to mental health care, and approximately 160,000 of these are hospitalised. In 2009, mental health settings in England reported 38,688 incidents; in Wales, 12,314 incidents were reported. In England, one-third (32 per cent) of all reported incidents were accidents, followed by disruptive/ aggressive behaviour (21 per cent), self-harming behaviour (17 per cent), access/admission/transfer/discharge (11 per cent) and medication (7 per cent). Reports from mental health settings in England also showed that 1,282 people died and another 913 people suffered severe harm or permanent injury after adverse events such as self-harm (including suicide), accidents, disruptive/aggressive behaviour and errors in medication. In Wales, a similar profile was found.

In the area of mental illness, many medication errors can be serious. For example, failure to monitor a patient who is prescribed a psychotropic drug (antidepressant, sedative, stimulant or tranquiliser) may result in sometimes serious side effects not being identified. A British study examining 12 mental health trusts[4] reported that 579 medical errors were reported per month. A counteractive factor is that pharmacists have been shown to efficiently identify and correct such errors.[5]

These figures show a commitment to reporting safety incidents; another positive marker is that patient safety reports are submitted from mental health settings across the NHS.[6] A potential problem, however, is the under-reporting of incidents. To illustrate, one study has showed that fewer than half (45.6 per cent) of 983 nurses stated that all medication errors were being reported.[7] The nurses explained that causes of omitting to report incidents were fear of the reactions of co-workers or the management, difficulties in reading the doctor's handwriting and fatigue in nurses.

As we have seen, patient safety incidents reported from mental health settings within the NHS are in many ways qualitatively different from those reported from other health care settings. Whilst some of the incidents reported from a mental health setting may be preventable, for example medication related errors, other events may not be foreseeable. For example, no one factor has been shown to predict self-harm.[8] Thus, because of the many factors that may trigger self-harming behaviour in a patient, the mental health care staff may not be able to prevent self-harm despite being aware that a patient is prone to self-harm.

Patient safety from the patient's perspective

Understanding patient safety from the patient's perspective can provide valuable insight into causes of patient safety issues and thereby contribute to improving quality of care. This important issue has been discussed for a number of years. For example, in 2002 Vincent and Coulter[9] pointed out that patients can make valuable contributions to enhancing safety. In particular, patients can assist in reaching an accurate diagnosis; choosing a healthcare provider; participating in treatment decision making; and reporting medical errors and adverse events. A complication here is that patients' experiences may be complex combinations of issues to do with quality of care and safety issues, and these experiences may not be readily translatable to clinical terms like 'medical error' or 'adverse event'.[10] Thus treatment and care issues that can contribute to medical errors or adverse events may, from the patient perspective, be experienced as a safety risk.

For example, a study of cancer outpatients found that one in five patients reported an unsafe experience.[11] However, the researchers' analysis of the data showed that only 31 per cent of these reports actually could be identified as a close call, medical error or injury. The remainder (almost 70 per cent) were categorised as quality of care problems (long waits, miscommunication with clinicians or dissatisfaction with the environment and amenities). What does this suggest about the association between quality of care, on the one hand, and patient safety, on the other, in patients' experience? Gilburt *et al.* suggested that patients and professionals have entirely different views on what variables and themes are important, and therefore most studies provide 'a poor representation of the user perspective'.[12]

To date there is little research on the patient perspective on safety in health care, both internationally and in England and Wales.[13] This dearth of research especially applies to the mental health sector. UK studies in this area have mainly used either qualitative or survey method.[14] In order to summarise what we know about patient perceptions of safety and factors that are related to safety issues in mental health services in England and Wales, we will begin by exploring four large surveys that have asked patients and staff in mental health services about their experiences of safety and quality of care. The summary of survey data will then be supplemented by results from qualitative studies that can illustrate and support the survey findings.

Four surveys on patient perceptions of safety and quality of care in mental health services

All four surveys were undertaken in the period 2004–2009. In the brief summary below, details for each survey are presented.

A   *The Care Quality Commission Mental Health Acute In-patient Survey* for 2009 (CQC)[15] is the most recent survey. The CQC included reports on experiences of treatment and care from more than 7,500 patients who had received hospital care in 64 NHS trusts across England.

B   *The National Audit of Violence* collected data from patients, staff and visitors at 265 English and Welsh mental health and learning disability wards[16] (Healthcare Commission, 2005). The audit collected more than 6,500 anonymous questionnaires from participants about their views on the extent to which the wards had routines in place to effectively prevent and manage violence.

C   *Acute Care 2004: A National Survey of Adult Psychiatric Wards in England*, by the National Institute for Mental Health in England (NIMHE),[17] gathered questionnaire data from ward managers on 303 mental health wards, relating to various aspects of staffing, environment and local policy and practice.

D   The *Ward Watch* report by the mental health charity Mind summarises the experiences of 335 people who were current or recent users of in-patient mental health services.[18]

The four surveys: patient perceptions of factors that can contribute to safety problems

In CQC's survey (Care Quality Commission, 2009), fewer than half (45 per cent) of the participating patients reported that they *always* felt safe on the ward; 16 per cent *did not feel safe at all*. These findings are similar to those reported in Mind's study (2004), where almost one-third (27 per cent) of respondents reported that they *rarely* felt safe during their stay in hospital.

What can data from the four surveys tell us about potential sources of the widespread experience of not being safe in the hospital environment? To examine this, significant adverse events reported in each of the four surveys will be compared and discussed. In our discussion of survey findings, both issues to do with safety and issues that relate to quality of care will be included. The rationale for this choice is that patients may not distinguish between safety and quality of care; rather, the two may be part of the same patient experience. This view seems to be reflected in the following declaration from the UK Department of Health:

> Poor standards of design, lack of space and access to basic amenities and comforts in much of our current inpatient provision have contributed to and reinforced service *users' negative experiences of inpatient care as unsafe,* uncomfortable and untherapeutic.
>
> (Department of Health, 2002;[19] emphasis added)

In order to give a brief account of information related to patient experience of factors that contribute to safety issues, four general factors were pulled from the survey results: the environment; overcrowding; access to stimulating and meaningful activities and violent behaviour; seclusion, restraint and medication

Environmental safety

The National Audit of Violence found that many wards failed to meet basic safety standards (Healthcare Commission, 2005). For example, frequent reports told of unacceptably high noise levels in the daytime; and more than half the wards reported that they did not have sufficient quiet spaces for patients and staff. This finding was consistent with the *Acute Care 2004* survey, where reports showed that fewer than half of the wards had sufficient quiet areas for patients and also sufficient quiet areas for patients to meet with relatives and friends.

The Mind *Ward Watch* report (2004) data indicated that respondents of both sexes were dissatisfied with mixed-sex accommodation. Also, a slightly larger proportion of respondents who did not have access to single-sex bathroom facilities *rarely* felt safe in hospital (37 per cent) compared with those who did (37 per cent versus 23 per cent). A larger proportion of respondents who had access to single-sex daytime facilities felt safe *all* or *most of the time* compared with respondents who did not have access to single-sex daytime facilities (53 per cent versus 40 per cent).

Last year's CQC survey reported that every tenth respondent had stayed in the same room as patients of the opposite sex during their most recent hospital stay. This is a smaller proportion than in Mind's study (2004), which showed that almost one-quarter (23 per cent) of respondents were accommodated in mixed-sex rooms. This decrease is in line with the Department of Health's mandate to NHS services to eliminate mixed-sex accommodation as far as possible.

Overcrowding

The National Audit of Violence found that many mental health services struggled to work with an increasing population, some of whom had both a mental health and a substance use disorder. Similar findings were reported in Mind's survey.

Boredom and violence

The link between boredom and violence is well documented, and so is the connection between violent and aggressive behaviour and anxiety.[20]

The recent CQC survey showed that there was a general lack of activities available to patients; more than one-third (35 per cent) of the patients perceived that there was too little to do on weekdays and more than half (54 per cent) reported the same for weekends and evenings. These reports echo the findings of *The National Audit of Violence* and *Acute Care 2004*. Furthermore, all the three surveys found that a lack of things for inpatients to do was associated with more frequent incidents of violence. Many of the respondents in *The National Violence Audit* commented on the lack of activities:

'I get bored stiff. Only option seems to be TV or sleep.'

(patient)

'Evenings and weekends stretch out before you, with no organised activities on offer and effectively a weekend lasts from Friday lunch to Mon 2.30pm.'

(patient)

'There is nothing to do here at all, except watch TV. The art room has lots of paint but no paintbrushes. I find boredom gives me far too much time to think, which doesn't help the depression.'

(patient)

The CQC survey found that a fairly large proportion of the participants wanted talking therapies (counselling, cognitive behavioural therapy and anxiety management); however, fewer than half of these patients were offered the opportunity for such interventions. In *Acute Care 2004*, ward managers reported similar findings, and despite the strong support for treatments such as cognitive behavioural therapy and solution focused behavioural therapy for this patient population, these interventions were only routinely available on fewer than 20 per cent of wards. Thus shortage of psychological interventions was related to the situation in many wards, where nurses and occupational therapists provided the largest proportion of input into therapies and activities whilst a small proportion (one-quarter) of the wards had input from psychologists.

VIOLENCE

In *The National Audit of Violence*, almost half (45 per cent) of respondents reported experiences of violence that had upset or distressed them, one-third (34 per cent) reported that they had felt threatened or unsafe, and almost one-fifth (18 per cent) reported that they had been actually assaulted on the ward. In Mind's study a large proportion of the female respondents reported that they felt unsafe in psychiatric hospitals: more than half of the women (51 per cent) reported that they had been verbally or physically threatened during their stay in hospital. Every fifth woman (20 per cent) said she had been physically assaulted.

According to participating patients' comments, violence on the ward was triggered by lack of space and shortages of staff on the ward:

> 'Unavailability of staff to take you out on escort so you are cooped up in a noisy, hot, unpleasant environment.'
>
> (patient)

> 'There are not enough staff on the ward, in other words too many patients and not enough staff. This makes it impossible for staff to satisfy all patients' needs and they become aggressive.'
>
> (patient)

Another factor that was thought to contribute to violence on the ward was the mix of patients with different illnesses and at varying stages of illness on the ward:

> 'Very ill patients and recovering patients on same ward, too many areas where very ill and recovering patients interact without supervision.'
>
> (staff member)

Several respondents made an explicit link between the high prevalence of alcohol and drug misuse among inpatients and violence. Respondents also thought that access to cigarettes played a part in violent and aggressive behaviour on the ward:

> 'Not being able to go out for cigarettes when they [want] or short of it.'
>
> (patient)

The audit also reported inappropriate use of beds, which was confirmed by *Acute Care 2004*, where it was found that 4.2 per cent of acute beds were being used solely for the purposes of detoxification.

Seclusion, restraint, and medication

Seclusion involves isolating an individual from others, and restraint involves either personally holding the individual or securing the individual in a mechanical restraint that restricts his or her activities. Both procedures are used in mental health services for a specified brief period of time to interrupt severe problem behaviour that places the individual or others at risk of harm.

In the *Acute Care 2004* survey, almost one-third (28 per cent) of the ward managers reported that seclusion was used on their ward; however, many ward managers (25 per cent) did not know if they had a policy on the use and recording of seclusion. Patients and staff who participated in *The National Audit of Violence* agreed that seclusion and medication were used to control patients' disruptive behaviours, with this sometimes necessitated by a lack of staff and/or training.

> 'Medication is often the only option felt to be available. There is a desperate lack of experienced staff on the ward. The staffing levels are not adequate to deal with aggression that we face.'
>
> (staff member)

> 'I have been involved in numerous violent incidents and restraints. I have requested training and they have refused it on the grounds of cost. I feel that staff are under a great deal of pressure and are not adequately trained.'
>
> (staff member)

> 'Lack of staff training in managing violence leaves staff unaware of what to do.'
>
> (staff member)

In *The National Audit of Violence*, a small proportion of staff members reported that neither medication, seclusion nor restraint were being used too quickly, whilst around one-third of the patients thought these interventions were used too quickly.

> 'My son can usually be talked out of being violent. Most of my family can do this and we have not received any training. At sixteen, my son is very frightened; often he needs reassurance not restraint.'
>
> (visitor)

Qualitative studies of patient perceptions of safety and quality of care in mental health services

In the interview study by Gilburt and co-workers,[21] 19 former patients in an inpatient mental health service reported experiences that were in line with the survey findings that many patients experienced a *lack of feeling safe* during their stay in hospital. In this study, all but three participants reported a *lack of feeling safe* in the hospital environment. Not feeling safe was related to fear, whilst feelings of fear were closely related to violent behaviour, perpetrated by themselves or by other patients or staff members. Another finding in this study that is reminiscent of the survey data is that several women felt unsafe on wards with both men and women.

However, in Gilburt *et al.*'s study,[22] men too described being attacked by other men; in other words, both men and women felt vulnerable on wards where the majority of patients were men. A study of 31 women patients in single-sex and mixed-sex medium secure units showed that women in both types of treatment units reported threats and physical violence from other patients.[23] The researchers concluded that single-sex mental health care units for women may not solve the safety issues.

As we have seen, much of the research – survey studies and qualitative studies alike – views patients as potentially at risk of harming themselves, other patients or staff members. However, other researchers have found that patients themselves sometimes are active in making inpatient environments safer for themselves. They do this by avoiding potentially risky situations and fellow patients, warning other patients about their unpredictability, and seeking assistance from staff.[24] These research findings clearly demonstrate the importance of fully involving patients in safety initiatives.

Conclusion

This chapter has shown that many NHS mental health care trusts and units have formed the habit of submitting reports from patient safety incidents. This means that the trusts are developing a patient safety culture from which the NHS can continue to learn and better prevent future incidents. In addition, by encouraging all staff members to share experiences of good practice with others across mental health settings in England and Wales, an open atmosphere may be created which in turn may act as a foundation from which a patient safety culture can continue to flourish and grow.

From a patient perspective, it is perhaps evident that patients want to know about errors that affect them. But, do they also want to be involved in developing and improving patient safety? From the review of studies on patient experiences of patient safety and quality of care in this chapter, we have seen that patients often have a different understanding of what patient safety entails compared to the official view. Therefore it might be that patients' willingness to become involved in patient safety to some extent depends on the degree to which they can recognise their experiences in the official patient safety language and terminology. Other factors that can play a role in patients' active involvement in improving patient safety are the patient's age and ethnicity, the nature and level of severity of the patient's condition and its treatment, and issues around perceived vulnerability to harm and confidence in challenging health care staff.

Another important question to ask is: what happens with the patient when error or medical injury occurs? Up until now, relatively little work has been done to understand how patients experience medical errors. However,

ments. Other issues in this context that need to be addressed are the reason(s)
severely if the medical staff do not come forward when error or medical
way in which the injury is managed. Thus, patients are likely to suffer more

Notes

1 World Health Organization (2001) *World Health Report 2001 – Mental Health: New Understanding, New Hope*, Geneva, WHO. Online. Available HTTP http://www. who.int/whr/2001/en/.
2 World Health Organization Europe (2005) *Facing the Challenges, Building Solutions. Report from the WHO European Ministerial Conference*, Geneva, WHO. p. 46. Online. Available HTTP http://www.euro.who.int/document/E87301.pdf.
3 National Patient Safety Agency (2006) *With Safety in Mind: Mental Health Services and Patient Safety*, Patient Safety Observatory Report 2. Online. Available HTTP http://www.nrls.npsa.nhs.uk/resources/clinical-specialty/mental-health/?entryid45=59801&p=2.
4 Paton, C. and Gill-Banham, S. (2003) 'Prescribing Errors in Psychiatry', *Psychiatric Bulletin* 27, pp. 208–210.
5 Stubbs, J., Haw, C. and Cahill, C. (2004) 'Auditing Prescribing Errors in a Psychiatric Hospital: Are Pharmacists' interventions Effective?', *Hospital Pharmacist* 11, pp. 203–206.
6 O'Dowd, A. (2008) 'Only a Minority of Serious Patient Safety Incidents Are Reported, MPs Hear', *British Medical Journal* 337, p. 2384.
7 Mayo, A.M. and Duncan, D. (2004) 'Nurse Perceptions of Medication Errors: What We Need to Know for Patient Safety', *Journal of Nursing Care Quality* 19, pp. 209–217.
8 House, A., Owens, D. and Patchett, L. (1999) 'Deliberate Self-harm', *Quality in Health Care* 8, pp. 137–143.
9 Vincent, C.A. and Coulter, A. (2002) 'Patient Safety: What about the Patient?', *Quality and Safety in Health Care* 11, pp. 76–80.
10 Gilburt, H., Rose, D. and Slade, M. (2008) 'The Importance of Relationships in Mental Health Care: A Qualitative Study of Service Users' Experiences of Psychiatric Hospital Admission in the UK', *BMC Health Services Research* 8, p. 92.
11 Weingart, S.N., Price, J., Duncombe, D., Connor, M., Sommer, K., Conley, K., Bierer, B.E. and Reid, Ponte P. (2007) 'Patient-reported Safety and Quality of Care in Outpatient Oncology', *Joint Commission Journal on Quality and Patient Safety* 33, pp. 83–94.
12 Gilburt et al. 'The Importance of Relationships', p. 94
13 Brickell, T.A., Nicholls, T.L., Procyshyn, R.M., McLean, C., Dempster, R.J., Lavoie, J.A.A., Sahlstrom, K.J., Tomita, T.M. and Wang, E. (2009) *Patient safety in mental health*, Edmonton, Alberta: Canadian Patient Safety Institute and Ontario Hospital Association. Online. Available HTTP http://www.patientsafetyinstitute.

ca/English/research/commissionedResearch/mentalHealthAndPatientSafety/ Documents/Mental per cent20Health per cent20Paper.pdf.

14 Quirk, A. and Lelliott, P. (2001) 'What Do We Know about Life on Acute Psychiatric Wards in the UK? A Review of the Research Evidence', *Social Science & Medicine* 53, pp. 1565–1574.

15 Care Quality Commission (2009) 'Supporting Briefing Note: Issues Highlighted by 2009 Survey of Mental Health Acute Inpatient Services'. Online. Available HTTP http://www.cqc.org.uk/_db/_documents/2009_survey_of_mental_health_ acute_inpatient_services_Briefing_note_200909230047.pdf.

16 Healthcare Commission (2005) *National Audit of Violence (2003–2005). Final Report*, London, Healthcare Commission. Online. Available HTTP http://www. wales. nhs.uk/documents/FinalReport-violence.pdf.

17 Garcia, I., Kennet, C., Quarishi, M. and Duncan, G. (2005) *Acute Care 2004: A National Survey of Adult Psychiatric Wards in England*, London, Sainsbury Centre for Mental Health. Online. Available HTTP http://www.scmh.org.uk/pdfs/ Acute_care_2004.pdf.

18 Mind (2004) *Ward Watch: Mind's Campaign to Improve Hospital Conditions for Mental Health Patients*. Online. Available HTTP http://www.mind.org.uk/ assets/0000/0353/ ward_watch_report.pdf (accessed 21 August 2009).

19 Department of Health (2002) *Mental Health Policy Implementation Guide: Adult Acute Inpatient Care Provision*, London, Department of Health. Online. Available HTTP www.dh.gov.uk.

20 Daffern, M. and Howells, K. (2002) 'Psychiatric Inpatient Aggression: A Review of Structural and Functional Assessment Approaches', *Aggression and Violent Behavior* 7, pp. 477–497.

21 Gilburt et al. 'The Importance of Relationships'.

22 Gilburt et al. 'The Importance of Relationships'.

23 Mezey, G., Hassell, Y. and Bartlett, A. (2005) 'Safety of Women in Mixed-sex and Single-sex Medium Secure Units: Staff and Patient Perceptions', *British Journal of Psychiatry* 187, pp. 579–582.

24 Quirk, A., Lelliott, P. and Seale, C. (2005) 'Risk Management by Patients on Psychiatric Wards in London: An Ethnographic Study', *Health, Risk and Society* 7, pp. 85–91.

25 Vincent et al. 'Patient Safety: What about the Patient?'

26 Department of Health (2005) 'Delivering Race Equality in Mental Health Care: An Action Plan for Reform Inside and Outside Services'. Online. Available HTTP http://www.dh.gov.uk/prod_consum_dh/groups/dh_digitalassets/@dh/@en/ documents/digitalasset/dh_4100775.pdf.

10 Regulating patient safety in the European Union

Realistic aspiration or unattainable goal?

Jean V. McHale

Introduction

Patient safety is an issue which has been the source of much concern over recent years, both at domestic and international level. In the UK a report of an expert group chaired by the Chief Medical Officer's 'An Organisation with a Memory' in 2000 highlighted how patient safety was a serious concern.[1] It has been suggested that in the European Union (EU) itself somewhere between 8 and 12 per cent of patients suffer adverse effects while receiving healthcare.[2] It is thus unsurprising that the EU has become increasingly concerned with issues of patient safety.

Patient safety was identified as an area for action by the European Commission in the White Paper *Together for Health: A Strategic Approach for the EU 2008–2013*.[3] This broad document confirms the EU's commitment to health in all policies. The EU has recently confirmed its commitment to addressing issues of patient safety in a Commission Communication to the Parliament and Council.[4] This Communication highlighted the Commission's concerns on a range of issues, including the rise of healthcare associated infections such as MSRA. The Commission undertook a consultation on patient safety in 2008 which revealed that of the 185 respondents to the consultation some 20 per cent had suffered a healthcare related adverse event. The Commission in its 2008 Communication stated that its aim was that of 'an integrated approach, placing patient safety at the core of high quality health care systems by bringing together all factors that have an impact on the safety of patients'.[5]

This chapter explores the role of the EU, past, present and in the future in the area of 'patient safety'. It provides the backdrop to the EU's engagement in this area and the drive to regulate at EU level driven by patient safety concerns flowing from scandals such as those in relation to contaminated blood leading to the EU Blood Safety Directive.[6] It explores how other areas of EU law, notably the impact of a number of recent free movement cases, have begun to lead to a re-evaluation of the provision of healthcare services across member states at EU level. It explores whether the prospect of an expansion in the number of patients travelling to another EU member state to access medical services will provide a trigger for comprehensive regulation of patient safety questions at EU level in the future, with 'EU' standards for patient safety and the advantages and disadvantages of such an approach. It notes how patient safety issues are something which also cannot be seen solely in the context of the EU as the global interface between the EU and other organisations such as the World Health Organisation (WHO) may become increasingly important in developing law and policy in this area. Finally, it questions whether the proposed measures constitute an effective package for reform or whether the complexity and the diversity of the EU mean that ultimately many of these measures may prove an unattainable goal.

Engaging with health and patient safety

Given the increasing involvement of the EU in matters of health law it is unsurprising that the EU has also increasingly become involved in issues concerning patient safety.[7] This can be seen demonstrated through different aspects of EU competence. Provisions concerning public health were incorporated in EU law by the Maastricht Treaty, which introduced Article 129 into the Treaty of Rome. This took effect in 1993. This provision was subsequently amended by the Treaty of Amsterdam. The amendments to the Treaty were triggered by some concerns following the rise of BSE and controversies in relation to blood safety.[8] A new Treaty provision, Article 152 EC, which was introduced by the Treaty of Amsterdam, placed public health centre stage. This provision has now been amended by the Lisbon Treaty, which inserts a new Article 168. This now provides that

> A high level of human health protection shall be ensured in the definition and implementation of all Union policies and activities.
>
> Union action, which shall complement national policies, shall be directed towards improving public health, preventing physical and mental illness and diseases, and obviating sources of danger to physical and mental health. Such action shall cover the fight against the major health scourges, by promoting research into their causes, their transmission and their prevention, as well as health information and education, and monitoring, early warning of and combating serious cross-border threats to health.
>
> The Union shall complement the Member States' action in reducing drugs-related health damage, including information and prevention.

The Treaty provisions, however, stop short of mandating convergence in health policy. Instead they state that while incentive measures can be used to take action, this cannot amount to harmonisation of the laws across states (Article 168(5)). Nonetheless it is the case that laws and 'soft' law such as policy documents may over time work towards a convergence of legislative measures at member state level.[9] In addition EU funded research may facilitate the engagement between experts across the EU in the area and the resulting sharing of information can lead to changes in expectation as to what constitutes 'best practice' in relation to a particular issue. This in time may also impact upon perceptions if member states themselves decide to address patient safety issues through legislation. Patient safety has been safeguarded through health itself being placed firmly upon the EU agenda. There is competence in relation to provisions concerning the internal market. Article 114(3) of the Treaty, as amended by the Treaty of Lisbon, provides that 'the Commission must "take as a base a high level of protection" where this relates to legislative proposals concerning "health, safety, environmental protection and consumer protection"'. The EU has subsequently confirmed that it is committed to the mainstreaming of health objectives in all Community policies and activities.[10]

Patient safety is something which has been promoted through the EU public health programmes. Several programmes operated in relation to HIV and AIDS. For example, Decision 91/317/EEC of the Council and Ministers of Health of the Member States adopting a plan of action in the framework of the 'Europe against AIDS' programme 1991–1993.[11] The scope of this programme concerned training, research, information provision. In addition it also addressed measures to ensure blood safety. This was followed by the 'Europe against AIDS' programme 1996–2000. This aimed at reducing mortality from AIDS and also constraining the spread of the disease.[12] The programme promoted co-operation between national policies and also non-governmental organisations. First, it addressed the surveillance and monitoring of communicable diseases. Second, it was concerned with combating transmissions. Third, it had a focus on information, education and training. Fourth, it provided that there would be support for those persons who had developed HIV or AIDS and also support in relation to combating consequent discrimination.

Communicable diseases are no respecters of national borders and this is reflected by measures taken at EU level. In relation to the prospect of the adverse effect of communicable diseases upon patient safety the EU established the European Centre for Disease Prevention and Control.[13] Its mission under the Regulation which establishes the organisation is to 'identify, assess and communicate current and emerging threats to human health posed by infectious diseases'.[14] Its role includes the collection and evaluation of scientific data, which it then distributes. It also provides both scientific advice and assistance and undertakes training. It is charged with providing 'timely information' to member states, to the Commission and also to those agencies of the Community and relevant international organisations which operate in the area of public health.[15] It is involved in exchanging information, relevant expertise and also best practice information. The European Centre operates surveillance networks. It also has the task of assisting the European Commission through the operation of 'early warning systems' for emergencies.[16]

Patient safety questions are also fundamentally important in the context of EU regulation of pharmaceuticals and also of the regulation of medical devices.[17] Thus, from Treaty provisions to establishment of specific agencies such as the European Centre for Disease Protection and Control the EU is increasingly concerned with health in general and patient safety in particular. We now go on to consider two areas where the EU's involvement has impacted upon or has the potential to have a considerable impact upon patient safety issues: first, the regulation of standards of quality and safety in the use of blood, tissue and cells; and, second, in the area free movement.

Regulating the safety of blood, tissues and cells

Using Article 152 (now Article 168) as its legal basis, the EU has enacted a number of Directives concerning patient safety issues. First, the EU enacted the Blood Safety Directive. Second, the EU became concerned to engage with issues of quality and safety concerning organs and tissue from humans. This subsequently led to the EU Tissue and Cells Directive.[18] The characteristic of the Directives in this area is that they are new model harmonisation directives. Rather than attempting to totally regulate the area, they provide standards and structures while leaving some issues for member states themselves to determine.

The background to these Directives can be seen in terms of major international patient safety scandals. From the mid-1980s there was reporting of major controversies concerning blood safety. In France incidents were reported of some 4,000 persons receiving blood which was infected with HIV.[19] Similarly, in 1993 there were reports of haemophiliacs in Germany becoming infected with HIV through blood products.[20] Concerns regarding blood safety have a particularly international dimension due to the fact that individual member states will import blood and blood products. Some research indicated that there was a greater chance that individuals would not declare the fact that they were carrying HIV where the donation was paid.[21] It was unsurprising that such developments were followed by the enactment of Article 152 of the Treaty. The EU decided to specifically regulate in this area in the light of these perceived concerns regarding safety. The Blood Safety Directive concerns the collection and testing of human blood and of blood components;[22] it also relates to processing, storage and distribution where blood is intended for transfusion.[23] Only establishments which are accredited, authorised or licensed can collect and test human blood.[24] Establishments must designate a 'responsible person' for ensuring that the collection, testing of blood and blood components shall be in accordance with the laws of the member states.[25] The responsible person is also to provide the competent authority with information, where necessary, concerning, for example, designation, authorisation and licensing procedures.[26] The Directive provides for requirements in relation to inspection and quality control.[27] These include record keeping and traceability.[28] This is in order that blood and blood components can be traced from donor to recipient. It also requires that procedures be established for the notification of serious adverse events (these are defined as 'accidents and errors') which are 'related to the collection, testing, processing, storage and distribution of blood and blood components which may have an influence on their quality and safety as well as any serious adverse reactions observed during or after transfusion which may be attributed to the quality and the safety of blood and blood components'.[29]

The Blood Directive aims to ensure that information is available about donors.[30] Blood donors are required to provide identification, their history of health and a signature.[31] Before giving blood the Directive requires that donors must be interviewed and subject to examination by a qualified health professional.[32] The Directive does not preclude individual member states including standards which are more stringent than those contained in the Directive itself. This leaves scope for more rigorous regimes concerned with patient safety at domestic level. The Directive also provides that

> Member states shall take the necessary measures to encourage voluntary and unpaid blood donations with a view to ensuring that blood and blood components are in so far as possible provided from such donations.[33]

This links more generally to concerns expressed at EU level and beyond regarding the commoditisation of human material, something which extends beyond the scope of this chapter.[34]

The EU then subsequently enacted Directive 2004/23/EC on setting standards of quality and safety for the donation, procurement, testing, processing, preservation, storage and distribution of human tissues and cells (referred to here subsequently as the Tissue and Cells Directive.[35] This, as its name suggests, is concerned with quality and safety in relation to tissue and cells. As with the Blood Safety Directive, it is concerned with issues of procurement, donation, testing, preservation and also distribution of tissues and cells. The Directive itself has a very broad application. Its scope covers 'haematopoietic peripheral blood, umbilical cord blood and bone marrow stem cells; reproductive cells (i.e. sperm and eggs), foetal tissues and cells, adult and embryonic stem cells'.[36] Excluded from the Directive are blood and blood products, 'organs or parts of organs if their function is to be used for the same person as the entire organ on or in the human body'.[37] In addition it also excludes material which is used as an autologous graft (i.e. where material is removed from and is then applied to that person).[38] As with the Blood Safety Directive, member states are also required to ensure that persons who procure tissue must have 'appropriate training and experience'.[39] In addition those organisations which preserve, process, store or distribute such material must be in some form accredited or licensed by a 'competent body'.[40] The member state must establish such a body to regulate, inspect and control and maintain a register of those bodies which are accredited.[41] Accredited bodies also have to supply information to the competent body on an annual basis. In addition states are required to set up procedures which relate to notification and recording of adverse events and reactions.[42] Importantly, the member states are required to take necessary measures to ensure that tissue establish tissues establishments mechanisms which ensure quality and safety of tissues and cells.[43]Again, further safeguards relate to the fact that there is exclusion of material from deceased persons in certain situations, e.g. where the cause of death is not known. As with blood safety, emphasis is placed upon the importance of donations being both voluntary and not subject to payment. One of the challenges in relation to implementation of such measures is to ensure that member states comply with the provision of the Directive. Reports from the Commission indicate that currently compliance remains somewhat sporadic.[44]

Free movement and patient safety

Over the last few years litigants have increasingly been using their free movement rights in EU law to assert claims to medical treatment. Article 56 of the EC Treaty provides that

> Restrictions on the freedom to provide services within the Community shall be prohibited in respect of nationals of Member States who are established in a State of the Community other than that of the person for whom the services are intended.

Article 57 further provides that

> Services shall be considered to be 'services' within the meaning of this Treaty where they are normally provided for remuneration.
> 'Services' shall in particular include … (d) activities of the professions.

Claims under the Treaty have been combined with Article 22 of Regulation No. 1408/71, which concerns social security provisions. This enables EU citizens to seek to access medical treatment in another member state and claim reimbursement for the cost of that treatment. While member states have some discretion under this regulation to determine reimbursement, Article 22 provides that authorisation

> may not be refused where the treatment in question is among the benefits provided for by the legislation of the Member State on whose territory the person concerned resides and where he cannot be given such treatment within the time normally necessary for obtaining the treatment in question in the Member State of residence, taking account of his current state of health and the probable course of the disease.

Over time individuals challenged the refusal of national social insurance systems to reimburse costs of treatment in another member state. In *Kohll* a refusal by the Luxembourg social insurance scheme to refund the cost of orthodontic treatment in Germany was held to be contrary to free movement principles and not objectively justifiable,[45] an approach later extended to hospital services.[46] Nonetheless the European Court of Justice indicated that member states could impose some forms of restriction such as prior authorisation in those situations where otherwise there might be consequent instability to the operation of national health systems. However, the court drew the distinction in difference in approach between extra-mural and hospital care: in the former prior authorisation was not needed, whereas its use in relation to hospital care was upheld.[47] Subsequently, in the well known case of *Watts* a litigant successfully claimed that the Treaty provisions could extend to enable reimbursement of treatment costs by the NHS, in this case reimbursement for the cost of a hip operation, and avoid the standard NHS waiting time of 12 months.[48]

These freedom of movement cases sparked considerable concern.[49] Most obvious was the fear that the resource allocation policy of individual member states could be undermined by individuals seeking to by-pass waiting lists and seek treatment abroad. But more pertinent for the issue under consideration in this chapter was the prospect of problems arising in relation to differential standards of care being provided across different member states, with the consequent possibility that litigation might result.[50] Furthermore, there was a real possibility that home member states would be left to deal with the consequences if something went wrong in another member state, as continuing care would fall inevitably within the province of the home member state.

Interestingly, as early as 2001 Nys suggested that this line of free movement cases might result in development of a 'harmonised package' of comparable healthcare services across the EU.[51] It appears that gradually the EU is moving in that direction in its most recent proposals. Following the raft of free movement cases the EU published a proposed Directive in relation to patients' rights in cross-border care.[52] This Directive was agreed by the Council of the European Union on 8 June 2010.[53] This is a wide-ranging document which responds to the free movement cases. Some of the provisions are of particular interest in relation to questions of patient safety. The proposal recommends common principles across all EU systems. It introduces a 'duty of co-operation' under Article 13 of the Draft Directive. The proposal states that '[r]ealising the potential of the internal market for cross-border healthcare requires co-operation between providers, purchasers and regulators of different Member states at national, regional or local level in order to ensure safe, high quality and efficient care across borders'.[54] This is with the aim of making clear which member state is responsible for compliance with common principles for healthcare. There is to be appropriate provision of patient information on access to cross-border healthcare and national contact points for such information.[55] This is also to be linked to other measures such as the Commission and Council recommendation on Patient Safety and Quality of Health Services (discussed in the introduction [p. 150] and concluding section to this chapter [p. 160]). The proposals state that

Whenever healthcare is provided it is vital for patients to ensure:

- clear information that enables people to make informed choices about their healthcare
- mechanisms for ensuring the quality and safety of healthcare that is provided
- continuity of care between different treating professionals and organizations
- and mechanisms to ensure appropriate remedies and compensation for harm arising from healthcare.[56]

The aim is to ensure clarify in responsibilities of member states in relation to quality and safety of care.

The proposals also include a legal framework for cross-border care clarifying the case law in this area. The Directive will establish a co-operation framework, which will include such things as health technology assessment, data collection and quality and safety. This proposes new 'European reference networks'. These would aim to join on a voluntary basis specialised healthcare centres across member states. The aim would be that such networks could provide 'focal points' for purposes such as research, evaluation and the dissemination of information.[57] Pilot projects are being funded to test the concept of such networks. Furthermore, the EU is currently providing support for a pilot network considering health technology assessment, EUnetHTA.[58] The Commission also noted the potential for information and communication technologies to improve the quality, safety and efficiency of healthcare.[59]

There are also recommendations on e-health contained in the Draft Directive. Concerns regarding the use of such technologies include the different types of technology and formats, and it is recommended that harmonisation is needed across the EU to facilitate use of such technologies.[60]

The proposed Directive, while indicating how transfer of medical records may be necessary to facilitate patient care, also illustrates the problems with such an approach in that there remain tensions between access to data and protection of personal data, which is also required under EU law through Directive 95/46/EC of the European Parliament and of the Council of 24 October 1995 on the protection of individuals with regards to the processing of personal data and on the free movement of such data. Following the Draft Directive a Recommendation has been published on the cross-border interoperability of electronic health systems.[61] This is aimed at facilitating access to patient data when the patient is being treated in another member state, but the issue of data security will inevitably remain a fundamental concern for individuals and member states.

One further recommendation of the Directive is that there should be mechanisms in place to provide compensation for harm, although the precise forms of such mechanisms are left to the individual member states to determine.[62] This is inevitable given the wide-ranging differences in complaints and civil litigation procedures across member states. In the UK responses to this recommendation contained in the Draft Directive have been critical. The General Medical Council stated that 'there have to be effective systems that lead to regulatory action or redress for patients if they have been harmed.'[63] The then UK government minister Dawn Primarolo, also criticised this provision and stated that '[o]ur view is that Article 5 is not clear enough with regards to how complaints, liability and negligence fit together'.[64] Nonetheless this provision in the Draft Directive also raises the question of whether transfer of information on such issues could in the longer term lead to greater alignment across the EU, both in relation to complaints processes and also more generally in relation to civil compensation.

The use of the language of rights in the context of the proposed Directive is also interesting. There is no EU document of patient rights in force to date but this may come in the future. Certainly for those member states who are signatories what is also relevant post-Lisbon is the new enforceability under the EU Treaty of the EU Charter of Fundamental Rights.[65] This is a document which was until recently simply of 'soft-law' status but now is enforceable save in relation to those member states – Poland and the UK – which have exercised their right to opt out. This is a wide-ranging document whose provisions range from rights to dignity in Article 1, through consent to treatment in Article 3, to the right to 'healthcare' in Article 35. This document does not enable challenges to be brought in areas where the EU does not already have competence – it does not have a freestanding ability to wholly reframe EU law. Yet its very existence could yet prove influential in reframing the debate as to whether there is a fundamental right to a safe system of healthcare within member states.

The proposed Patients Rights Directive contains wide-ranging proposals. Their implications may be that the delivery of healthcare services in the longer term becomes increasingly aligned across member states. In practice, however, while this may be the aim, ensuring that this becomes a reality, as we shall see in the concluding section (p. 160), is something which is fraught with considerable practical difficulties.

Taking 'patient safety' policy forward

The Commission communication in 2008, as noted earlier, highlighted not only concerns relating to patient safety but also the potential for EU engagement. This Communication highlighted the fact that different EU countries were at different stages of engagement with the issue of patient safety. It saw the EU as playing an important role in relation to collecting information and also disseminating 'best practice' across member states, and facilitating momentum here even when specific projects have come to an end. The Communication also recommended that member states should first

(1) Support the establishment and development of national policies and programmers on patient safety in general terms.
(2) Inform and empower patients by involving them in the patient safety policy process by informing them of levels of safety and, if things go wrong how they can find accessible and comprehensible information on complaints and redress systems.
(3) Set up or improve comprehensive blame-free reporting and learning systems so that the extent and type and causes of adverse events are captured to enable resources to be sufficiently channelled into developing solutions and interventions which can then be shared at EU level. Such reporting on adverse events should be done in a constructive rather than punitive or repressive manner so that healthcare providers feel confident that they can report without fear of negative consequences.
(4) Ensure that patient safety is embedded into the education and training of healthcare workers as the providers of care.[66]

The Commission itself was also to work on the development of common 'definitions, terminology and indicators' on patient safety.[67] It also would facilitate sharing of information, best practice and the promotion of EU research programmes in relation to patient safety. In addition it would consider how member states could best collaborate in relation to patient safety issues in the future.

In addition the EU published in 2009 the Council Recommendation on patient safety, including prevention and control of healthcare associated infections, which was adopted by the member states on 9 June 2009.[68] In this recommendation the Council states that

Patients should be informed and empowered by involving them in the patient safety process. They should be informed of patient safety standards, best practices and/or safety measures in place and on how they can find accessible and comprehensible information on complaints and redress systems.[69]

The Recommendation also provides that states should establish reporting and learning systems in relation to adverse events. In addition, interestingly, it recommends that 'Patient Safety should be embedded in the education and training of healthcare workers as the providers of care'.[70] The recommendation states the need for the collection of relevant data to establish patient safety programmes and also the need for common terminology and indicators across the member states.[71] The Recommendation also states that there is a need for national strategies to incorporate the control and prevention of healthcare associated infections within healthcare institutions.[72] Furthermore, it emphasises the need to make control and prevention of such infections a long-term strategic priority for healthcare institutions.[73] There was also a need for surveillance systems in relation to such infections either to be established or to be strengthened at institutional, regional and national level.[74] The proposals also suggest that healthcare professionals specialising in information control should be encouraged. States are also encouraged to work with the health technology industry to reduce the prospect of adverse events.[75] The Recommendation is nonetheless consistent with the principle that it is for member states themselves to have responsibility for the organisation and delivery of health services and medical care.

A Patient Safety and Quality of Care Working Group has also been established under the auspices of the High Level Group on Health Services and Medical Care. One issue which it is currently addressing is the interface between the work of the EU in this area and other initiatives. In particular, there are two developments, one from the OECD and the other from the WHO, which are worthy of note.[76] The WHO has asked the EU through its resolution on Patient Safety to establish a quality programme which will, first, develop global norms and standards.[77] Second, the programme will 'frame evidenced based policies'. Third, it will have the task of supporting the project EU Nepal. There is also international collaboration in the production of an International Classification for Patient Safety between participating centres across the world. The OCED also has an ongoing 'Health Care Quality Indicator Project'. This has been operational since 2002 and currently involves 37 countries. It led to the publication of *Healthcare at a Glance* in 2002 and 2007. Topics considered include patient safety, prevention, primary care and mental health.

These developments and programmes highlight how many patient safety issues simply cannot be seen through the prism of a single jurisdiction or even that of the EU if they are effectively to be resolved. Patient mobility and the ease of cross-border disease transmission illustrate that one of the challenges for the EU is to effectively engage with the international position in terms of developing policy and law in this area.

Conclusions

The EU is engaging with a range of areas which can facilitate the improvement of patient safety. As in other areas, the EU's impact upon health law and health policy at member state level seems likely to increase. However, how fundamental this impact will be remains to be seen. One major challenge here is the diversity of healthcare provision across member states. Despite the developments highlighted in the chapter it appears that much remains to be done across the EU as a whole. A Eurobarometer survey published in April 2010 noted concerns across the EU countries surveyed that harm can arise through infections contracted in hospital or through incorrect or missed diagnosis or diagnosis which was delayed.[78] The survey indicated that over one-quarter of those responding or family members had suffered some form of adverse health event. It was noted that these generally were unreported. Furthermore, some 29 per cent of those who responded were not aware where the responsibility for patient safety lay in their member state. There was significant variation in responses across member states as to perceptions of the quality of healthcare. So, for example, healthcare was rated good by 97 per cent of respondents in Belgium and by 95 per cent of respondents in Austria. In contrast, only 25 per cent of those responding in Greece rated the quality of healthcare good or very good and only 30 per cent of those responding in Poland. As the survey notes, '[i]t is clear that there is room for reflection on how to reduce observed disparities between countries'.[79] This highlights the major challenge for the EU in this area. There is simply not a level playing field in the types of healthcare provision across member states. Levels of funding between member states in relation to healthcare vary considerably and this is likely to continue in the short to medium term. Similarly, the nature of facilities from primary care to hospitals is disparate across member states. So too, the provision of healthcare professionals and the training provided to such health professionals differ. These disparities have only increased following the expansion in EU member states in recent years. There are thus what appear to be almost irreconcilable tensions in achieving some of the proposed aims. Throw in here the interface with patient rights statements and the situation becomes yet more complex. There is a danger that it becomes simply unrealistic to operate effectively what is being proposed in an expanded EU. That is not to say that aspirations to engage with and improve standards of patient safety are wrong – far from it. Rather, it means that we need to be realistic as to what can be achieved, at least in the short term.

Patient safety at EU level, as elsewhere, is thus a multifaceted issue. It raises questions of standards of healthcare and how these can and indeed should be framed. It highlights the fact that patient safety and standards are no respecters of borders. It illustrates further the challenges of patient mobility across the EU, whether by patients seeking treatment and claiming reimbursement or by those undertaking cosmetic procedures in the private sector in member states where healthcare infrastructures are less well developed and where there is a danger that safety standards may be compromised. The EU is looking at healthcare more 'holistically today', as the EU Health White Paper indicates, and patient safety is a multifaceted issue which can only be effectively dealt with by such a 'holistic' approach. Such engagement is to be welcomed, but given the diversity of approaches to healthcare standards and quality and modes of delivery across the EU we are still some way off translating such approaches into coherent law and policy over the member states as a whole.

Notes

1 Department of Health Expert Group, *An Organization without a Memory: 'Report of an Expert Group on Learning from Adverse Events in the NHS*, London, Department of Health, 2008.
2 'Communication from the Commission to the European Parliament and Council on Patient Safety Including the Prevention and Control of Healthcare Associated Infections', COM (2008) 837 final, para. 3.1.
3 Of 23 October 2007.
4 'Communication from the Commission to the European Parliament and Council on Patient Safety ...' COM (2008) 837 final.
5 Ibid., para 1.
6 Directive 2002/98/EC of the European Parliament and Council, 27 January 2002.
7 See, generally, T.K. Hervey and J.V. McHale, *Health Law and the EU*, Cambridge, Cambridge University Press, 2004.
8 Case C-180/96-R *UK v. Commission* [1996] ECR I-3903.
9 Hervey and McHale, *Health Law and the EU*.
10 Decision No. 1350/2007/EC of the European Parliament and of the Council of 23 October 2007.
11 OJ 1991 L 175/26.
12 Decision 647/96/EC of the European Parliament and Council, OJ 1996 L 95/16.
13 http://www.ecdc.europa.eu/en/healthtopics/Pages/Healthcare-associated_Infections_%28HCAI%29.aspx.
14 Regulation (EC) No. 851/2004 of the European Parliament and of the Council of 21 April 2004 establishing a European Centre for disease prevention and control, OJ L 142, 8.2.2003, Article 3.
15 Ibid.
16 Ibid., p. 30.
17 See, further, Hervey and McHale, *Health Law and the EU*, ch. 8.
18 (2004), Directive 2004/23/EC.
19 See, further, A.M. Farrell 'Is the Gift Still Good: Examining the Politics and Regulation of Blood Safety in the European Union', *Medical Law Review* 14:2, 2006, p. 155.
20 J. Abraham and G. Lewis, *Regulating Medicines in Europe: Competition, Expertise and Public Health*, London, Routledge, 2000.
21 P.J. Hagen, *Blood Transfusion in Europe: A 'White Paper'*, Strasbourg, Council of Europe, 1993.
22 Directive 2002/98/EC, Article 2 of the European Parliament and Council of 27th January 2003 setting standards of quality and safety for the collection, testing, processing and storage and distribution of human blood and blood components and amending Directive 2001/83/EC.
23 Article 2(3) and see also Commission Directive 2004/33/EC of 22 March 2004 implementing Directive 2002/98/EC of the European Parliament and Council as regards certain technical requirements for blood and blood components. Commission Directive 2005/61/EC of 30 September 2005 Implementing Directive 2002/98/EC of the European Parliament and Council as regards traceability requirements and modifications of serious adverse reaction events; and Commission Directive 2005/62/EC of 30 September 2005 Implementing Directive 2002/98/EC of the European Parliament and Council as regards common standards and specifically relating to a quality system for blood establishments.
24 Directive 2002/98/EC, Article 5.
25 Ibid., Article 9(1).

26 Ibid.
27 Ibid., Article 8.
28 Ibid., Articles 13 and 14.
29 Ibid., Article 2(3).
30 Ibid., Article 17.
31 Ibid., Article 29(3).
32 Ibid., Article 19.
33 Ibid., Article 20.
34 See, generally, e.g., N. Duxbury 'Do Markets Degrade?', *Modern Law Review* 55, 1996, p. 33. R. Titmus, *The Gift Relationship: From Human Blood to Social Policy*, London, Allen and Unwin, 1970; S. Wilkinson, *Bodies for Sale: Ethics and Exploitation in the Human Body Trade*, London, Routledge, 2003.
35 Directive 2004/23/EC of the European Parliament and of the Council of 31 March 2004 on setting standards of quality and safety for the donation, procurement, testing, processing, preservation, storage and distribution of human tissue and cells. Commission Directive 2006/17/EC of the European Parliament and of the Council as regards certain technical requirements for the donation, procurement and testing of human tissues and cells. Commission Directive 2006/86/EC of the European Parliament and of the Council as regards traceability requirements, notification of serious adverse reactions and events and certain technical requirements for the coding, processing, preservation, storage and distribution of human tissue and cells.
36 Preamble, Article 7.
37 Directive 2004/23/EC, Article 2(2).
38 Ibid.
39 Ibid., Article 5.
40 Ibid., Article 6.
41 Ibid., Article 10.
42 Ibid., Article 11.
43 Ibid., Article 16.
44 Communication from the Commission to the Council, the European Parliament, the European Economic and Social Committee and the Committee of the Regions on the application of Directive 2004/23/EC on setting standards of quality and safety for the donation, procurement, testing, processing, preservation, storage and distribution of human tissues and cells, COM/2009/0708 final.
45 Case C-158/96 *Kohll* [1998] ECR-I-1935.
46 Case C-157/99 Judgement of 21 July 2001; and see also Case C-368/98 *Vanbraekel* [2001] ECR-I-5363.
47 Case C-385/99 *Muller-Faure and van Riet* [2003] ECR I-I-4509.
48 Case C-372/04 *R (on the application of Watts) v. Bedford Primary Care Trust, Secretary of State for Health* [2006] ECR I-4325; and see further on this case A. du Bois-Pedain, 'Seeking Healthcare Elsewhere', *Cambridge Law Journal* (2007) 66; G. Davies 'The Effect of Mrs Watts Trip to France on the National Health Service', *Kings Law Journal* 18, 2007, p. 160. J.V. McHale 'The Right to Medical Treatment in EU Law', *Medical Law Review* 15, 2007, p. 99.
49 See, further, C. Newdick, 'Citizenship, Free Movement and Healthcare: Cementing Individual Rights by Coroding Social Solidarity', *Common Market Law Review* 43, 2006, p. 1661.
50 J.V. McHale and M.Bell, 'Traveller's Checks', *Health Service Journal* 60, 2002, p. 39.
51 H. Nys, 'Comparative Health Law and the Harmonization of Patients' Rights in Europe', *European Journal of Health Law* 8, 2001, p. 317.
52 'Proposal for a Directive of the European Parliament and of the Council on the Application of Patients' Rights in Cross-border Healthcare', COM (2008) 414.

53 Council of the European Union, 'Council Agrees on New Rules for Patients' Rights in Cross-border Healthcare', Luxembourg, 8 June 2010.

54 'Proposal for a Directive of the European Parliament and of the Council on the Application of Patients' Rights in Cross-border Healthcare', COM (2008) 414, para. 8.1.

55 'Proposal for a Directive of the European Parliament and of the Council on the Application of Patients' Rights in Cross-border Healthcare', COM (2008) 414, para. 7.5.

56 Ibid., para 4.

57 'Proposal for a Directive of the European Parliament and of the Council on the Application of Patients' Rights in Cross-border Healthcare', COM (2008) 414, para. 2.3.1.

58 Ibid., para. 2.32.

59 Ibid., para. 2.3.2.

60 Ibid., para. 8.4.

61 Commission recommendation C (2008) 3282 of 2 July 2008 on cross-border interoperability of electronic health record systems.

62 Ibid., para. 8.6(16).

63 House of Lords, *'Healthcare across EU Borders: A Safe Framework'*, London, The Stationery Office, 2009.

64 Ibid., para. 144.

65 J.V. McHale, 'Fundamental Rights in the EU', in E. Mossialos *et al.*, *Health Systems Governance in the EU: The Role of EU Law and Policy*, Cambridge, Cambridge University Press, 2010.

66 'Communication from the Commission to the European Parliament and Council on Patient Safety including the Prevention and Control of Health-care Associated Infections.' COM (2008) 837 final, para. 6.

67 Ibid., para. 7.

68 Council of the European Union, Brussels, 5 June 2009.

69 Ibid., 5 June 2009, para. 9.

70 Ibid., para. 10.

71 Ibid., para. 11.

72 Ibid., para. 13.

73 Ibid., para. 14.

74 Ibid., para. 15.

75 Ibid., para. 17.

76 World Health Alliance for Patient Safety Forward Programme 2008–9, WHO.

77 WHA 55.18.

78 Eurobarometer, *'Patient Safety and Quality of Health Care'*, Brussels, European Commission, April 2010.

79 Ibid., p. 67.

11 Patient safety and clinical risk management in Germany

Marc Stauch

Introduction: health care in Germany

Organisation and Regulation

In Germany, as in the United Kingdom, there is mass health care provision based on the principle of treatment according to need, and provided more or less free at the point of delivery. Bismarck's social reforms of the 1880s established a system of statutory health insurance funds (*Gesetzliche Krankenkassen*) for workers financed partly by the employer and partly by deductions from their salary.[1] In subsequent years the scope of the system was gradually extended to other groups in society, so that nowadays virtually every citizen has health insurance cover: some 90 per cent of the population are members of one of the statutory funds, while the remainder – typically citizens on higher incomes, who are allowed to opt out of the public insurance scheme – will usually carry private insurance.

Under this approach, and particularly as compared to the UK with its centralised NHS scheme, the involvement of the German state in health care remains at 'arms length'. It provides the underlying statutory framework,[2] but then leaves the detailed ordering and running of the system to the key non-state actors in the area. Thus the financing of treatment remains a matter for the insurance funds, contracting with doctors and hospitals to provide the necessary health care. Doctors, operating alone or in partnerships and providing primary health care, are private actors, remunerated on a fee-for-service basis by the insurance funds. For their part, the hospitals may be either public institutions (run by a given regional municipality or other public body) or private bodies. Of the latter, some are charitable in nature, including hospitals run by various religious orders, while others are commercial, for-profit enterprises.[3]

A further significant factor, contributing to the more devolved nature of health care provision in Germany is the federal character of the political system. Thus, in relation to hospitals, the applicable law regulating them is a matter for each of the individual states (*Länder*) as opposed to the federal government (*Bund*). Doctors, both in primary care and in hospitals, are subject to a dual system of control. First, they must be licensed to practise by the federal level approbation (licensing) authority; second, they are obliged to join, and are subject to the professional rules of, the relevant regional medical council (*Landesärztekammer*) for the particular state (*Land*) in which they practise.[4]

In terms of ensuring patient safety, these regulatory bodies have an important preventative function. Under the federal level *Bundesärzteordnung* the approbation authority may remove doctors who are found to be 'unworthy' of or 'unreliable' in exercising their calling: this includes cases where the doctor poses a risk to patients.[5] Similarly, failure to abide by the rules of the *Landesärztekammer* will result in the doctor having to answer before a professional tribunal. The rules in question, collectively known as *Standesrecht*, include duties of continuing professional training and development to ensure that doctors are aware of new developments in their field, and to participate in quality assurance initiatives run by the *Landesärztekammer*.[6] Other *Standesrecht*-based duties of doctors, with patient safety implications, include the careful documentation of the treatments they carry out and the reporting of undesired side-effects from pharmaceutical products.[7]

The issue of patient safety

In recent years, and particularly in the last decade, the issue of patient safety has gained increasing prominence in Germany. There, as elsewhere, it has become clear that unacceptably high levels of avoidable medical injuries are occurring, particularly in hospital care. In 2007 an expert committee charged with monitoring developments in health care presented statistics (compiled on the basis of 184 studies) suggesting an annual rate in German hospitals of 2–4 per cent preventable adverse events (*vermeidbare unerwünschte Ereignisse*) and a preventable adverse event (PAE) related mortality rate of 0.1 per cent. Given that there are around 17 million in-patient treatments in Germany each year, this corresponds to roughly half a million PAEs and 17,000 preventable deaths.[8]

Insofar as injury occurs in a given case, there are various legal consequences that may follow. These include professional sanctions applied by the *Landesärztekammer* and/or federal approbation authority, as well as the possibility in some cases of criminal liability.[9] However, in practice the main accountability mechanism takes the form of the doctor's and/or hospital's liability under civil law to compensate the injured patient or, in case of death, his or her dependants. In fact the number of cases in Germany in which patients instigate legal proceedings for medical negligence appears to be several times higher than in the UK: while reliable statistics are hard to come by, one reputable commentator has estimated the number of such actions as lying somewhere between 20,000 and 35,000 each year.[10]

In dealing with such claims, the role of the civil courts has been supplemented by the work of special 'arbitration boards', which are designed to facilitate out of court settlements. We shall look in more detail at how these civil law mechanisms operate, before going on to ask how far they contribute to improving patient safety.

The consequences of medical injury

Civil law compensation

In terms of the overall framework, and also as regards many of the detailed rules, there is much similarity between the German and UK approaches to holding doctors and hospitals to account for medical injury.[11] Admittedly, in Germany the patient will typically bring his claim in contract law rather than the tort of negligence. However, this difference (stemming from the absence in German contract law of consideration as a formal element) is in itself of little import. This is because a contract for medical treatment will be classified as a contract for services, in which there is no obligation to achieve a particular result (nor a guarantee that injury will not occur), but merely a duty of careful performance.

Accordingly to recover for medical injury, it remains necessary for the patient to prove this resulted from negligent treatment by the doctor/hospital. Under § 276 II of the *Bürgerliches Gesetzbuch* (civil code), negligence is defined as an actor's failure to observe the socially required level of care (*die im Verkehr erforderliche Sorgfalt*), an approach that – as applied to doctors – has much similarity to the 'reasonable doctor' standard in English law. Furthermore, the courts have accepted that, to decide if a given doctor was negligent, they must be guided in the first instance by the opinion evidence of other doctors as to whether his or her conduct was justified.[12] Nonetheless, against this background, the German courts have developed medical negligence law in a relatively 'patient friendly' direction, and allowed for liability findings and compensation for injury in a significant number of cases. This has been achieved in a number of ways.

First, the courts have taken a proactive approach to identifying instances of negligence. Thus they have been more willing than their English counterparts to look critically at practices accepted by the medical experts and sometimes find them wanting. As the Federal Supreme Court (*Bundesgerichtshof*) stated in a medical negligence case from 1964, 'the fact a given practice is customary will not be sufficient to negate negligence if at the same time there is a failure to do all that is necessary, according to the rules and experience of medical science, to safeguard the patient from bodily harm'.[13] Moreover, in cases where the harm stemmed from a risk in the treatment environment rather than one inherent in the patient's condition, the courts have developed a doctrine of 'fully masterable risks' (*voll beherrschbare Risiken*). Under this the burden from the outset will be on the doctor/hospital to justify their conduct by showing they took all reasonably possible precautions to avoid the risk. Failing this, they will be held negligent.[14]

A second way that German courts have revealed a claimant-friendly stance in dealing with medical injury claims is in fashioning a number of special proof rules in order to mitigate evidentiary problems the patient may face. This includes formal presumptions – in cases where there is inadequate record-keeping by the doctor/ hospital as to the course of diagnosis and treatment – that non-documented tests and/or treatment measures were omitted, permitting a straightforward finding of negligence on that basis.[15] Another striking device deployed by the courts in medical negligence cases is the full reversal of proof of causation allowed for in case of 'gross' negligence. Pursuant to this, once the patient establishes that the doctor/hospital committed a particularly grave treatment error, and that this created a more than negligible risk of the injury he suffered, the onus will pass to the defence to disprove that the error caused the injury – normally an impossible task. The upshot is compensation in many cases where the patient would likely have suffered the injury anyway, i.e. quite apart from negligence.[16]

Third, the stringent rules in Germany relating to the disclosure of treatment risks should be mentioned. Here the courts have adopted a highly subjective approach to the information the patient must be provided with at the time of consenting to treatment: every matter that may conceivably affect the decision of the particular patient must be divulged, including utterly negligible risks.[17] Moreover, in every case where disclosure is inadequate (through a failure to mention risks) the treatment will amount to an unlawful battery. The upshot is that when such a risk materialises and causes injury the patient will generally be entitled to compensation without further ado. He is not required to show that had he known of the risk he would actually have declined the treatment.[18]

The work of the arbitration boards

As noted, the role of the courts in this area is augmented by the work of special 'arbitration boards'. The formation of these boards began on the initiative of the regional medical councils (*Landesärztekammer*) in the mid-1970s as a response to an upsurge in malpractice actions. A growing climate of distrust was becoming apparent between doctors and patients, including the tendency for patients – frustrated by lack of information – to report doctors to the police, leading to criminal investigations for unlawful bodily injury. By establishing the boards, the profession aimed to defuse these tensions and demonstrate openess; in particular, they hoped to assist the patient in making good well-founded claims, while encouraging the abandonment of unmerited claims.[19] Since then, twelve such boards, attached to the *Landesärztekammer*, have been set up across Germany. Their general remit is to offer an expert report (*Gutachten*) outside the formal process of litigation, as to whether there was faulty treatment causative of injury. The proceedings remains cost-free for the patient, being financed by the *Landesärztekammer*, with contributions from the relevant hospital authorities. Typically a claim will be assessed by expert panels of between three and five members, one of whom is legally qualified and the others doctors (including one from the relevant specialty).[20] The majority of boards, known as *Gutachterkommissionen*, will confine themselves to issuing a report; others – termed *Schlichtungsstellen* – will also seek to mediate a settlement in appropriate cases.

The boards have won a reputation for neutrality and efficiency, and the take-up on them has increased steadily over time. Statistics published on the website of the German Medical Association (*Bundesärztekammer*), the umbrella organisation for the *Landesärztekammer*, show that in 2008 nearly 11,000 new applications were made.[21] On average the boards identify medical negligence as the cause of injury in around one-quarter of the cases they investigate, and in around 70 per cent of these the doctor's liability insurer will then proceed to settle. Conversely, where no error is found, the large majority of patients will abandon their claim. As well as thus facilitating the resolution of claims, the boards have been credited with having a positive effect on patient safety – with their reports, where errors are found, being passed on to the *Landesärztekammer* for use in continuing professional training programmes.[22]

Assessing the civil law redress rules

In general, there is probably greater satisfaction in Germany with the way in which the civil law operates in the area of medical negligence than in the UK. There is a sense that the law generally works well in providing for compensation in appropriate cases;[23] moreover, the operation of the overall civil litigation system in Germany, and availability of the cost-free arbitration boards, appears to have contributed to a reasonable level of access to justice for injured patients.[24] This satisfaction is reflected in the relative lack of interest in replacing the present approach with compensation for medical injury via other options, such as a 'no-fault' insurance-based scheme. Though there were, as in the UK, some initiatives in this direction in the 1970s, the consensus today is that such a scheme would be both difficult to design equitably and too expensive.[25] Indeed, when Germany reunified in 1990, the partial no-fault scheme of 'additional support for victims of medical injury' that had operated in the former German Democratic Republic was wound up.[26]

Importantly, too, in contrast with the UK,[27] there appear to be fewer concerns that the workings of the civil law may have counterproductive effects for patient safety, by encouraging doctors to 'hush up' accidents and/or engage in secretive settlements. One reason for this may be due the more inquisitorial character of legal proceedings in Germany, in which the courts play an active part (aided by neutral, court-appointed medical experts) in seeking the independent truth of what occurred in a given case.[28] Second, the system of arbitration boards, in which, as we saw earlier, the profession has demonstrated its openness to self-examination, has gone some way towards allaying concerns.

That is not to say that medical cover-ups do not occur in Germany: a well-known scandal from the 1980s – with parallels with the Bristol Royal Infirmary scandal in the UK – was the *Barmbek/Bernbeck* case, which concerned an eminent orthopaedic surgeon at a Hamburg hospital who continued to practise despite unsatisfactory hygienic conditions and an excessive rate of patient injuries. Nonetheless, the subsequent committee of enquiry, set up by the Hamburg state parliament, did not identify the system of civil litigation as a contributory factor; instead, the finger was pointed at the strong hierarchies and collegiality at the hospital.[29]

In fact, commentators have suggested a number of ways in which the civil law of medical negligence has had a positive influence upon patient safety in Germany.[30] First, as noted, the courts have adopted a critical approach to expert testimony on approved medical practice and have long been prepared to find practices negligent, when (in the court's view) they contain undue risks for the patient. In such cases a finding of negligence will provide a spur to the medical profession to improve the practices in question. The same effect may be observed in relation to the ancillary duty of doctors to keep careful documentation of treatment given. Initially, this was prescribed by the courts (backed up by a procedural sanction; that non-documented procedures would count, evidentially, as not performed). Subsequently, as noted, the duty has found its way into the doctors' own professional rules (*Standesrecht*).[31]

Probably, though, the most important effect that German medical negligence law has in relation to patient safety is at the level of the organisational or institutional liability of hospitals. In particular, as discussed on p. 167, the courts have developed the doctrine of 'fully masterable risks', which will apply whenever a patient's injury can be linked to a risk factor in the treatment environment, rather than one inherent in his illness. There are frequent examples of the approach in the case law, including in relation to injuries stemming from co-ordination problems among the medical team, staffing decisions by the hospital (the use of inexperienced or non-specialist personnel), equipment failures and medicinal contamination.[32] In all these cases it will be for the hospital to negate the inference of negligence by demonstrating that it took the greatest possible precautions against the risks in question. Legally, this provides a powerful incentive for hospitals to engage in well-considered risk management strategies, to improve both the quality of their second order planning and the underlying safety of the physical treatment environment.[33]

Even so, and notwithstanding the last points, it remains clear that on its own the civil law does not do enough to promote patient safety. One problem is that the working of the law depends on the patient 'reporting' safety problems (by bringing a legal action); however, only a fraction of problems can be identified in this way. Thus near-misses (*Beinahe-Schäden*) are excluded from consideration, as are cases where the patient – though injured – does not consider litigation worthwhile, for example due to concerns about costs or evidential difficulties. In other cases he may simply be unaware that his injury was preventable.[34] The realisation of the true numbers of such injuries that occur each year in German hospitals has spawned a huge recent interest in other mechanisms for addressing patient safety, which will be considered below.

Development of patient safety and clinical risk management

Background in public law and Standesrecht

In the last twenty years the patient safety movement has become increasingly important in Germany, quite apart from concerns about civil liability connected to medical injury. Instead, two main sources of impetus for the movement can be identified. First, it has developed as part of a wider drive on the part of the state to introduce quality assurance (*Qualitätssicherung*) into the health care system, as reflected in reforms to the statutory framework of health provision. Second, the role of the medical profession itself has been of great significance, with important duties relevant to quality assurance now anchored in *Standesrecht*, and the formation of new profession-led institutions directed at improving safety.

Looking first at quality assurance initiatives on the part of the state, these began in the late 1980s to improve the cost-effectiveness and financing of health care delivery. This was expressed in a series of reforms to Book V of the *Sozialgesetzbuch* (social security code), in 1989 and more substantially in 2000,[35] imposing quality assurance duties on delivers of health care to publicly insured patients. In this context §§ 135 ff SGB Book V require hospitals and primary practices to introduce internal quality management and compile regular reports detailing their initiatives and achievements in this area. In addition, they are obliged to participate in external quality auditing by the health care purchasers (public and private health insurance funds) that compare treatments and health outcomes across different hospitals and practices.[36] Another obligation is to abide by regulations (*Richtlinien*) emanating from the federal level *Gemeinsames Bundesausschuss* (G-BA), which aim to standardise therapies and associated clinical procedures. In developing these, the G-BA draws on the findings of evidence-based medicine as to the efficacy and cost-effectiveness of relevant treatments.[37]

Quality assurance in health care and the issue of patient safety are not identical; thus, as suggested, the former has an economic dimension, aiming in part to eradicate treatments that, while they may not positively injure the patient (or may even do some good), do not provide sufficient benefits in terms of their cost.[38] Furthermore, quality assurance may extend to aspects of a patient's experience of health care not directly related to his safety, such as the time taken by the doctor to discuss inevitable risks and side-effects of treatment. Nonetheless there is a sense in which patient safety can be subsumed within the broader domain of quality assurance: an injured patient is clearly neither a good qualitative outcome nor an effective use of resources.

This common ground is evident also in terms of the methodology of quality assurance, particularly the reliance on systematic, large-scale studies to assess the quality of structures, processes and outcomes in health care.[39] This often leads directly to identifying deficits in patient safety: thus, a quality assurance survey commissioned in 2000 by the *Zentrum für Krankenhaus-Management* revealed a serious lack of communication among medical staff, and between them and administrative personnel, in hospitals, with attendant risks to patients from co-ordination errors; another study demonstrated the high level of post-operative hospital infections, and the potential for costs savings through effective hygiene management.[40] In addition, the quality auditing by the health insurance funds pursuant to § 135 SGB V operates as a general warning system by showing when patient outcomes in a given hospital (or a department within it) diverge in a statistically relevant manner from those elsewhere, and seeking the explanation.[41]

As noted on p. 171, the other major impetus in the directions of quality assurance and improved patient safety in German health care has come from within the medical profession itself.[42] As regards quality assurance, expert groups within the profession have been engaged in disseminating clinical 'best practice' guidance (*Leitlinien*; *Empfehlungen*) since the 1970s. More specific concerns as to patient safety began to be voiced by critical health care professionals in the 1980s, and duties on doctors to participate in the quality assurance initiatives of the *Landesärztekammer* were introduced into the doctors' *Standesrecht* in 1988.[43] It was apparent to the profession that, in view of the medical and technical knowledge required in devising effective risk management strategies in the area, it was uniquely placed to address the issue. Moreover, doing so was recognised as a medico-ethical obligation, in line with the Hippocratic maxim of '*primum non nocere*'.[44]

In the following years the patient safety movement in the medical profession has gained steadily in momentum. This is echoed in the various profession-led bodies that have sprung up with the specific remit of addressing patient safety. Thus in 1995 the *Bundesärztekammer* and the *Kassenärztliche Bundesvereinigung* (association of public health insurance doctors) formed the Centre for Quality in Medicine (*Ärztliches Zentrum für Qualität in der Medizin*); in 2005 the Centre inaugurated a Forum for Patient Safety (*Forum Patientensicherheit*) to conduct further research in the area, and develop a critical incident reporting system (CIRS).[45] Another significant development in 2005 was the formation of the German Coalition for Patient Safety (*Aktionsbündnis Patientensicherheit*), a charitable association whose membership comprises doctors, professional organisations, health care institutions, insurers and patient organisations.[46]

Current safety initiatives

Central to patient safety is gathering information on incidents, systematic analysis, and the formulation and dissemination of strategies to reduce recurrence in the future.[47] As regards information gathering and analysis, important initiatives have been undertaken by both the *Forum Patienten- sicherheit* and the German Coalition for Patient Safety in developing CIRS systems. Germany now has two main systems of this kind, which allow health care professionals to register near-misses anonymously online: – cirsmedical.de, which is aimed mainly at health professionals working in hospitals, and jeder-fehler-zaehlt.de ('every mistake counts'), directed at doctors in primary care.[48]

Furthermore, as regards the analysis of PAEs, the Coalition and the *Forum* have been active in the evaluation of relevant data. The Coalition begins its report on its activities each year with a lengthy analysis of studies of medical accidents from countries around the world.[49] Another important source of information about such accidents in Germany is represented by the records of the arbitration boards attached to the *Landesärztekammer*, which cover a significant proportion of cases where patients suspect negligence. Most of the boards publish regular case studies, bringing particular incidents that they have dealt with to the attention of doctors in the region. Furthermore, since 2006, data on all cases dealt with by the boards have been sent to the *Norddeutschen Schlichtungsstelle* in Hanover for systematic collation and analysis.[50]

In relation to the prevention of future adverse events, a significant role is played by the German Coalition for Patient Safety. This is manifested not least by its ongoing efforts to foster a change of culture among medical pro- fessionals, so they are more open to admitting and learning from mistakes. In 2008 the Coalition published a brochure, *Aus Fehlern lernen* ('learning from mistakes'),[51] which attracted national media attention. In it a number of doctors, including some of the highest eminence, candidly discussed errors they had made in the course of their careers and the ensuing conse- quences for their patients. An ongoing project is the building up of a special Institute for Patient Safety, based at the University of Bonn, which will do further research, employing systems and root-cause analysis, into the background of medical injuries.[52]

In the course of its work, the German Coalition for Patient Safety has also established dedicated working groups to develop risk management strategies for specific sources of mishap/injury: these include patient identity mix-ups, 'wrong-site' surgery and pharmaceutical errors. The clinical proto- cols drafted by the groups are subsequently made available as downloads on the Coalition's website.[53] The Coalition is also involved in the project *Aktion 'Saubere Hände'* (action on clean hands), sponsored by the federal health ministry and designed to reduce the number of infections in hospi- tals. In 2008 it, together with the *Ärztliches Zentrum für Qualität in der Medizin*, was designated Lead Technical Agency, responsible for the imple- mentation of the World Health Organisation's 'High 5s' patient safety project in Germany.[54]

Conclusions

The growth of a patient safety culture in Germany, particularly in the last few years, shows significant parallels with developments in the UK. Indeed, the efforts in both countries can be seen as part of an international movement among developed nations with comprehensive health care systems to reduce the level of preventable injury in medical care, motivated in part by resource concerns. Nevertheless, there are some distinctive features of the German experience. In contrast to the UK, the civil law governing liability for medical injury has not been identified as having a negative impact upon patient safety: it is seen broadly as performing its compensation function satisfactorily, and having had some positive effects on safe practices in health care. There appear to be few concerns that doctors may be inhibited by the relevant law from admitting and thereby learning from mistakes. In fact, the medical profession has shown a clear willingness to be proactive and engage in critical self-examination in this area. As noted, the *Landesärztekammer* set up arbitration boards over thirty years ago that provide patients with a cost-free medical report from other doctors as to whether they were the victim of negligent care. Today it remains the profession that plays the pre-eminent role in driving forward action on patient safety, with the state retaining a supervisory role in the background.

As to the success of the patient safety movement in reducing PAEs in German health care, this is something that is ultimately hard to assess. On the one hand, the chairman of the quality assurance committee of the *Bundesärztekammer* recently described the present state of activity in this field in Germany as 'exemplary'.[55] On the other, the numbers of medical injuries resulting in litigation and/or reported to the arbitration boards appear to be as high as ever. One difficulty is the fluidity of the notion of a preventable adverse outcome, with developments in both medicine and risk management leading to events, once seen as inevitable, being reclassified as preventable. Overall, though, it is likely that improvements in the organisation and co-ordination of care have at least reduced the number of 'clearly avoidable' mishaps that occur.

Notes

1 *Krankenversicherungsgesetz*, 1883.
2 This is contained in Book V of the *Sozialgesetzbuch* (social security code).
3 E. Deutsch and A. Spickhoff, *Medizinrecht*, 5th edn, Berlin, Springer, 2003, pp. 26–27.
4 Ibid., pp. 15–17.
5 § 5 II 1 Bundesärzteordnung; Deutsch and Spickhoff, *Medizinrecht*, p. 16.
6 See § 4 and § 5 of the *Musterberufsordnung für Ärzte* (MBO), the model professional rules for doctors, which the rules of the individual *Landesärztekammer* are based upon.
7 § 6 and § 10 I MBO.
8 *Sachverständigenrat zur Begutachtung der Entwicklung im Gesundheitswesen*, 2007 Report: *Cooperation and Responsibility*, para. 107. Online. Available HTTP http://www.svr-gesundheit.de/Gutachten/Gutacht07/KF2007-engl.pdf.

9 Criminal proceedings against doctors are more frequent than in the UK, due partly to there being an offence of 'negligent bodily injury': §229 *Strafgesetzbuch* (criminal code). It has been estimated that annually some 3,000 investigations begin, albeit the great majority are discontinued for lack of evidence or public interest: see K. Ulsenheimer in A. Laufs (ed.), *Die Entwicklung der deutschen Arzthaftungsrecht*, Berlin, Springer, 1997, pp. 27 ff.

10 C. Katzenmeier, *Arzthaftung*, Tübingen, Mohr Siebeck, 2002, pp. 39–42.

11 M. Stauch, *The Law of Medical Negligence in England and Germany*, Oxford, Hart, 2008, pp. 25 ff.

12 Ibid., p. 43.

13 *Bundesgerichtshof*, 13 October 1964, *Neue juristische Wochenschrift* 1965, 345 (346).

14 Stauch, *The Law of Medical Negligence in England and Germany*, pp. 45–46.

15 Ibid., pp. 68–70.

16 Ibid., pp. 87 ff.

17 Ibid., pp. 107 ff.

18 Ibid., p. 125.

19 I. Weizel, *Gutachterkommissionen und Schlichtungsstellen*, Hamburg, Kovac, 1999, pp. 13 ff.

20 Ibid.

21 *Bundesärztekammer, Statistische Erhebung der Gutachterkommissionen und Schlichtungs-stellen* (2008). Online. Available HTTP http://www.bundesaerztekammer.de/downloads/Statistische_Erhebung_2008_edg.pdf.

22 C. Meurer, *Außergerichtliche Streitbelegung in Arzthaftungssachen*, Berlin, Springer, 2008, p. 145.

23 What counts as 'appropriate' here differs from in the UK; thus German law, less influenced by concerns about limited health resources, has engaged in a degree of social risk-shifting: see Stauch, *The Law of Medical Negligence in England and Germany*, pp. 159–160.

24 Generally the relevant legal costs are lower in Germany. One reason may be that patient lawyers receive more help from the court, and hence require less expertise than in the UK.

25 Katzenmeier, *Arzthaftung*, pp. 266 ff; Stauch, *The Law of Medical Negligence in England and Germany*, pp. 144 ff.

26 Katzenmeier, *Arzthaftung*, pp. 229–230.

27 See *Final Report: Learning from Bristol: The Report of the Public Inquiry into Children's Heart Surgery at the Bristol Royal Infirmary 1984–1995*, Command Paper, CM 5207, at p. 33.

28 Stauch, *The Law of Medical Negligence in England and Germany*, pp. 64 ff.

29 B. Beyerle, *Rechtsfragen medizinischer Qualitätskontrolle*, Heidelberg: Müller, 2004, p. 11.

30 See D. Hart, 'Patientensicherheit, Risikomanagement, Arzneimittelbehandlung und Arzthaftungsrecht' (2007) 25 *Medizinrecht* 383, at pp. 389 ff.

31 See note 7.

32 Stauch, *The Law of Medical Negligence in England and Germany*, pp. 74 ff.

33 Hart, 'Patientensicherheit, Risikomanagement, Arzneimittelbehandlung und Arzthaftungsrecht', at p. 391; B.-R. Kern, 'Organisationsverschulden in der Judikatur', in D. Berg and K. Ulsenheimer (eds), *Patientensicherheit, Arzthaftung, Praxis- und Krankenhausorganisation*, Berlin, Springer, 2006, pp. 59 ff.

34 This appears to be particularly true of pharmaceutical errors, which empirically make up a substantial proportion of PAEs, but are seldom litigated: Hart, 'Patientensicherheit, Risikomanagement, Arzneimittelbehandlung und Arzthaftungsrecht', at p. 392.

35 The latter reforms were set out in the *GKV-Gesundheitsreformgesetz* 2000.

36 Pursuant to § 137 I SGB, failure to comply with these duties will result in financial penalties.
37 The G-BA, comprising representatives from the medical professions, public insurance funds and hospital associations, is assisted in this task by the Institute for Quality and Economy in Health (*IQWiG*).
38 Deutsch and Spickhoff, *Medizinrecht*, p. 294.
39 Ibid., p. 296.
40 H. Kastenholz and B. Both, 'Qualitätssicherung der medizinischen Versorgung aus Sicht des Bundesministeriums für Gesundheit' (2002) 45 *Bundesgesundheitsblatt* 215, at p. 217.
41 K. Goerke, 'Qualitätssicherung nach SGB V', in Berg and Ulsenheimer, *Patientensicherheit, Arzthaftung, Praxis- und Krankenhausorganisation*, p. 20.
42 Hart, 'Patientensicherheit, Risikomanagement, Arzneimittelbehandlung und Arzthaftungsrecht', at p.385.
43 R. Ratzel and H.-D. Lippert, *Kommentar zur Musterberufsordnung der deutschen Ärzte* (MBO), 4th edn, Berlin, Springer, 2006, p. 65. For other aspects of *Standesrecht* relevant to patient safety, see notes 6 and 7 above.
44 Hart, 'Patientensicherheit, Risikomanagement, Arzneimittelbehandlung und Arzthaftungsrecht', at p. 385.
45 Information (in English) about the ÄZQ and its *Forum Patientensicherheit* can be found on the Centre's website, at http://www.forum-patientensicherheit.de/english.
46 See, further, the Coalition's website at http://www.german-coalition-for-patient-safety.org/.
47 Hart, 'Patientensicherheit, Risikomanagement, Arzneimittelbehandlung und Arzthaftungsrecht', at p. 383.
48 See, further, the systems' websites, located respectively at http://www.cirsmedical.de/ and http://www.jeder-fehler-zaehlt.de/.
49 See, for 2008, the Coalition's Report, *Agenda Patientensicherheit 2008*, pp. 3–80. Online. Available HTTP http://www.aktionsbuendnis-patientensicherheit.de/apsside/Agenda_2008.pdf.
50 Meurer, *Außergerichtliche Streitbelegung in Arzthaftungssachen*, pp. 142 ff.
51 See http://www.aktionsbuendnis-patientensicherheit.de/apsside/Aus_Fehlern_lernen_0.pdf.
52 See the Coalition's Report, *Agenda Patientensicherheit 2008*, pp. 110–111.
53 See, e.g., for 'wrong-site' surgery, http://www.german-coalition-for-patient-safety.org/apsside/07-07-25-EV_Handlungsempfehlungen.pdf.
54 See http://www.forum-patientensicherheit.de/high5s.
55 'Jonitz: Deutschland bei Patientensicherheit vorbildlich', *Pressemitteilung der Bundesärztekammer*, Berlin, 17 November 2009. Online. Available HTTP http://www.forum-patientensicherheit.de/aktuelles/news2009-11-17.

12 Patient safety and the law in Canada

Joan M. Gilmour

Introduction

Patient safety initiatives are increasingly at the forefront in health policy and health care, sparked initially by the 1999 release of the Institute of Medicine's influential report, *To Err Is Human*, in the United States.[1] That report highlighted not only the frequency and gravity of preventable patient injury, but also the need to address the role played by systemic factors in order to improve the safety and quality of health care. Its insights into the genesis of error soon prevailed in policy discourse in other countries as well, reframing the debate about how to make care safer. However, the extent to which this approach can be incorporated into legal reasoning and how best to do so are still unclear. Lawsuits remain the primary means to resolve claims for harm caused by deficient care, and in negligence law, liability and entitlement to recover damages are premised on a finding of fault. The disjunction between law and patient safety is significant, because law plays a large part in shaping the environment for the provision of health care, assessment of risks, and responses to adverse events by all concerned.

It has been more than a decade since the Institute of Medicine's report. News of egregious errors and widespread patient injury has continued to make headlines in many countries, shaking assumptions about the safety of health care and highlighting the need for change. In response, numerous initiatives to improve patient safety have been undertaken. Yet for the most part, law reform has lagged behind. This affects uptake of patient safety advocates' recommendations, because in many ways law conditions the solutions that can be implemented—people are guided in their conduct by underlying legal frameworks.

Concerted attention to the extent of patient harm and the role played by systemic factors came somewhat later in Canada than elsewhere. A study of the incidence of adverse events and patient injury in acute care hospitals in Canada published in 2004 (the Canadian Adverse Events Study) identified an incidence rate of 7.5 per cent.[2] Expert reviewers considered 36.9 per cent of theses highly preventable.[3] Most (64.4 per cent) resulted in no or minimal to moderate impairment, with recovery within six months. However,

5.2 per cent of adverse events resulted in permanent disability, and 15.9 per cent in death. Extrapolating from this data, the authors estimated that in 2000, of the almost 2.5 million annual admissions to similar hospitals in Canada, about 185,000 were associated with an adverse event, of which 70,000 were potentially preventable, and that 9,250 to 23,750 deaths could have been prevented.[4] The Canadian Institute for Health Information noted that this made preventable adverse events in health care one of the leading causes of death in Canada.[5]

This chapter assesses the relation between legal systems and patient safety initiatives in Canada. It focuses on the law governing delivery of health care and responsibility for harm, to determine whether the legal system reflects developments in our understanding of how error occurs, and what is needed to prevent or reduce harm. While there are significant distinctions among health care systems in different countries, as well as in social, political, economic, and legal environments, comparative analysis can provide important insights that are useful to inform policy development in both health and law. I begin the chapter with an explanation of the Canadian context, explaining the relevant legal frameworks, how health care delivery is governed, and the civil litigation process in negligence claims. In the subsequent section, I review the rise of a patient safety sensibility in Canada, and reflect on the continued toll taken by patient injury despite the many initiatives meant to reduce it. The following section analyzes the extent to which recommendations made by patient safety advocates have affected the law. Finally, I consider progress made and problems that remain.

Canadian legal and health care systems

Constitutional jurisdiction

Canada is a federal system, with constitutional jurisdiction divided among the federal, and provincial or territorial governments. While "health" is not a single matter assigned exclusively to one level of government, the provinces and territories have jurisdiction within their boundaries over most aspects of health care, as well as the administration of justice and the tort system.[6] The federal government has jurisdiction over limited aspects of health care,[7] but its primary ability to influence health systems and policy is indirect, exerted through its spending power.[8] In evaluating developments and law reform proposals meant to enhance patient safety, the realities of the Canadian federation and divisions in jurisdiction must be borne in mind.

With the exception of the province of Quebec, which is a civil law system, the other nine provinces and three territories in Canada are governed by common law, and the review of civil liability for substandard health care in this chapter is limited to common law.[9] The discussion of regulatory reform, however, draws on examples from across the country.

The Canadian health care system

Canada has a publicly funded universal health insurance system. The provinces and territories are each responsible for developing and administering their own public health insurance plans, subject to certain criteria and conditions set by federal legislation. Each plan must comply with these requirements in order to qualify for federal transfer payments that assist provinces to meet the cost of publicly insured health services.[10] Coverage under provincial public health insurance plans is primarily focused on physician services and hospital care.[11] Each jurisdiction also insures additional services such as home care, outpatient prescription drugs or services provided by non-physicians (dentists, physiotherapists, chiropractors, and others). Coverage for non-physician, non-hospital services is limited, and varies among jurisdictions.[12] It is often subject to additional requirements, such as means testing, age limits, or other conditions.

Approximately 70 per cent of Canadian health expenditures are public, while 30 per cent of expenditures are paid privately, either through private insurance or by individuals.[13]

Most health services in Canada are provided by health practitioners who work either as independent professionals or as employees of health care institutions, such as hospitals or privately owned clinics or firms.[14] Most physicians work as independent professionals. Even when they practice solely or primarily in hospitals, few are employees; instead, hospitals grant them privileges. Others working in hospitals, such as nurses or physiotherapists, are generally hospital employees. Most hospitals are public, but although heavily reliant on government funding and extensively regulated, they are not considered to be part of government *per se*.[15] Public hospitals are generally non-profit institutions, and are typically owned by religious orders, lay institutions, municipalities, or government.[16] Other types of privately owned health care entities include nursing homes and clinics; these may be operated on a for-profit or non-profit basis.[17]

Although governments do not deliver care directly to patients, they have substantial responsibilities with respect to health care. They fund delivery of insured health care, both through public health insurance plans that pay health care providers for insured services rendered to patients, and through funds transferred to public hospitals and other organizations, such as clinics, to cover the costs associated with insured services they provide. Governments also regulate the quality of health services and providers, although each province and territory has delegated a substantial portion of its responsibility regarding health practitioners to self-regulated professions.[18] They have broader governance responsibilities as well, for "system governance or stewardship ... establishing the general objectives of the system, for monitoring and evaluating the system's success ... for ensuring coordination and continuity between the different parts of the system, and for ensuring reasonable access to health care services either through public funding or other means."[19] Despite the extent of governments' practical and legal powers over the health system, attempts to hold government civilly liable for alleged shortcomings—for instance inadequately funding services, or failing to protect health workers from exposure to infectious disease—have failed. Courts have generally held that in such instances governments do not owe a private law duty of care to individuals that can be enforced by means of a civil lawsuit.[20]

Health care and legal liability

Most lawsuits against health professionals, hospitals and their employees are based on allegations of negligence—i.e. that health care providers or institutions acted in ways that were substandard or deficient, causing harm to patients that justifies compensation.[21] Legal liability for negligence is contingent on a finding of fault. While courts certainly recognize that events have multiple causes,[22] most negligence actions tend to be focused on the individuals directly concerned in the events giving rise to the lawsuit, even in cases involving several defendants. They do not generally engage in at-large analyses of the role that more diffuse, systemic factors played in the plaintiff's injuries.[23]

The basic tenets of negligence law are very similar in Canada, the United Kingdom and other common law countries—a plaintiff must establish that a duty of care was owed, the standard of care was breached, and the breach caused injury to the plaintiff that is compensable in law. However, some characteristics of Canadian substantive and procedural law and practice are distinctive. I comment on four, to highlight differences in the legal environment that affect patient safety initiatives: hospital liability, qualified privilege, the civil litigation process, and liability insurance arrangements.

Hospital liability

Hospitals owe duties of care to their patients, and are directly liable for their own negligence (for instance, in monitoring staff competence or establishing systems needed to operate the hospital safely), and vicariously liable for wrongdoing by those for whom they are legally responsible, such as their employees. However, unlike those in a number of other countries, Canadian hospitals are not generally liable for the negligence of independent professionals, most notably non-employed physicians.[24] The insights of the patient safety movement into the role of systemic factors in causing medical errors and patient injury, and, in particular, the ways in which constraints imposed at the "blunt end" of institutional decision-making shape decisions at the "sharp end" of practitioners and patients, lend considerable force to arguments for extending hospitals' liability to include negligence by non-employed physicians.[25] Expanding hospital liability would also reflect changes in the organization and delivery of care more accurately. In many instances, physicians' services cannot be evaluated properly in isolation from the institutional environment and treatment provided by the rest of the health care team. Justifications for relieving hospitals from liability for non-employed physician negligence are becoming increasingly strained.[26] In a few cases, courts have taken the evolving nature of health care delivery into account in determining liability.[27] Otherwise, the law on this point has remained unaltered for years.

Qualified privilege

Hospitals have long employed formal and informal processes to review the safety and quality of care. Because of concerns that confidentiality was essential to encourage disclosure, most provinces and territories shielded at least some quality assurance (QA) processes from disclosure in lawsuits by means of qualified privilege legislation.[28] Patient safety advocates consider this information key to accurate analysis of factors contributing to injuries, and to developing effective strategies to prevent or reduce recurrence. Recognizing that health care providers are reluctant to make such disclosure if doing so carries the risk of negative repercussions (i.e. "blame and shame"), they, too, argue that the public interest in facilitating initiatives to make health care safer justifies non-disclosure outside the "safe harbor" of quality assurance activities. In response, statutory protection for QA activities has continued to expand. Increasingly, it has been extended to information reported to regional health authorities and government ministries, and applied in more types of legal proceedings.[29] The nature, scope, and availability of the protection afforded this information varies among jurisdictions. Factual information not available elsewhere is generally still accessible to patients.[30] Otherwise, information disclosed as part of QA processes is protected.[31] If the statutory protection is inapplicable, production in civil proceedings can sometimes be resisted on the basis that the information is protected by common law privilege. Determinations are made case by case.[32] While these laws may increase disclosure about errors and injury, they can also affect access to justice, because restricting information about how and why a patient has been harmed can make it more difficult to establish entitlement to compensation in legal proceedings.

The litigation process

It has been estimated that in Canada fewer than 10 per cent of viable claims attributable to negligence in health services have resulted in payment.[33] As described earlier, the Canadian Adverse Events Study established that approximately 5.2 per cent of preventable adverse events resulted in permanent disability, and 15.9 per cent in death.[34] While not all adverse events are attributable to negligence, some are. The number of negligent adverse events is certainly considerably larger than the number of people who sue or recover for negligence. In 2008, only 88 lawsuits against physicians went to trial in Canada, and, of these, plaintiffs were successful in only 13; defendant physicians prevailed and were found not liable in the remaining 75.[35] These figures are typical of results in prior years as well. Some claims settle before trial, but overall the numbers are not large.

Access to the justice system is problematic for a number of reasons. Information asymmetries between patients, providers and institutions mean that there is no assurance a patient will know or be able to obtain and appreciate the information needed to understand that he or she has been the victim of a medical error. Lawsuits are slow and, despite the possibility of contingency fee arrangements, remain very expensive. Causation can be particularly difficult to prove in medical malpractice cases.[36] Almost invariably, expert opinions are required even to assess the viability of a claim, adding to the cost of deciding whether to sue. While Canada does have legal aid systems in each province and territory, legal aid certificates are not generally granted in civil lawsuits for medical malpractice. Finally, as noted earlier, most medical malpractice lawsuits that proceed to trial are unsuccessful. As in the UK, costs "follow the event," meaning that the loser is liable to pay a portion of the winner's costs—a daunting prospect for plaintiffs, especially given the low likelihood of winning. The Canadian Medical Protective Association (CMPA), the physicians' mutual defense organization that provides liability coverage for approximately 95 per cent of Canada's physicians, has reported declining incidence of malpractice lawsuits against its more than 75,000 members for the last ten years.[37]

Liability insurance

Although the great majority of physicians are independent professionals, most are remunerated on a fee-for-service basis by provincial public health insurance plans for the services they provide to patients. Fees for publicly insured services are negotiated between provincial medical associations and governments. They are meant to cover remuneration for physicians' services as well as overheads, including the cost of liability coverage (generally, the fees paid to CMPA). Consequently, increased costs for liability coverage cannot simply be passed on to patients by charging more for insured services. Recognizing this, and wanting to ensure both continued access to health services and the availability of compensation when patients have been negligently injured and damages awarded, provincial governments and medical associations have negotiated agreements pursuant to which governments contribute to the cost of physicians' liability coverage. These arrangements vary among provinces, but the total amount of government contributions and the proportion of individual physicians' costs paid are substantial.[38]

Hospital insurance arrangements resemble more traditional contracts of insurance. More than 500 Canadian health care facilities obtain liability coverage through participation in the Health Insurance Reciprocal of

Canada (HIROC), a member-owned non-profit insurance reciprocal exchange.[39] Hospitals receive the great majority of their funding from governments, and the bulk of the services they provide are publicly insured. Thus hospitals, too, cover the cost of liability coverage with funds provided by government.

Patient safety and clinical risk

As in other countries, the rise of a patient safety sensibility led health policy-makers, practitioners and institutions in Canada to recognize that solutions to error and injuries required attention to systemic causes, and a con-comitant move away from "shaming and blaming" individual practitioners through civil liability, in-hospital processes, and professional discipline. In 2002, the National Steering Committee on Patient Safety released its report, *Building a Safer System: A National Integrated Strategy for Improving Patient Safety in Canadian Health Care*, which concluded that the extent of adverse events and consequent harm to patients is so significant that "it is no longer appropriate to think that previous and current processes to ensure safety are still effective in controlling adverse outcomes."[40] It recommended that efforts to reduce adverse events focus on systems analysis that would take into account the role played by the "blunt" or remote end of the system, i.e. regulators, administrators, policy-makers, and technology suppliers, who shape the environment in which practitioners work.[41] It made two recommendations about the legal system: first, that the statutory protection accorded data and opinions associated with patient safety and quality improvement discussions be strengthened to prevent their disclosure in legal proceedings, while preserving patients' ability to access factual information about the adverse event; second, it called for further consideration of the effects of the tort and health insurance systems on patient safety, with a view to formulating recommendations to promote a culture of patient safety.[42]

The Committee also recommended the formation of a Canadian Patient Safety Institute (CPSI). Government response was quick: in 2003, the federal government established CPSI and allocated $50 million in funding over five years to support patient safety initiatives, including $8 million annually for CPSI. The Institute is an independent, non-profit corporation with a mandate to work collaboratively with health professionals and organizations, regulatory bodies, and governments to build a safer health care system. Its role is facilitative and advisory; it has no power to require that action be taken. Since its inception, it has produced a framework for root cause analysis, developed the Canadian Disclosure Guidelines to facilitate disclosure to patients involved in adverse events, funded research, and undertaken or funded a number of other projects, often as part of partnerships.[43] Its funding was renewed for an additional five years in 2008.[44]

Across the country, governments, regional health authorities, accreditors, hospitals and health facilities, self-regulating professional bodies, practitioners and their professional associations, and researchers have all undertaken initiatives to improve patient safety. These are positive developments. Yet despite the burgeoning response, error and serious harm to patients remain distressingly frequent. Errors occur not only singly, as with unnecessary surgery or incorrect medication, but also in situations where the harm itself has been systemic and injuries widespread. There has been a troubling number of reports of large-scale errors in the work of pathology laboratories, radiologists, and others across the country.[45] I comment on two in particular, because the resulting loss of public confidence was so grave that Commissions of Inquiry were appointed to determine what had happened and why, and to recommend measures to avoid a recurrence and improve accountability.

In Newfoundland and Labrador, a Commission of Inquiry was appointed following the discovery that laboratory hormone receptor testing to determine whether hundreds of women diagnosed with breast cancer were candidates for anti-hormonal therapy was inaccurate, such that many women who should have received the therapy were incorrectly told it would not assist. The Commission clearly outlined how disparate systemic factors combined with each other and contributed to these injuries.[46] Many of its recommendations focused on systemic responses, to correct deficiencies ranging from quality control and monitoring in individual laboratories to structural changes needed in institutions, regional health authorities, and government.[47]

Errors in the work of a pediatric forensic pathologist in Ontario that resulted in parents, family members, and others being wrongfully convicted of criminal charges in the deaths of children also led to the appointment of a Commission of Inquiry.[48] While forensic analysis is associated with the justice system, it is closely tied to and relies on the health system. The credibility of the pathologist involved, who worked at a renowned pediatric hospital, depended on his (assumed) expertise in pediatric pathology. In turn, his formidable reputation in the field played a significant role in both the wrongful convictions and plea bargains some accused felt forced to accept despite their innocence. The Commission's recommendations highlight not only the pervasive role systemic factors played, but also how far beyond the health system such errors can reach.

Law reform

Civil liability

It is clear that many people injured by medical error go uncompensated. Nonetheless, lawsuits for negligence remain the primary means to resolve claims for harm caused by substandard care. Although several provinces have reformed their civil justice systems in recent years, changes have largely been focused on measures meant to reduce the cost of judgments, such as allowing courts to order periodic payment of damages awarded in personal injury cases, and the costs of accessing the civil justice system, such as simplified procedures for lower value claims, and expanded ability to seek summary judgment.[49] None has specifically targeted clinical negligence litigation, with the exception of legislation in a number of provinces strengthening legal protection from disclosure for information gathered in the context of quality assurance processes. Despite cogent criticism of the tort system's performance and recommendations for reform,[50] the civil litigation system is largely unchanged. The relatively stable claims environment, a well-established torts system, stakeholders' vested interests in its continuation, the lack of a liability insurance crisis, and the absence of significant, organized public or provider pressure for substantial tort reform mean that little substantial change to the tort system is likely in the near future.

Regulatory reform

Legislative activity meant to improve patient safety has instead focused on regulatory reform. The result has been regulatory environments that are increasingly complex and interconnected. I highlight and assess developments that have expanded and reduced access to information, and increased institutional accountability.

Expanding access to information

Disclosing harm

Disclosing harm to patients affected by adverse events is both an ethical and legal requirement.[51] Patient safety advocates have long emphasized the importance of openness when patients have been harmed by health care. Yet too often disclosure still does not occur, despite the obligation for it to do so.[52]

Increasingly, disclosure requirements are being made more explicit and given greater force, for instance through standards of practice established by professional self-regulating bodies.[53] Health professionals who fail to comply could potentially face disciplinary sanctions. Some provinces have legislated expanded disclosure requirements. Ontario now requires public hospital boards to ensure that administrators establish a system for disclosing all "critical incidents" to the patient or his or her substitute decision-maker. Disclosure must include actions taken or recommended to address the consequences to the patient. Additionally (although subject to qualified privilege legislation), hospital administrators must ensure that patients are told about what systemic steps, if any, the hospital is taking to avoid or reduce the risk of similar critical incidents.[54]

One difficulty with most disclosure policies is the distinction they attempt to draw between facts (which must be disclosed to patients), and opinions about what occurred (which the policies suggest should not be disclosed). The Commission of Inquiry on Hormone Receptor Testing in Newfoundland and Labrador rejected the narrow restriction that only "facts" about an adverse event should be revealed to patients. As Commissioner Cameron pointed out, given the subject matter of the Inquiry,[55]

> nearly every statement, including one that says that a result is positive or negative, is a statement of opinion. That there is poor fixation and that inadequate attention is being paid to internal controls are other examples. This is the kind of information that is necessary if one is going to tell a patient something about why the adverse event occurred and that must be done if possible ... If the health system is to have any credibility, patients must be given an explanation for why the mistake occurred and what is being done to ensure that it will not happen in the future.

The Commission recommended legislation be passed entrenching patients' right to disclosure, including relevant peer review or quality assurance reports about an adverse event, in priority to any statutory protection from disclosure accorded quality assurance information.

Apology legislation

Growing recognition of the importance of apologies to injured patients, coupled with the countervailing concern that an apology could be taken as an admission of liability and used against health care providers in legal proceedings, has led several jurisdictions to pass legislation encouraging apologies. In Canada, British Columbia was the first to do so, in 2006; a number of other provinces have since followed suit.[56] Generally, the legislation provides that an apology made by or on behalf of a person in relation to any civil matter does not constitute an admission or an acknowledgment of fault or liability, and is not admissible in judicial or quasi-judicial civil proceedings. Again, provinces vary in the scope and application of the statutory protection.

There was little to no indication in Canadian jurisprudence prior to passage of the legislation that apologies were actually being relied on in medical malpractice lawsuits as admissions of liability. However, to the extent this perception blocked apologies, such legislation should be useful in removing an impediment to openness with injured patients. The statutes are too new to assess their effectiveness in increasing the number of apologies or disclosure of harm.

Reporting requirements

Systems for reporting errors and near misses are becoming increasingly formalized and expansive within institutions, and are being extended to require reporting by more types of health facilities, and to more third parties, such as regional health authorities and/or government. Third party reporting may be mandated by statute or imposed by policy. For example, in Quebec the executive director of an institution or designate is required by law to report all accidents or incidents (essentially, near misses) in non-nominate form to the regional board. Quebec also requires creation of risk and quality management committees to identify incident or accident risks, ensure support to the victim, and establish monitoring systems to undertake causal analysis and prevent recurrence.[57] Other provinces have also created protected zones to enable information about adverse events to be shared beyond the bounds of the institution for patient safety purposes. [58]

The trend towards increased transparency is also apparent in laws imposing additional practitioner and institutional reporting requirements, and expanding patient and public access to information. Since 2005, Manitoba has required information about a physician's professional history to be publicly available, including disciplinary actions and judgments in medical malpractice cases in the preceding ten years. Ontario recently began requiring health professionals to report findings of professional negligence and malpractice to their professional governing bodies. This information must be posted on the organization's register, and is publicly available.[59] Hospitals are increasingly required to make information public, such as infection rates for certain diseases.[60] Legal obligations to share information among those responsible for ensuring the safety and quality of care (notably, health facilities and governing bodies of self-regulated health professions) have also been expanded.[61] These initiatives give an indication of the variety of approaches being taken to break down barriers among silos of information in the health care system, in order to make information more widely available to institutions, regulators, and the public. The goal is important, but the proliferation of reporting obligations raises concerns about the unintended consequences that may flow from resources required to comply, the fate of reports made, and the ongoing sustainability of a large number of reporting systems with broad and overlapping mandates.

Reducing access to information: a double-edged sword

Protecting quality assurance information

Statutory protection from disclosure for quality assurance information has been expanded or strengthened in a number of provinces, with a view to encouraging disclosure of error and harm within the health system. However, expanding statutory privilege comes at a cost: (1) to injured patients, in accessing information so they can find out what happened, and, if needed, establish legal entitlement to compensation when harmed by negligence; (2) to the public, in learning about and assessing health care delivery; (3) to policy-makers, who require accurate information as the basis for sound policy development; and (4) to the justice system, since non-disclosure of relevant information can reduce the likelihood of accurate fact-finding by courts and other decision-making bodies.

The risks were highlighted by the Newfoundland and Labrador Commission of Inquiry on Hormone Receptor Testing. The regional health authority,

Eastern Health, claimed that the Commission could not publish reports about laboratory services that outside experts had previously prepared for the authority, on the ground that they were protected by statutory and common law privilege. The Commission successfully challenged this position; the court held that the reports were neither privileged at common law, nor "quality assurance information" protected by statutory privilege.[62] As Commissioner Cameron astutely observed in her report, it is doubtful that health authorities will fail to ensure the preconditions for claiming statutory protection are met in future. She pointed out that, although some might argue this evidence could have been obtained in other ways, it would have been very difficult for the Commission to reconstruct events without these experts' opinions and observations.[63] The best evidence on crucial issues would not have been available if the claim of privilege had been upheld, seriously hampering the Commission's ability to accurately analyze what occurred and formulate solutions. This is precisely the kind of assessment and problem-solving that patient safety advocates want, and that (at least in theory) qualified privilege is meant to promote, although by health facilities rather than public inquiries. However, in this instance, the regional health authority's response was seriously deficient. In light of this history, the Commission concluded that the law governing qualified privilege should be revisited, to take account of the public interest in openness and accountability, and not just the public interest in protected disclosure.

Access to information can also be restricted by institutional policy such as hospital by-laws. These should support the provision of safe, quality health care. They can, however, be structured to discourage openness and reduce transparency. For instance, a protocol hospital by-law developed in Ontario could sharply limit the ability of physicians and staff to publicly disclose concerns about deficiencies in care or criticize hospital management.[64] A governance framework that puts the job security of critics at risk will not bolster public confidence; it is more likely to reinforce public concern that information is being inappropriately withheld.

Increasing institutional accountability for patient safety

Hospitals and other health care organizations are often in a better position to implement change than practitioners, because they control many of the systemic factors that affect patient safety. Recent changes in regulatory and accreditation requirements strengthen the "business case" for patient safety, by making it in hospitals' and administrators' interests to give it greater priority. Some examples follow.

Setting standards

Governments have begun to require hospitals to take explicit account of patient safety in their planning processes. They have also become increasingly active in establishing detailed patient safety standards for health services. For instance, in 2010 Ontario began requiring all hospitals to use a surgical checklist, covering operating room teams' most common tasks and items.[65]

Standards set by non-government entities such as Accreditation Canada, the private, non-profit organization that assesses hospitals and other health organizations, are also influential. Accreditation is voluntary in most jurisdictions, but is a *de facto* requirement for public hospitals. The agency's evaluation now includes explicit patient safety criteria, and patient safety considerations form part of its review of hospital governance.[66]

Compensation

The increasingly detailed responsibilities imposed on health facilities, boards and senior management to improve the quality and safety of care are being tied to institutional funding and executive pay. For instance, recent Ontario legislation, the Excellent Care for All Act introduced a limited form of pay for performance, linking a portion of executive compensation to achieving health care organizations' Quality Improvement Plan targets.[67]

Looking back, looking forward

The approaches adopted to making health care safer in Canada are similar to those undertaken in a number of other countries, although subject to the complication of divided constitutional jurisdiction over health care. While this makes it difficult to develop a uniform national approach, it allows for a range of responses, adapted to widely varying circumstances in a very large country. Few of the initiatives undertaken have been evaluated. The relation between patient safety and the law, the subject of this chapter, is only one part of the larger patient safety picture. In this section, I reflect on changes made, and what is still needed.

Given the number of preventable adverse events in Canadian health care, it is apparent that the incidence of negligence is significantly higher than the number of claims made, and much higher still than the even smaller number of people who actually recover any compensation.[68] Suing to recover compensation is not a realistic possibility for many who have been harmed by medical error. The extent to which the prospect of tort liability acts as a deterrent is unclear, but seems at best diffuse and indirect.[69] As presently structured, the medical liability system is inadequate in providing compensation or reducing the likelihood of harm, and requires substantial change.[70]

Options range from overhauling the tort system to introduce no-fault compensation for patients harmed by substandard health care, to adopting smaller-scale reforms that could be incorporated into existing law. There is little impetus in Canada for radical reform. However, smaller changes could improve both patient safety and accountability. I have developed proposals for reform in greater detail in earlier work.[71] Here, I mention some possibilities. These include expanding hospital liability to include responsibility for non-employed physicians' negligence on-site, and revising qualified privilege legislation to pay more heed to the public interest in access to information and accountability. Additionally, more use could be made of lawsuits as a learning resource, with insurers providing health care practitioners, institutions, and policy-makers with access to more information about how injuries occur. The substantial financial assistance governments provide to defray the costs of physicians' and hospitals' liability coverage should give them leverage to require that this information be made available to advance patient safety initiatives. Unfortunately, there is little indication even these moderate changes will be adopted.

Patient safety law reform has instead focused on regulatory changes rather than tort reform. A number of the initiatives described in this chapter evidence a more interventionist state. Examples include the requirement that hospital boards ensure critical incidents are disclosed to patients,[72] and the imposition of detailed minimum safety standards, such as the requirement to use surgical safety checklists in Ontario.[73] These developments could signal a shift in the state's role *vis-à-vis* institutions and health practitioners. Yet the reality of such initiatives is often more complicated because in order to set standards in complex and technical areas the state must still rely on clinical expertise. This preserves rather than displaces the power and influence of medical authority (or, at least, medical elites who are consulted in their formulation). Thus, even changes that seem to reinforce hierarchical, command and control governance by the state, such as requiring detailed clinical practice standards, are tempered by the need to rely on physicians to formulate and implement them.

Public trust in health care providers and systems, and in procedures to ensure accountability, is essential. A significant portion of the public, practitioners, and institutions resist simply "blaming the system,"[74] and there is considerable disagreement about when individual, as opposed to systemic, accountability is appropriate. These areas present some of the greatest challenges to public willingness to accept reforms proposed by patient safety advocates, practitioners, professions, and governments.

Acknowledgment

I am grateful for the research assistance of Natasha Razack.

Notes

1 Linda T. Kohn, Janet M. Corrigan, and Molla S. Donaldson (eds.), *To Err Is Human: Building a Safer Health System*, Washington, DC, National Academy Press, 2000.

2 Ross Baker *et al.*, "The Canadian Adverse Event Study: The Incidence of Adverse Events among Hospital Patients in Canada," (2004) 170:11 *Canadian Medical Association Journal* 1678.

3 Ibid., p. 1679. An adverse event was defined as "an unintended injury or complication that results in disability at the time of discharge, death or prolonged hospital stay and that is caused by health care management [including both individual hospital staff and broader systems and care processes] rather than by the patient's underlying disease."

4 Ibid., at pp. 1683–1684.

5 Canadian Institute for Health Information (CIHI), *Health Care in Canada in 2004*, Ottawa, CIHI, 2005, pp. 42–43. Online. Available HTTP http://www.cihi.ca/cihiweb/dispPage.jsp?cw_page=PG_263_E&cw_topic=263&cw_rel=AR_43_E.

6 The Constitution Act, 1982, being Schedule B to the Canada Act 1982 (U.K.), 1982, c. 11.

7 Peter Hogg, *Constitutional Law of Canada*, Toronto, Thomson Carswell, 2007, looseleaf.

8 Canada Health Act, R.S.C. 1985, c.C-6. Although public health insurance is a provincial responsibility, the federal government has imposed a requirement that all provincial public health insurance plans must meet five criteria—universality, accessibility, comprehensiveness, portability, and public administration—as well as ban extra billing by physicians, and user fees by hospitals. Provinces must comply in order to qualify for federal cash transfer payments, which assist them with the cost of publicly funded health services.

9 Regarding the law in Quebec, see Lara Khoury, *Uncertain Causation in Medical Liability*, Cowansville, Quebec, Yvon Blais, 2006.

10 Canada Health Act, R.S.C. 1985, c.C-6.

11 Ibid., s.2.

12 *Auton v. British Columbia*, [2004] 3 S.C.R. 657.

13 Canadian Institute for Health Information (CIHI), *Health Care in Canada 2008*, Ottawa, CIHI, 2008. Online. Available HTTP http://www.cihi.ca/cihiweb/dispPage.jsp?cw_page=PG_1472_E&cw_topic=1472&cw_rel=AR_43_E.

14 W. Lahey, "Medicare and the Law: Contours of an Evolving Relationship," in Jocelyn Downie,Timothy Caulfield and Colleen M. Flood (eds.), *Canadian Health Law and Policy*, 3rd edn., Markham, Lexis Nexis Canada, 2007, p. 1.

15 *Stoffman v. Vancouver General Hospital*, [1990] 3 S.C.R. 483; *Eldridge v. British Columbia*, [1997] 3 S.C.R. 624.

16 *Hospitals: Provincial and Territorial Legislation*, cited in CCH Canadian Ltd., *Canadian Health Facilities Law Guide*, North York, CCH Canadian Ltd., 1996–1997, looseleaf, pp. 512–520.

17 Lahey, "Medicare and the Law."

18 Joan M. Gilmour, Merrijoy Kelner, and Beverly Wellman, "Opening the Door to Complementary and Alternative Medicine: Self Regulation in Ontario" (2002) 24 *Law & Policy* 149.

19 Lahey, "Medicare and the Law," p. 15.

20 *Mitchell Estate v. Ontario* (2004), 71 O.R. (3d) 571 (Sup. Ct.); *Abarquez v. Ontario* (2009), 95 O.R. (3d) 414 (C.A.); but see *Taylor v. Canada (Minister of Health)* (2007), 285 D.L.R. (4th) 296 (On. Sup. Ct.).

21 Justice Ellen I. Picard and Gerald B. Robertson, *Legal Liability of Doctors and Hospitals in Canada*, 4th edn., Toronto, Carswell, 2007 [Picard and Robertson].

22 *Athey .v Leonati*, [1996] 3 S.C.R. 458, paras 17, 25.

23 J. M. Gilmour, "Duty of Care and Standard of Care," in Commission of Inquiry on Hormone Receptor Testing, *Looking Forward…Policy Papers*, vol. 2, St John's, Government of Newfoundland and Labrador, 2009, p. 35.

24 *Yepremian v. Scarborough General Hospital* (1980), 28 O.R. (2d) 494 (C.A.); Picard and Robertson, *Legal Liability of Doctors and Hospitals in Canada.*

25 Joan Gilmour, *Patient Safety, Medical Error and Tort Law: An International Comparison*, 2006. Online. Available HTTP www.osgoode.yorku.ca/faculty/ Gilmour_Joan_M.html, pp. 30, 59–61.

26 G.H.L. Fridman, *Introduction to the Canadian Law of Torts*, 2nd edn., Markham, Lexis Nexis Butterworths, 2003, p. 336; Philip Osborne, *The Law of Torts*, 3rd edn., Toronto, Irwing Law, 2007, p. 324; Gilmour, *Patient Safety, Medical Error and Tort Law*; and Picard and Robertson, *Legal Liability of Doctors and Hospitals in Canada.*

27 See, e.g. *LaChambre v. Nair*, [1989] 2 W.W.R. 749 (Sask. Q.B.) (defendant hospital liable for failing to ensure properly coordinated care between specialties); *Milne v. St. Joseph's Health Centre*, [2009] O.J. No. 4004 (Sup. Ct.) (nurse liable for harm caused by her poor communication with other members of health care team).

28 Gilmour, *Patient Safety, Medical Error and Tort Law*, p. 63.

29 See, e.g., Regional Health Services Act, S.S. 2002, c.R-8.2, s.58; Evidence Act, S.S. 2006, c. E-11.2, s. 10.

30 See, e.g., Quality of Care Information Protection Act, 2004, S.O. 2004, c.3, Sch. B.

31 Commission of Inquiry on Hormone Receptor Testing, *Investigation and Findings*, vol. 1 (M. Cameron, Commissioner), St John's: Government of Newfoundland and Labrador, 2009, p. 358.

32 Picard and Robertson, *Legal Liability of Doctors and Hospitals in Canada.*

33 R.S. Prichard, *Liability and Compensation in Health Care*, Toronto, University of Toronto Press, 1990, p. 17.

34 Baker *et al.*, "The Canadian Adverse Event Study."

35 The Canadian Medical Protective Association, "The CMPA Annual Report 2008," 2008, p. 9. Online. Available HTTP http://www.cmpa-acpm.ca/ cmpapd04/docs/about_cmpa/annual_report/2008/com_executive_report-e.cfm [CMPA Annual Report 2008].

36 Joan M. Gilmour, "The Multiple Meanings of Causation in the Supreme Court of Canada's Medical Malpractice Jurisprudence," in Jocelyn Downie and Elaine Gibson (eds.), *Health Law at the Supreme Court of Canada*, Toronto, Irwin Law, 2007, p. 111.

37 Canadian Medical Protective Association, "The CMPA Annual Report 2008," pp. 9–10.

38 Gilmour, *Patient Safety, Medical Error and Tort Law*, p.. 34; Matt Borsellino, "CMPA Fees Drop," *Medical Post* (September 4, 2007), p. 51; Canadian Medical Protective Association, "The CMPA Annual Report 2008"; Steve Buist, "Taxpayers Footing the Bill for Malpractice Insurance," February 7, 2009. Online. Available HTTP http://www.thespec.com/article/509183; Matt Borsellino, "CMPA Fees Set to Rise for Most," *Medical Post*, September 8, 2009, p. 7; Matt Borsellino, "Out-of-pocket CMPA Fees All Over the Map," *Medical Post*, January 12, 2010, p. 37.

39 Commission of Inquiry on Hormone Receptor Testing, *Investigation and Findings*, vol. 1, p. 365.

40 The National Steering Committee on Patient Safety, *Building a Safer System: A National Integrated Strategy for Improving Patient Safety in Canadian Health Care*, September 2002, p. 16. Online. Available HTTP http://www.patientsafetyinstitute. ca/English/toolsResources/patientSafetyPublications/Pages/NationalPublications. aspx.

41 Ibid., p. 19.

42 Ibid., p. 28; Gilmour, *Patient Safety, Medical Error and Tort Law*, p. 50.

43 Canadian Patient Safety Institute. Online. Available HTTP www.cpsi-icspa.ca.
44 Health Canada, "Health Canada Renews Funding to the Canadian Patient Safety Institute," July 2, 2008. Online. Available HTTP http://www.hc-sc.gc.ca/ahc-asc/media/nr-cp/_2008/2008_104-eng.php.
45 Myron Love, "Manitoba Committee Clears Pathology Lab," *Medical Post*, March 23, 2010, p. 2; Lisa Priest and Sarah Boesveld, "Ontario Launches Review of Pathology Reports," *Globe and Mail*, February 26, 2010, p. A6; The Health Quality Council of Alberta, Media Release, "Health Quality Council of Alberta Releases Findings of Follow-up Urban and Regional Emergency Department Patient Experience Report," January 25, 2010. Online. Available HTTP http://www.hqca.ca/assets/pdf/ED%20January%202010/HQCA_urban_and_regional_ED_report_release_FINAL.pdf; "Eastern Health uncovers lab testing problem," February 23, 2010. Online. Available HTTP http://www.cbc.ca/canada/newfoundland-labrador/story/2010/02/23/nl-lab-cyclosporine-230210.html; Karen Howlett, "Privileges Restored for Mastectomy MD," *Globe and Mail*, March 12, 2010, p. A11; The Canadian Press, "Work of Saskatchewan Radiologist Questioned," *CTV News*, May 21, 2009. Online. Available HTTP http://www.ctv.ca/servlet/ArticleNews/story/CTVNews/20090521/radiologist_090521/20090521?hub=Health; and CBC News, "30,000 Tests by N.B. Radiologist Probed," October 5, 2009. Online. Available HTTP http://www.cbc.ca/canada/newbrunswick/story/2009/10/05/nb-radiologist-review-201.html; Jessica Leeder, "Pathologists Appeal to Ottawa for Help," *Globe and Mail*, July 1, 2008, p. A13, "Commission of Inquiry into Pathology Services at the Miramichi Regional Health Authority," *A Report with Recommendations of a Commission of Inquiry into Pathology Services at the Miramichi Regional Health Authority* (P. Creaghan, Commissioner), New Brunswick, 2008.
46 Commission of Inquiry on Hormone Receptor Testing, *Investigation and Findings*, vol. 1.
47 Ibid.
48 Commission of Inquiry into Pediatric Forensic Pathology in Ontario, *Inquiry into Pediatric Forensic Pathology in Ontario Report* (S. Goudge, Commissioner), Toronto, Ontario Ministry of the Attorney General, 2008.
49 Gilmour, *Patient Safety, Medical Error and Tort Law*.
50 Ibid.; Prichard, , *Liability and Compensation in Health Care*; and Robert Elgie, Timothy Caulfield and Michael Christie, "Medical Injuries and Malpractice: Is It Time for No-Fault?" (1993) 1 *Health Law Journal* 97.
51 T.M. Bailey and Nola M. Ries, "Legal Issues in Patient Safety: The Example of Nosocomial Infection," (2005) 8 *Healthcare Quarterly* 140, citing An Act Respecting Health Services and Social Services, R.S.Q., c.S-4.2; Picard and Robertson, *Liability and Compensation in Health Care*, p. 171. The parameters of the legal duty—what must be disclosed, by whom, and in what circumstances—are not entirely settled.
52 Karen Davis *et al.*, "Mirror, Mirror on the Wall: An International Update on the Comparative Performance of American Health Care," May 2007. Online. Available HTTP http://www.commonwealthfund.org/Content/Publications/Fund-Reports/2007/May/Mirror—Mirror-on-the-Wall—An-International-Update-on-the-Comparative-Performance-of-American-Healt.aspx.
53 See, e.g., College of Physicians and Surgeons of Ontario, "Disclosure of Harm Policy Statement #5–10," May 2010. Online. Available HTTP http://www.cpso.on.ca/policies/policies/default.aspx?id=1578&terms=disclosure+of+harm.
54 O. Reg. 423/07, s.2, made under the Public Hospitals Act, R.S.O. 1990, c.P.40.
55 Commission of Inquiry on Hormone Receptor Testing, *Investigation and Findings*, vol. 1, p. 364.
56 At the time of writing seven provinces had passed apology laws, including: British Columbia (Apology Act, S.B.C. 2006, c. 19); Alberta (Alberta Evidence

Act, R.S.A. 2000, c.A-18); Nova Scotia (Apology Act, S.N.S. 2008, c.34); Newfoundland and Labrador (Apology Act, S.N.L. 2009, c.A-10.1); Ontario (Apology Act, 2009 S.O. 2009, ch. 3); Saskatchewan (Evidence Act, S.S. 2006, c. E-11.2); Manitoba (Apology Act, C.C.S.M. c. A98) More will likely follow suit.

57 Bailey and Ries, "Legal Issues in Patient Safety; An Act to Amend the Act Respecting Health Services and Social Services as Regards the Safe Provision of Health Services and Social Services, R.S.Q., c. S-4.2.

58 See, generally Gilmour, *Patient Safety, Medical Error and Tort Law*, pp. 63–65. For example, Saskatchewan requires health districts to report specified types of critical incidents to the Ministry of Health on a non-nominate basis, and health facilities to similarly report to the regional health authority. The authority must investigate the incident and determine how to prevent its recurrence. Its report is submitted to the minister, who can share it with other regional health authorities and facilities to disseminate lessons learned (Regional Health Services Act, S.S. 2002, c.R-8.2, Critical Incident Regulations, R.R.S. c. R-8.2 Reg. 3). In Manitoba, see Regional Health Authorities Act, C.C.S.M. c. R34.

59 *Health Professions Procedural Code*, being Sch. 2 to the Regulated Health Professions Act, 1991 S.O. 1991, c.18, s.23(2) 8.

60 See, e.g., O.Reg. 965, s.4(1)(e), made under the Public Hospitals Act, R.S.O. 1990, c.P.40, see also Health Protection and Promotion Act, R.S.O. 1990, c.H.7, s.21(1).

61 See, e.g., *Health Professions Procedural Code*, s.85.5, Public Hospitals Act, R.S.O. 1990, c.P.40, s.33. Hospitals, health facilities, and others employing health professionals in Ontario must report individuals whose employment has been terminated, or admit privileges restricted or revoked because of professional misconduct, incompetence, or incapacity, to their professional governing body.

62 Commission of Inquiry on Hormone Receptor Testing, *Investigation and Findings*, vol. 1, p. 361; *Eastern Regional Integrated Health Authority v. Newfoundland and Labrador (Commission of Inquiry on Hormone Receptor Testing)*, [2008] N.J. No. 47 (S.C.).

63 Ibid.

64 Province of Ontario, By-law No. 328, Hospital Prototype Corporate By-law; Karen Howlett, "Doctors Fear New Hospital Bylaws Will Keep Them Silent," *Globe and Mail*, May 12, 2010. But see Tom Blackwell, "Alberta Doctors Win Right to Free Speech," *National Post*, June 26, 2010, p. A18.

65 O.Reg. 965, s. 22.2, made under the Public Hospitals Act, R.S.O. 1990, c. P.40. Ontario recently passed legislation requiring health care organizations to prepare annual Quality Improvement Plans covering the following areas: results of the Annual Patient and Caregiver Satisfaction and Employee and Service Provider Satisfaction Surveys; data relating to patient relations processes; in the case of a public hospital, its aggregate critical incident data compiled based on disclosures of critical incidents pursuant to regulations under the Public Hospitals Act and information concerning indicators of quality of health care provided by the hospital disclosed pursuant to Regulations under the Public Hospitals Act, as well as annual performance improvement targets – Excellent Care for All Act, S.O. 2010, c.14, s.8.

66 Accreditation Canada, *2009 Canadian Health Accreditation Report: A Focus on Patient Safety—Using Qmentum to Enhance Quality and Strengthen Patient Safety*, Ottawa, Accreditation Canada, 2009. Online. Available HTTP http://www.accreditation.ca/news-and-publications/publications/canadian-health-accreditation-report/.

67 Excellent Care for All Act, S.O. 2010, c.14, s.9.

68 Gilmour, *Patient Safety, Medical Error and Tort Law*, p. 73; Picard and Robertson, *Legal Liability of Doctors and Hospitals in Canada*.

69 D. Dewees, D. Duff, and M. Trebilcock, *Exploring the Domain of Accident Law: Taking the Facts Seriously*, New York, Oxford University Press, 1996.

70 Law Society of Upper Canada, *Listening to Ontarians: Report of the Ontario Civil Legal Needs Project*, Toronto, The Ontario Civil Legal Needs Project Steering Committee, May 2010.

71 Gilmour, *Patient Safety, Medical Error and Tort Law*.

72 Commission of Inquiry on Hormone Receptor Testing, *Investigation and Findings*, vol. 1.

73 Bill 46, An Act Respecting the Care Provided by Health Care Organizations.

74 Gilmour, *Patient Safety, Medical Error and Tort Law*, p. 40; R.M. Wachter, "Patient Safety at Ten: Unmistakable Progress, Troubling Gaps," (2010) 29 *Health Affairs* 165, at p. 168.

13 New developments in the US

The Federal Patient Safety Act

Ronni P. Solomon

Introduction

In the US, a recently implemented law establishes innovative structures and processes for collecting national patient safety data with the goal of reducing medical error and improving patient safety. Under the law, called the Patient Safety Act,[1] healthcare providers may voluntarily submit information about adverse events to federally listed patient safety organizations (PSOs), newly established organizations that must meet certain criteria. PSOs perform analysis of aggregated data and, in turn, provide feedback with analysis and recommendations for improving patient safety and quality of care. As of March 21, 2010, there were 79 federally listed PSOs.[2]

The Patient Safety Act provides federal legal privilege and confidentiality—the first federal protections of this kind in the US—applicable across all states and to all healthcare providers who choose to participate.

The roots of the Patient Safety Act lie in the Institute of Medicine's 1999 landmark report *To Err Is Human: Building a Safer Health System* (IOM Report). The IOM Report found that in the United States between 44,000 and 98,000 people lose their lives every year in hospitals due to preventable medical errors.[3] Even using the low end of this range, medical error ranks as the eighth leading cause of death in the United States, significantly outnumbering deaths caused by car accidents, breast cancer, or AIDS.[4] The IOM Report stated that this "may be only the tip of the iceberg" in determining the full extent of injuries from medical error, and subsequent reports substantiate concern about the extent of harm. For example, the U.S. Centers for Disease Control estimate that 1.7 million hospital-acquired infections each year result in approximately 99,000 deaths and an estimated loss of $6 billion annually for the healthcare industry in 2007 dollars.[5] In 2008, the U.S. Office of Inspector General found that 15 per cent of hospitalized Medicare beneficiaries in two selected counties experienced an adverse event during their hospital stays and that another 15 per cent of Medicare beneficiaries experienced events that caused temporary harm that, while not comparable to the more serious adverse events included in the overall rate, may reflect patient care problems and learning opportunities.[6]

The IOM Report contained other significant findings, namely that the cost of these preventable events was approximately $17 billion per year and that most errors result from faulty systems, processes, and conditions rather than individual "bad apples." It recommended establishing a national focus to enhance the knowledge base on patient safety, developing reporting systems on adverse events and near misses, raising performance standards and expectations, and implementing a culture of safety at healthcare organizations.

Reaction to the IOM Report triggered congressional debate over medical error and how federal legislation might work to improve patient safety. Eventually, on July 29, 2005, after five years in the making, Congress passed the Patient Safety and Quality Improvement Act (the "Patient Safety Act").[7] The Patient Safety Act aims to provide for the improvement of patient safety and to reduce the incidence of events that adversely effect patient safety. To accomplish these goals, the Act sets up entities called patient safety organizations to serve as learning organizations, and incentives to encourage the submission of candid patient safety information by healthcare providers to PSOs. By using their expertise to evaluate data collected from many providers, PSOs spot problems and trends that an individual provider or hospital, with its limited pool of data, may be unable to detect. To encourage voluntary reporting, Congress provided federal legal privilege and confidentiality. In doing so, the Act codifies the IOM's findings that to foster participation in voluntary reporting systems Congress needed to enact laws to protect the confidentiality of certain information collected. Without such legislation, healthcare organizations and providers may be discouraged from participating out of worry that the information they provide might ultimately be subpoenaed and used in lawsuits.[8]

Although the law was passed in 2005, PSOs were unable to operate until the United States Department of Health and Human Services (HHS) issued regulations for the certification of PSOs. On February 12, 2008, the U.S. Department of Health and Human Services published proposed rules to implement the Patient Safety Act.[9] On November 21, 2008, the DHHS promulgated its final rule implementing the legislation, with an effective date of January 19, 2009.[10]

Key elements of the Patient Safety Act

Patient safety organizations

PSO eligibility and listing

A PSO can be a public or private organization, provided it maintains the structure, expertise, and operational procedures to analyze patient safety risks and make recommendations on how to improve healthcare safety and quality. First and foremost, the PSO's mission and primary activity must be to improve patient safety and the quality of healthcare delivery. To become listed as a PSO, the organization must attest on a tri-annual basis that it meets 15 requirements for certification—eight patient safety activities and seven operational activities.

The eight patient safety activities are as follows:

1   Engage in efforts to improve patient safety and the quality of healthcare delivery.
2   Collect and analyze patient safety work product.
3   Develop and disseminate information—such as recommendations, protocols, and suggested best practices—to improve patient safety.
4   Use patient safety work product to encourage a culture of safety, and provide feedback and assistance to minimize patient risk.
5   Maintain procedures to preserve the confidentiality of patient safety work product.
6   Implement appropriate security measures to protect patient safety work product.
7   Use qualified staff (the workforce can include employees, contractors, and others, whether or not they are paid by the PSO).
8   Operate a patient safety evaluation system, and provide feedback to participants within the patient safety evaluation system.

The seven operational activities are as follows:

1   Ensure that the mission and primary activity of the PSO is to conduct activities to improve patient safety and the quality of care.
2   Use appropriately qualified staff, including licensed or certified medical professionals.
3   Within the 24-month period after initial listing as a PSO, and within each sequential 24-month period thereafter, have at least two contracts with different providers for a reasonable period of time to receive and review patient safety work product.
4   Demonstrate that the PSO is not a health insurer or a component of a health insurer.
5   Make required disclosures to HHS, such as the number of contracts with providers and any relationships with contracting providers that extend beyond the activities of The Patient Safety and Quality Improvement Act aka Patient Safety Act.
6   Collect patient safety work product in a standardized manner to permit valid comparisons of similar cases among similar providers.
7   Use patient safety work product to provide direct feedback and assistance to providers to minimize patient risk. A component PSO must also certify that it meets three other requirements demonstrating that there is a firewall between the component PSO and the parent organization.

PSOs can create a *component* organization and seek PSO listing for the component and, if so, must certify that it meets three additional requirements to demonstrate that there is a firewall between the component PSO and the parent organization.[11]

Certain organizations, called excluded entities, are prohibited from becoming PSOs. A health insurer is an excluded entity and is prohibited from establishing a component PSO. Accrediting organizations and state regulatory agencies—such as those that operate mandatory event reporting programs—are prohibited from becoming PSOs; however, these organizations may establish component PSOs that are subject to more stringent privacy and security requirements than components of non-excluded organizations.

PSOs are listed for a period of three years. HHS requires a PSO to seek relisting no later than 75 days before the expiration of its three-year listing. This ensures that providers are aware in advance of a PSO's intent to "go out of business" and gives providers time to confirm the PSO's plans to cease operations and to identify an alternative PSO to analyze their patient safety work product. Additionally, HHS will send a PSO a notice of "imminent expiration" at least 60 days before its certificate expires. The Agency for Healthcare Research and Quality (AHRQ) will post the notice on its website so that providers are made aware of the situation and can consider whether to identify alternative PSOs to review their patient safety work product. If a PSO decides to voluntarily relinquish its certification, it must follow procedures to notify providers that submit patient safety work product to it and explain how its patient safety work product will be disposed of. If HHS decides to revoke a PSO's certificate—after giving the PSO an opportunity to make its case—the PSO must "take all reasonable action" to notify each provider whose patient safety work product it collected or analyzed of its status and inform the provider how its patient safety work product and any data submitted during the 30 days after loss of the PSO's listing will be disposed of. In their contracts with PSOs, providers can impose more stringent provisions for the disposition of patient safety work product.

If a PSO loses its listing, it must dispose of all patient safety work product with identifiable and nonidentifiable information within 90 days. The regulation says that data submitted as patient safety work product continues to receive confidentiality and privilege protections during the 30 days after loss of a PSO's listing. The PSO must dispose of the data by transferring it, with the provider's approval, to a PSO that will receive the information; returning it to the source from which it was submitted; or, if return is not feasible, destroying the information.

Oversight of PSOs

Two agencies within HHS implement the PSO system. The AHRQ certifies PSOs and oversees PSO compliance with statutory and regulatory requirements. The Office for Civil Rights (OCR) oversees compliance with the confidentiality provisions of the Act and Regulations, and is authorized to levy civil monetary penalties against PSOs for each breach of the Act or the Regulations.

To assess compliance, AHRQ performs random site visits for about 5–10 per cent of all PSOs each year. Rather than adopt a punitive approach, HHS will work with a PSO to correct its deficiencies. However, if a PSO fails to work with HHS to correct its deficiencies the department will require the PSO to correct its deficiencies. If HHS's mandatory approach fails, it will begin a process to revoke the PSO's listing. Also, HHS can fine a PSO for "knowing or reckless" breaches of confidential patient safety work product. HHS will follow an expedited process to revoke the PSO's certification if the PSO is or is about to become an entity excluded from listing as a PSO, the parent organization of the PSO is an excluded entity, such as an accrediting organization, and cannot be listed as a PSO but uses its authority over providers to require them to use the services of its component PSO, or the failure to act promptly would lead to serious adverse consequences.

Each time a PSO seeks a new listing or relisting, AHRQ reviews any previous findings regarding the PSO or its senior managers and officials. AHRQ will consider any current activities or history reflecting noncompliance. The federal government may seek additional information from the PSO to increase its confidence that, despite the entity's history or the history of its senior managers and officials, the entity can be relied upon to comply with its statutory and regulatory obligations.

Network of patient safety databases

As set forth under the Act, AHRQ is creating the Network of Patient Safety Databases (NPSD) to provide an "evidence-based management resource for providers, patient safety organizations, and other entities." PSOs will submit adverse event information received from hospitals to the NPSD through "Common Formats," which are standardized data collection forms that AHRQ is developing. To support aggregation and learning, the HHS's Agency for Healthcare Research and Quality developed Common Formats to facilitate the collection and reporting of patient safety events. The broad use of Common Formats presents significant advantages, namely that by using standardized terms PSOs and providers get meaningful aggregation and analysis of patient safety data. AHRQ developed Common Formats for use by healthcare providers and PSOs, the first set of which address patient safety reporting by acute care hospitals. Future versions will be developed for other settings, such as nursing homes, ambulatory surgery centers, and physician and practitioner offices.

The Common Formats apply to all patient safety concerns, including: incidents—patient safety events that reached the patient, whether or not there was harm; near misses or close calls—patient safety events that did not reach the patient; and unsafe conditions—circumstances that increase the probability of a patient safety event. They include event descriptions, delineation of data elements, specifications for patient safety population reports, and technical specifications for electronic data collection and reporting.

At present, some PSOs use AHRQ's Common Formats, and others do not. The extent to which HHS accepts alternate approaches remains to be seen. The Patient Safety Act requires that PSOs, to the extent practical and appropriate, collect patient safety work product in a standardized manner.[12] The regulations state that the PSO must either: (1) certify that the PSO uses the Common Formats and definitions in its collection of patient safety work product; (2) certify and satisfactorily demonstrate to HHS that the PSO is using an alternative system of formats and definitions that permits valid comparisons of similar cases among similar providers; or (3) provide a clear explanation that satisfactorily demonstrates to HHS why it is not practical or appropriate for the PSO to comply with either of those options.

AHRQ plans to use aggregated PSO data from the NPSD to identify national and regional trends of adverse events, and to make this information available to the public. AHRQ's plans include generating two public reports, as required by the Patient Safety Act: a report about effective strategies for reducing medical errors and increasing patient safety, and a report containing trend analysis results.[13] PSO data will be de-identified before submission to the NPSD.

Federal legal privilege and confidentiality

The Act provides privilege and confidentiality protections for *patient safety work product* collected within a *patient safety evaluation system* for the purpose of reporting to a PSO (the italicized terms are discussed later in this chapter). Specifically, the Act states that, notwithstanding any other provision of federal, state, or local law, patient safety work product shall be privileged and shall not be:

1 subject to a federal, state, or local civil, criminal, or administrative subpoena or order, including in a federal, state, or local civil or administrative disciplinary proceeding against a provider;
2 subject to discovery in connection with a federal, state, or local civil, criminal, or administrative proceeding, including in a federal, state, or local civil or administrative disciplinary proceeding against a provider;
3 subject to disclosure pursuant to section 552 of title 5, United States Code (commonly known as the Freedom of Information Act) or any other similar federal, state, or local law;
4 admitted as evidence in any federal, state, or local governmental civil proceeding, criminal proceeding, administrative rulemaking proceeding, or administrative adjudicatory proceeding, including any such proceeding against a provider; or
5 admitted in a professional disciplinary proceeding of a professional disciplinary body established or specifically authorized under state law.

It is up to the courts and disciplinary bodies to apply the privilege protections; this is not something HHS has the authority to interpret and enforce.

In addition to privilege, patient safety work product is confidential and must not be disclosed by anyone holding the information except for permissible purposes outlined in the Act and the Regulations. However, the privilege and confidentiality protections remain in place even if patient safety work product is impermissibly disclosed.

EXCEPTIONS TO PRIVILEGE AND CONFIDENTIALITY

Limited exceptions to privilege and confidentiality apply. Disclosures of patient safety work product (PSWP) will not violate either confidentiality or privilege in the following four situations:

1   For use in criminal proceedings after a court screens the material and determines that the PSWP contains evidence of a criminal act, is relevant to the case, and is "not reasonably available from any other source."
2   To the extent required to provide "equitable relief" to an employee who reported information in "good faith"—much like a whistleblower— directly to a PSO or to a provider for intended disclosure to a PSO but was subject to an adverse employment action because of the report. A protective order is required to protect the confidentiality of the patient safety work product during a court or administrative proceeding.
3   If authorized in writing by each provider identified in the PSWP prior to the disclosure. The disclosing entity must retain a record of the authorization for six years.
4   If the PSWP meets specified de-identification standards—that is, it does not identify any providers, patients or reporters.[14]

PERMISSIBLE DISCLOSURES

Disclosure of PSWP is *permissible* in the following situations. The Act continues to protect the PSWP even when the information is disclosed under these circumstances—so the privilege remains.

1   For patient safety activities

    •   between a provider and a PSO, or to contractors that undertake patient safety activities on their behalf;
    •   among affiliated providers;
    •   by a PSO to another PSO or to another provider that has reported to the PSO, or by a provider to an unaffiliated provider, so long as the data are anonymized.[15]

2   For research authorized, funded, certified, or otherwise sanctioned by HHS.

3 By a provider to the Food and Drug Administration (FDA) or to entities required to report to FDA.

4 Voluntary disclosure to the organization accrediting the provider. Any provider identified in the patient safety work product must agree to the disclosure; otherwise, identifiers must be removed. The accrediting body may not further disclose the patient safety work product, and it cannot require the provider to reveal its communications with any PSO.

5 To the provider's or PSO's lawyer, accountant, or other professional in the course of business operations.

6 To law enforcement authorities, if the PSWP is related to an event that the discloser "reasonably believes" constitutes a crime, and that the discloser believes is necessary for criminal law enforcement.

7 To HHS to conduct compliance reviews and investigations of a PSO.

Patient safety work product that is permissibly disclosed shall continue to be privileged and confidential, and such disclosure shall not be treated as a waiver of privilege or confidentiality, and the privileged and confidential nature of such work product shall also apply to such work product in the possession or control of a person to whom such work product was disclosed.

The regulation also creates a narrow "safe harbor" for inadvertent mistakes in disclosing patient safety work product so that legal protections are not lost. This safe harbor applies only to providers and their responsible parties, such as employees—not to PSOs. The Act prevents a PSO from being compelled to disclose information collected or developed unless such information is identified, is not work product, and is not reasonably available from another source.

Patient safety work product

To obtain privilege and confidentiality under the Patient Safety Act, documents must meet the definition of *patient safety work product* (PSWP). The types of documents that can qualify as PSWP are quite broad and include any data, reports, records, memoranda, analyses (such as root cause analyses), or written or oral statements that can improve patient safety, healthcare quality, or healthcare outcomes. To qualify as PSWP, provider documents must be developed for the purpose of reporting to a PSO. To meet this requirement, providers must establish and use a *patient safety evaluation system* (PSES), the mechanism by which a provider collects, manages, and/or analyzes information for reporting to a PSO. Finally, documents that identify or constitute the deliberations of a patient safety evaluation system also are PSWP.

Documents developed by a PSO for the conduct of patient safety activities also are PSWP and therefore confidential and privileged. The Rule defines "patient safety activities" broadly enough to encompass virtually all activities a PSO might take in the course of its work with PSWP.

Patient safety work product does not include a patient's medical record, billing and discharge information, or any other original patient or provider record. Patient safety work product does not include a patient's medical record, billing and discharge information, or any other original patient or provider record; nor does it include information that is collected, maintained, or developed separately, or exists separately, from a patient safety evaluation system. Such separate information or copies thereof are not PSWP even if they are reported to the PSO.

If, upon analysis, the provider determines that data collected within the patient safety evaluation system does not constitute patient safety work product (e.g. because it is needed to fulfill external reporting obligations), the provider can remove the information from the system if it has not yet been reported to the PSO. Once removed from the patient safety evaluation system, the information is no longer patient safety work product, although information that is not patient safety work product can still be submitted to a PSO. The reason for removing PSWP from the PSES is to permit disclosure. Once information is reported to the PSO, it can only be disclosed by the provider for the limited purposes set forth in the regulations (see the discussion of permissible disclosures on p. 202). Thus, for example, mandatory events reports to a state regulatory agency are not permissible. Once shared with a PSO, that same report cannot be used to fulfill a mandatory reporting requirement. However, copies of such reports may still be disclosed to the PSO after submission to a state agency. The mandatory report sent to the agency will not become PSWP by virtue of submitting a copy to the PSO. However, the copy and any further analysis that occurs within the PSES or the PSO will be PSWP.

It may be possible to use PSWP as evidence in a malpractice case. To do so, each provider identified in the patient safety work product intended to be used as evidence must authorize and permit the disclosure.

Key definitions

Affiliated provider: A legally separate provider that is the parent organization of a provider. The affiliated provider is under common ownership, management, or control with the provider or is owned, managed, or controlled by the provider. The final regulation implementing the Act allows disclosures of identifiable, nonanonymous patient safety work product among affiliated providers.

Common formats: The U.S. Department of Health and Human Services' (HHS) Agency for Healthcare Research and Quality (AHRQ) has issued common definitions and reporting formats to allow PSOs to collect information from providers and standardize how patient safety events are represented. AHRQ expects PSOs to indicate their intent to adopt the Common Formats at initial listing and to certify that they are using the Common Formats when their listing is renewed. Common formats apply to the following types of patient safety concerns:

- incidents that reached the patient—whether or not harm occurred;
- near misses, or events that that did not reach the patient;
- unsafe conditions or circumstances that increase the probability of a patient safety event.

The initial release of the Common Formats also provides for reporting of specific information on nine types of events, including falls, healthcare-associated infections, medication events, pressure ulcers, and surgical events. PSO use of Common Formats ensures that PSOs will be able to compare similar events reported by similar providers and that data can be aggregated (with identifiers removed) to allow analysis of patient safety trends. AHRQ has issued a paper version of its Common Formats for hospital reporting (available online at https://www.psoppc.org/web/patientsafety/paperforms) and expects to update the formats based on feedback. The agency will then provide technical specifications for electronic use of the Common Formats. Once the Common Formats are in a more final stage, AHRQ will update them annually. In the future, AHRQ intends to develop Common Formats for other settings, such as long-term care organizations and ambulatory settings.

Component organization: This definition establishes the types of organizations that can operate component PSOs. A component organization is a unit or division of a legal entity. The entity can be a corporation, a partnership, or a federal, state, local, or tribal agency or organization. A component organization can also be an organization that is owned, managed, or controlled by one or more legally separate parent organizations. The defining feature of a component organization is management or control by others. For example, a component PSO could be a unit or division of a professional society that controls or manages the PSO. A component PSO can contract with its parent organization; for example, a component PSO established by a multifacility system can have a contract with the system. The definition of a component organization is broad enough to apply to entities created by corporate organizations and other legal entities. Additionally, a component organization can be created by public agencies such as the U.S. Department of Defense, the U.S. Department of Veterans Affairs, the Indian Health Service, and other state, local, and tribal organizations that manage or deliver healthcare services. An accrediting organization is also permitted to establish a component PSO provided that all requirements for ensuring that a firewall exists between the parent organization and the component PSO are met.

Disclosure: Disclosure is specifically defined in the regulations implementing the Act, although the definition used in the rule may differ from many providers' typical use of the word "disclosure." Disclosure, as defined by the Act, refers to the release of, transfer of, provision of access to, or divulgence of patient safety work product, in any manner, by an entity or person maintaining that patient safety work product to another legally separate entity or person. Impermissible disclosures—such as PSO divulgence of a provider's patient safety work product to another provider not entitled to the information—could result in revocation of the PSO's listing and financial penalties. The regulation outlines limited instances in which disclosures are permissible, such as disclosure to the U.S. Food and Drug Administration or to law enforcement when the event prompting the disclosure is the reason for law enforcement activity. Nothing prohibits the use or sharing of patient safety work product within a single legal entity. For example, a hospital can allow physicians on its staff to discuss patient safety work product for internal purposes, such as morbidity and mortality rounds. This distinction between *disclosure* and *use* is more specifically addressed in the Health Insurance Portability and Accountability Act of 1996. The Act's definition of the word "disclosure" is unlike the definition of "disclosure" typically used by providers. Most providers understand "disclosure" to mean a factual, but compassionate, recounting of a patient safety event with the patient involved—and, possibly, family members. This understanding of "disclosure" is not affected by the regulations implementing the Act.

Excluded entity: Thisprohibits certain types of organizations from becoming listed as a PSO. Two groups are excluded: entities in the first group, health insurers, are barred from becoming a PSO or a component PSO; entities in the second group, while barred from creating a PSO, may create a component PSO through a parent organization provided that they meet very strict requirements regarding separation of staff and data. The second group includes any entity that accredits or licenses healthcare providers or is an agent of an entity that oversees or enforces statutory or regulatory requirements governing the delivery of healthcare services.

Functional reporting: A provider and a PSO can design a flexible reporting mechanism that allows the PSO to access the provider's patient safety work product so that the arrangement is mutually useful and results in a suitable reporting relationship. Such functional reporting enables the PSO, as defined by a contract or agreement between the PSO and provider, to access specific information in the patient safety evaluation system for processing and analysis. This can be done without requiring the provider to physically transmit the information to the PSO. The arrangement should establish the mechanism for control of the information reported or the information to which the PSO has access and the scope of the PSO's authority to use the information.

Network of patient safety databases: The Act authorizes the creation of a network of patient safety databases to receive nonidentifiable data regarding patient safety events from PSOs and to perform analysis on the aggregated data. The goal is to create a learning system to develop quality improvement strategies for PSOs and healthcare providers. The PSO Privacy Protection Center, an organization funded by AHRQ to support the implementation of the Act, will assist PSOs in submitting the data to the network.

Parent organization: This term defines the types of organizations that can establish a component PSO. A parent organization owns a controlling or majority interest in the component PSO, can manage or control the component, and has the authority to review and overrule the component's decisions. The ownership of a component PSO can be shared with other organizations, as in a joint venture; however, each of the parent organizations must disclose contact information (the parent organization's name, address, phone number, and website address) when the component PSO seeks listing from AHRQ.

Patient safety activities: To become certified as a PSO, an organization must perform eight patient safety activities on behalf of a PSO or a provider. The obligations for conducting patient safety activities rest with PSOs, not providers. The eight activities, as listed in the final rule implementing the Act, are as follows:

1 Engage in efforts to improve patient safety and the quality of healthcare delivery.
2 Collect and analyze patient safety work product.
3 Develop and disseminate information—such as recommendations, protocols, and suggested best practices—to improve patient safety.
4 Use patient safety work product to encourage a culture of safety, and provide feedback and assistance to minimize patient risk.
5 Maintain procedures to preserve the confidentiality of patient safety work product.
6 Implement appropriate security measures to protect patient safety work product.
7 Use qualified staff (the workforce can include employees, contractors, and others, whether or not they are paid by the PSO).
8 Operate a patient safety evaluation system, and provide feedback to participants within the patient safety evaluation system.

Patient safety evaluation system (PSES): A patient safety evaluation system is the mechanism for collecting, managing, and analyzing information for reporting to or by a PSO. The system provides a protected environment for candid consideration and analysis of quality and safety information and is flexible and scalable to meet the needs of the specific hospital. For a multi-provider entity, the final rule permits the establishment of a single patient safety evaluation system or the sharing of patient safety work product among affiliated providers. Regardless of the scope or design of the system, hospitals must continue to fulfill mandatory reporting obligations, such as reporting of patient safety events to state reporting programs. Such information is not considered patient safety work product even though it may be collected by the patient safety evaluation system. A provider may not maintain its patient safety evaluation system within a PSO.

Patient safety organization (PSO): A PSO can be a public or private entity. Its mission and primary activity must be to improve patient safety and the quality of healthcare delivery. To become certified as a PSO, the organization must attest that it meets 15 requirements for certification—eight patient safety activities and seven operational activities. To continue its listing, a PSO must repeat the process every three years thereafter. A PSO must have at least two written contracts with different providers in effect at some point during a 24-month reporting period. AHRQ is responsible for listing PSOs and overseeing their compliance with statutory and regulatory requirements.

Patient safety work product (PSWP): Patient safety work product maintained by the provider and the PSO is subject to federal statutory legal privilege and confidentiality. Information becomes patient safety work product in any of three ways: (1) it is assembled or developed by a provider within a patient safety evaluation system for the purpose of reporting to a PSO and is reported to the PSO; (2) the information is developed by the PSO for the conduct of patient safety work activities; or (3) the information constitutes deliberations or analysis conducted within the scope of the patient safety evaluation system. Federal protections of patient safety work product begin at the time of collection within the patient safety evaluation system for reporting to the PSO. AHRQ stated in the preamble to the final regulations that this period of collection may extend as far back as to passage of the Act in July 2005. Patient safety work product can include data, reports, records, memoranda, analyses (e.g. root cause analyses), and written and oral statements—all of which can be used and analyzed to improve patient safety, healthcare quality, and healthcare outcomes. Excluded from patient safety work product are original patient or provider records, such as a patient's original medical record, and billing and discharge information. Certain protections may still apply even though the original record is not patient safety work product. For example, a patient's medical record is considered confidential, although it may not be protected from legal discovery. Patient safety work product does not include information that is collected, maintained, or developed separately from, or exists separately from, a patient safety evaluation system. Also, facts about corrective measures that a provider adopts to improve patient safety based on feedback from a PSO are not considered patient safety work product.

Provider: Providers, as defined by the Act and its implementing regulations, are eligible to work with PSOs or component PSOs by submitting patient safety work product for analysis by the PSO and receiving feedback to improve patient safety—all within an environment offering privilege and confidentiality protections. HHS defines a provider as (1) an entity or individual licensed or authorized by state law to provide healthcare services; (2) an agency, organization, or individual within a federal, state, local, or tribal government that delivers healthcare services or an organization or individual engaged as a contractor to one of these governments to deliver healthcare; or (3) a parent organization (as defined on pp. 206–207) of a provider or a federal, state, local, or tribal government unit providing healthcare services. HHS's final rule implementing the Act offers an extensive list of examples of providers but notes that the list is not exhaustive. Providers can be not-for-profit or for-profit entities. In its preamble to the final rule, HHS clarifies that a medical product vendor, pharmaceutical company, medical device company, or health insurer cannot be considered a provider.

Notes

1 Patient Safety and Quality Improvement Act of 2005, Pub. L. No. 109-41, *119 Stat. 424 (2005)* (codified at *42 U.S.C. §§299b-21* to -26 (2006)).

2 The Agency for Healthcare Research and Quality (AHRQ), an agency of the US Department of Health and Human Services, administers the provisions of the Patient Safety Act and maintains a publically available listing of PSOs on the AHRQ website at http://www.pso.ahrq.gov/listing/psolist.htm (accessed March 21, 2010).

3 L.T. Kohn, J. M. Corrigan, and M. S. Donaldson (eds.), *To Err Is Human: Building a Safer Health System, A Report of the Committee on Quality of Health Care in America*, Institute of Medicine, 1999) [hereinafter IOM Report].

4 Ibid. at 1.

5 R.D. Scott, "Direct Medical Costs of Healthcare-Associated Infections in U.S. Hospitals and the Benefits of Prevention," Atlanta, Centers for Disease Control and Prevention, 2009.

6 US Department of Health and Human Services (DHHS), Office of Inspector General (OIG), *Adverse Events in Hospitals: Case Study of Incidence Among Medicare Beneficiaries in Two Counties*, OEI-06-08-00220, December 2008. The OIG continues to study the incidence of adverse events and will issue reports.

7 Patient Safety and Quality Improvement Act of 2005, Pub. L. No. 109-41, *119 Stat. 424 (2005)* (codified at *42 U.S.C. §§299b-21* to -26 (2006)).

8 Although many states in the US provide statutory protection for peer review activities, the scope of the privilege and specific requirements for the privilege vary greatly. In many states, the privilege is waived if the protected data are disclosed outside of an individual hospital, which effectively prevents data aggregation and learning across multiple institutions. Also, most state peer review statutes apply only to hospitals, not other types of healthcare settings such as long-term care that stand to benefit from the Patient Safety Act.

9 Patient Safety and Quality Improvement, *73 Fed. Reg. 8112, 8112* (February 12, 2008).

10 43 CFR Part 3.

11 The three requirements are as follows:

    1 Separate patient safety work product from the rest of the parent organization. The rule prohibits the parent organization and individuals in the parent organization from having unauthorized access to patient safety work product. The component PSO must still establish appropriate security measures to maintain the confidentiality of patient safety work product.

    2 Require that members of the component PSO workforce and contractors not make unauthorized disclosures of patient safety work product to the parent organization.

    3 Ensure that the mission of the component PSO does not create a conflict of interest with the parent organization.

12 42 U.S.C. 299b–24(b)(1)(F).

13 DHHS, OIG. *Memorandum Report: Adverse Events in Hospitals: Public Disclosure of Information About Events*, OEI-06-09-00360, January 5, 2010, p. 9

14 The standards for rendering PSWP nonidentifiable are set forth in section 3.212 of the regulations.

15 The standard for making PSWP anonymous is set forth in section 3.206(b)(4)(iv).

14 Patient safety in American health care

Regulatory models

Barry R. Furrow

Introduction

Provider-caused injury is a predictable feature of health care, particularly in hospitals, in the United States and elsewhere. It is only since 2000, with the publication of the Institute of Medicine's report *To Err Is Human*, that American policymakers have started to pay serious attention to patient safety. The Institute of Medicine's projection of 44,000 to 98,000 deaths per year, and hundreds of thousands of avoidable injuries and extra days of hospitalization,[1] has fueled the patient safety movement in the United States.

A patient safety analysis begins with several basic propositions. First, much patient injury occurs through poor quality, unsafe, and ineffective practices. Second, we need more data on what works in medicine in order to provide better care. Third, even when we know what works to improve health care, the fragmented nature of health care delivery often blocks the application of effective approaches to treatment. Hospitals (and their physicians) all too often continue to practice bad medicine in spite of what is known about good practice. Fourth, in light of the above, we need to fund more research on what works. Fifth, and finally, we need to force more integration and coordination in health care delivery through financial incentives and tougher federal rules.

The general strategies to date have included state legislative initiatives to force disclosure of hospital adverse events and "near misses" to patients along with an apology; publication of hospital performance data about relative risks; modest "pay-for-performance" initiatives from corporate groups and tentative Medicare payment reforms; and legal tools ranging from warranties of performance by some providers to patients to improvements in tort liability rules of disclosure of physician performance. The field of Patient Safety is rapidly growing in the United States as a subspecialty within health law as a result of this burst of regulatory activity.[2]

The passage of the Patient Protection and Affordable Care Act of 2010 (PPACA) promises to take patient safety to the next level of regulatory intensity in American health care delivery. The PPACA has an astonishing variety of provisions aimed at improving the quality of the U.S. health care system, reducing errors, and generally promoting patient safety. These provisions include new centers, demonstration projects, and funding awards for a wide range of quality improvement projects. The PPACA sets out an ambitious research agenda for the United States and provides funding and other incentives to accomplish its goals. It establishes a mandate of continuous, data-driven testing of the performance of health care professionals and facilities. The PPACA also launches "demonstration projects" through which the federal government funds particular forms of health care or health care delivery systems, with a requirement that their performance be studied, often with the intent of examining their potential for wider adoption.[3]

The baseline of effective care: outcome measures, best practices, practice guidelines

Quality priorities and measurement

Several sections of PPACA discuss quality and its measurement in extensive detail, as part of implementing major funding programs that will focus on research on outcomes, best practice, comparative effectiveness, and other aspects of getting what works out to clinicians and hospitals. A national strategy for quality improvement is articulated in section 3011 of PPACA. This strategy has the goal of "improv[ing] the delivery of health care services, patient health outcomes, and population health." The priorities identified include: improving health outcomes, efficiency, and patient-centered health care for all populations; identifying areas with the potential for rapid improvement; addressing gaps in quality, efficiency, comparative effectiveness information, and health outcomes measures and data aggregation techniques; improving federal payment policy to emphasize quality and efficiency; enhancing the use of health care data to improve quality, efficiency, transparency, and outcomes; and improving research and dissemination of strategies and best practices to improve patient safety and reduce medical errors, preventable admissions and readmissions, and health care-associated infections.

Quality measure development is mandated by section 3013. A "quality measure" is defined as "a standard for measuring the performance and improvement of population health or of health plans, providers of services, and other clinicians in the delivery of health care services." Such quality measures will include, among others, health outcomes and functional status of patients; the management and coordination of health care across episodes of care and care transitions for patients across the continuum of providers, health care settings, and health plans; the quality of information provided to patients; use of health information technology; and the safety, effectiveness, patient-centeredness, appropriateness, timeliness and efficiency of care.

Research on outcomes and outcome measures

Section 10303 of the PPACA instructs the Secretary of Health and Human Services (HHS) to develop provider-level outcome measures for both hospitals and physicians, as well as other providers. Such measures will include at least 10 outcome measurements for acute and chronic diseases, including the five most prevalent and resource-intensive conditions, within two years; and for primary and preventative care, 10 measurements for distinct populations, within three years.

Section 6301 mandates patient-centered outcomes research as part of the larger goal of developing comparative clinical effectiveness research. The section defines "comparative clinical effectiveness research" and "research" to mean research evaluating and comparing health outcomes and the clinical effectiveness, risks, and benefits of two or more medical treatments, services, and items described in subparagraph (B). They are defined as "health care interventions, protocols for treatment, care management, and delivery, procedures, medical devices, diagnostic tools, pharmaceuticals (including drugs and biologicals), integrative health practices, and any other strategies or items being used in the treatment, management, and diagnosis or prevention of illness or injury in individuals."

The Patient-Centered Outcomes Research Institute is created by section 6301 as a non-profit institute which is not an agency of the government. This Institute's purpose is:

> to assist patients, clinicians, purchasers, and policy-makers in making informed health decisions by advancing the quality and relevance of evidence concerning the manner in which diseases, disorders, and other health conditions can effectively and appropriately be prevented, diagnosed, treated, monitored, and managed through research and evidence synthesis that considers variations in patient subpopulations, and the dissemination of research findings with respect to the relative health outcomes, clinical effectiveness, and appropriateness of the medical treatments, services, and items described in subsection (a)(2)(B).

The Institute will establish priorities for research in light of evidence gaps in clinical outcomes, medical practice variation, and other quality issues articulated in the national Strategy for Quality Care. The Institute is mandated to make its research findings available to clinicians, patients, and the public not later than 90 days after the conduct or receipt of such findings. It will disclose its findings through the official public website of the Institute.

Research on best practice

A new Center for Quality Improvement and Patient Safety is created by section 10303 to "identify, develop, evaluate, disseminate, and provide training in innovative methodologies and strategies for quality improvement practices in the delivery of health care services that represent best practices in health care quality, safety, and value" in collaboration with other federal agencies.

This Center will support the development of best practices for quality improvement practices in the delivery of health care services; system redesign to improve outcomes, improve patient safety, and reduce medical errors; identify high quality providers; assess research and rapidly disseminate information into practice. It will support, through contracts or other means, research on system improvements and the development of tools "to facilitate adoption of best practices that improve the quality, safety, and efficiency of health care delivery services. Such support may include establishing a *Quality Improvement Network Research* Program for the purpose of testing, scaling, and disseminating of interventions to improve quality and efficiency in health care." Findings will be disseminated through multiple media, and linked with the Office of the National Coordinator of Health Information Technology and used to "inform the activities of the health information technology extension program under section 3012, as well as any relevant standards, certification criteria, or implementation specifications."

Dissemination of outcomes, best practice and practice guidelines

The PPACA establishes a wide range of demonstration projects and awards to fund research on outcomes and effectiveness. Once those data begin to be available, the Act mandates their dissemination widely to other government agencies, to providers, and to the public generally.

The Center for Quality Improvement and Patient Safety, created by section 3013, shall make its findings available to the public "through multiple media and appropriate formats to reflect the varying needs of health care providers and consumers and diverse levels of health literacy." Its research findings shall also be shared with the Office of the National Coordinator of Health Information Technology "and used to inform the activities of the health information technology extension program under section 3012, as well as any relevant standards, certification criteria, or implementation specifications." Section 3014 mandates the collection of data on quality and resource use measures in order to "implement the public reporting of performance information," by awarding grants to collect such data.

Section 6301 requires broad dissemination of comparative effectiveness research findings. The Office of Communication and Knowledge Transfer at the Agency for Healthcare Research and Quality will disseminate the research findings that are published by the Patient-Centered Outcomes Research Institute and other agencies that are relevant to comparative clinical effectiveness research. The Office will create informational tools that organize and disseminate research findings for physicians, health care providers, patients, payers, and policymakers. The Office will also develop a publicly available resource database that collects and contains government-funded evidence and research from public, private, not-for profit, and academic sources. It will help users of health information technology "focused on clinical decision support to promote the timely incorporation of research findings disseminated under subsection (a) into clinical practices and to promote the ease of use of such incorporation."

Section 6301 also provides that the Secretary shall

> provide for the coordination of relevant Federal health programs to build data capacity for comparative clinical effectiveness research, including the development and use of clinical registries and health outcomes research data networks, in order to develop and maintain a comprehensive, interoperable data network to collect, link, and analyze data on outcomes and effectiveness from multiple sources, including electronic health records.

Section 3502 provides for quality improvement technical assistance and implementation. The Center for Quality Improvement and Patient Safety will award technical assistance and implementation grants or contracts for technical support to institutions that deliver health care and health care providers so that "such institutions and providers understand, adapt, and implement the models and practices identified in the research conducted by the Center, including the Quality Improvement Networks Research Program."

Section 1303 (c), Clinical Practice Guidelines, amends section 304(b) of the Medicare Improvements for Patients and Providers Act of 2008. It requires the Secretary of HHS to identify existing and new clinical practice guidelines.

Performance findings for consumers

Reporting of comparative outcomes of hospitals can be valuable to patients as they try to choose the best provider for their operations.[4] Such data needs to be carefully extracted and presented. It may not be easy to evaluate and compare institutions, but, like so many quality measures, the technologies of data comparison can only improve under external pressure to disclose such data. It may not be easy to evaluate and compare institutions, but, like so many quality measures, the technologies of data comparison can only improve under external pressure to disclose such data.[5]

Disclosing adverse events to patients: the Veterans Administration and Joint Commission models

Adverse event reporting is often coupled with disclosure of classes of bad outcomes to patients and their families. This disclosure idea developed as the result of a program begun by a Veterans Administration (VA) hospital, and has been adopted by the VA system. It served as the model for Pennsylvania's legislation creating the Patient Safety Authority. The Veterans Administration as of 2005 requires disclosure of adverse events to patients and their representatives, including adverse events that have or are expected to have a clinical effect on the patient or necessitate a change in the patient's care.[6]

The Joint Commission, the accrediting body for most U.S. hospitals, has imposed a disclosure standard that requires that "patients, and when appropriate, their families, are informed about the outcomes of care, including unanticipated outcomes."[7]

Pennsylvania created a Patient Safety Authority that mandates reports to the Authority by hospitals of all "serious events."[8] Fines may be levied for failures to report, and that statute provides for whistleblower protections, among other things.[9] Pennsylvania also adopted a patient notification requirement.[10]

The patient notification requirements of the Joint Commission and the Veterans Administration raise the issue that patients will become aware of errors for the first time. We see again a developing regulatory duty, both state and federal, to force hospitals to gather data and share it with the public.

The PPACA and disclosure

Section 3015 provides for performance websites, to make available to the public

> performance information summarizing data on quality measures. Such information shall be tailored to respond to the differing needs of hospitals and other institutional health care providers, physicians and other clinicians, patients, consumers, researchers, policymakers, States, and other stakeholders, as the Secretary may specify.

This performance information "shall include information regarding clinical conditions to the extent such information is available, and the information shall, where appropriate, be provider-specific and sufficiently disaggregated and specific to meet the needs of patients with different clinical conditions."

Section 10331 provides that physician performance information will be available to consumers through website information. Section 10331 creates a *Physician Compare* internet website based on the model of the *Hospital Compare* site now in operation. This will allow the public to compare physicians on performance measures. Content will include measures collected under the Physician Quality Reporting Initiative and assessments of: patient health outcomes and the functional status of patients; continuity and coordination of care and care transitions, including episodes of care and risk-adjusted resource use; efficiency; patient experience and patient, caregiver, and family engagement; safety, effectiveness, and timeliness of care. Physicians will be able to review their results before they are publicly reported, and the Secretary of HHS is admonished to assure: that the data is statistically valid and reliable, including risk-adjustment mechanisms; that it "provides a robust and accurate portrayal of a physician's performance"; that it provides "a more accurate portrayal of physician performance"; that appropriate attribution of care can be done when multiple physicians and other providers are involved in care; that "timely statistical performance feedback" is provided; and that the Centers for Medicare and Medicaid Services (CMS) have computer and data systems capable of supporting "valid, reliable, and accurate public reporting activities authorized under this section."

PPACA also mandates the reporting of outcome measures for hospital-acquired infections. Section 10303 (b) mandates that the Secretary shall "publicly report on measures for hospital acquired conditions that are currently utilized by the Centers for Medicare & Medicaid Services for the adjustment of the amount of payment to hospitals based on rates of hospital-acquired infections."

The assumption of such public posting of outcome and performance information on an internet site is that consumers will access the site and use it to make choices among providers. Section 10331 goes one step further by providing financial incentives to Medicare patients to choose high quality providers. Dissemination of information about quality may promote improvements in quality as consumer demand selects higher quality providers. There has also been a shift toward evaluating providers based on efficiency.[11] Consumer oriented performance websites raise interesting issues as to likely effects on consumer choices of providers. The studies of consumer behavior have found, for example, that consumers have rarely used comparative assessment that were available, and that quality may even be reduced.[12] On the other hand, quality information—presented in terms of what a patient might reasonably expect—might create a new set of pressures on providers to guarantee their work. Quality improvement can be stimulated by the publication of performance information.[13]

Pay-for-performance initiatives

Treatment costs induced by errors and adverse events are usually either covered by insurance or absorbed by patients, families, insurers, employers, and state and private disability and income-support programs. This means that the adverse outcomes are externalized to other payers and not internalized by providers best able to reduce these hazards or prevent them. The added costs of a failed intervention caused either by error or by a failure to use an effective approach include added acute care costs, lost income, lost household production, and extra pain for patients. As Leape and Berwick note,

> in most industries, defects cost money and generate warranty claims. In health care, perversely, under most forms of payment, health care

professionals receive a premium for a defective product; physicians and hospitals can bill for the additional services that are needed when patients are injured by their mistakes.[14]

Only tort suits have traditionally imposed these excess costs on the hospital or provider that was responsible for the patient's injury.[15]

One American integrated health system has offered warranties.[16] The Geisinger Clinic, an integrated healthcare delivery system in north-eastern Pennsylvania, has a "warranty" program which promises that 40 key processes will be completed for every patient who undergoes elective coronary artery bypass graft surgery (CABG)—even though several of the "benchmarks" are to be reached before or after hospitalization. Geisinger does not guarantee good clinical outcomes but it charges a standard flat rate that covers care for related complications during the 90 days after surgery.

Early regulatory efforts

"Never events"[17]

The concept of "never events" was first developed by the National Quality Forum (NQF)[18] to describe gross medical errors, errors in medical care that are clearly identifiable, preventable, and serious in their consequences for patients, and that indicate a real problem in the safety and credibility of a health care facility. Examples of never events include: surgery on the wrong body part; a foreign body left in a patient after surgery; mismatched blood transfusion; a major medication error; a severe "pressure ulcer" acquired in the hospital; and preventable post-operative deaths.

The never events development in twenty-odd states is a major step, forcing providers to disclose adverse outcomes on the list to the state department responsible, with the goal of improving their operations. It is more than just information disclosure. It allows for systematic recording and tracking of errors, for purposes of analysis of patterns of adverse events, feedback to hospitals, and, in some states, information for consumers as to the relative performance of hospitals and other providers. Many states have enacted legislation requiring reporting of incidents on the NQF list. Minnesota in 2003 was one of the first to pass a statute requiring mandatory reporting of 27 never events, with corrective action taken by the hospital and information shared with other states.[19] Other states, including New Jersey, Connecticut, and Illinois, have adopted reporting requirements for never events.

The CMS has adopted a non-payment strategy that is based on the never event approach, recognizing the added costs to the Medicare program in treating the consequences of such events. This CMS position on never events and payment is a significant step toward "pay for performance."

Infections

Medicare also has begun to adjust payments for 2008 for hospital-acquired infections.[20] CMS then launched a national Quality Initiative in 2002, in which hospitals are ranked in deciles by performance.[21] The top hospitals, in the top 10 and 20 per cent, will receive a two per cent bonus payment. If hospital performance falls below the payment-adjustment threshold by year three, the hospital will receive reduced Medicare reimbursement. The Medicare payment could be reduced by one or two per cent. This is the start of pay-for-performance initiatives that the PPACA continues more aggressively.

The PPACA coordination initiatives

The PPACA offers up a range of coordination models to reduce fee-for-service medicine and decrease fragmentation in the U.S. health care system, aimed at moving the fragmented U.S. system closer to the integration of the Mayo and Geisinger Clinics, among others. Some of these are listed below.

Centers

Centers can fund research, disseminate findings, and create a powerful force for the diffusion of effective models. Section 3021 establishes a new Center for Medicare and Medicaid Innovation (CMI) within the Centers for Medicare and Medicaid Services. The purpose of the Center will be to research, develop, test, and expand innovative payment and delivery arrangements to improve the quality and reduce the cost of care provided to patients in each program. Dedicated funding is provided to allow for testing of models that require benefits not currently covered by Medicare. Because centers such as the CMI can channel millions of dollars toward research and expansion of payment and delivery reforms, their output is likely to be influential on the future of medical practice.

Healthcare innovation zones

Section 3210 (xviii) aims to create such zones, comprised of groups of providers that include a teaching hospital, physicians, and other clinical entities that can deliver a full spectrum of integrated and comprehensive health care services to applicable individuals.

Accountable care organizations

Section 3022, the Medicare Shared Savings Program, creates a program that "promotes accountability for a patient population and coordinates items and services under parts A and B, and encourages investment in infrastructure and redesigned care processes for high quality and efficient service delivery." Accountable care organizations (ACOs) are groups of providers of services and suppliers who work together to manage and coordinate care for Medicare fee-for-service beneficiaries. These will typically be a collection of primary care physicians, specialists, and potentially other health professionals (and may or may not include hospitals) who accept joint responsibility for the quality and cost of care provided to its patients. If the ACO meets certain targets, its members receive a financial bonus. At the heart of the ACO concept is the expectation that when groups of providers are collectively accountable for meeting cost and quality targets, internal peer review and peer pressure will drive the identification and implementation of best practices systemically, which in turn could lead to better cost controls and outcomes.

ACOs will most likely operate as mini health plans, building the infrastructure to manage utilization and insure quality care delivery. To establish targets, cost trends, and provider payment and incentive distribution models, ACOs will require sophisticated financial and actuarial analyses. To control demand and improve the quality of care delivery, ACOs will need to have the tools, processes, and reporting for chronic disease management, complex case management, and wellness/prevention services. To control medically unnecessary services, ACOs will need to have the tools, processes, and reporting for preauthorization, hospital utilization review, high-tech radiology management, specialty referral management, and pharmacy management. They will in fact look like a new and improved version of the best managed care organizations of old.

Performance-based care coordination

Section 3021 provides a number of possible coordination reforms. These innovative payment and delivery arrangements include, among others, the promotion of various models of integration that reduce or eliminate fee-for-service payment systems, for example patient-centered medical home models and other models that "transition primary care practices away from fee-for-service based reimbursement and toward comprehensive payment or salary-based payment (i). Other models include direct contracting with groups of providers to promote new delivery models "through risk-based comprehensive payment or salary-based payment" (ii) and coordinated care models that "transition health care providers away from fee-for-service based reimbursement and toward salary-based payment" (iv). Section 3021 (ix) most explicitly allows for testing of all-payer payment reform for the medical care of residents of the state. Physicians earn a bonus for curtailing growth in the cost of health services by better managing treatment across care settings and by pursuing quality targets. A care-coordination model may be structured differently from an ACO and may also use different methods to calculate shared savings.

Payment bundling

Similar services are grouped together and are compensated using a single or global payment. Services could be grouped according to the care provided by a single doctor or multiple doctors. Patient bundling is another piece of the incentive program, under section 3023. Section 3023 mandates a pilot program on payment bundling, to integrate hospital care for a Medicare beneficiary based on episodes of care "to improve the coordination, quality, and efficiency of health care services under this title." An episode of care means a period of time that includes three days prior to admission to a hospital for a condition, the length of stay in the hospital, and 30 days after discharge. Bundled payments must include "payment for the furnishing of applicable services and other appropriate services, such as care coordination, medication reconciliation, discharge planning, transitional care services, and other patient-centered activities as determined appropriate by the Secretary." These bundled payments shall be "comprehensive, covering the costs of applicable services and other appropriate services furnished to an individual during an episode of care (as determined by the Secretary); and be made to the entity which is participating in the pilot program."

Patient-centered medical homes

Primary care physicians receive additional monthly payments for effectively using health information technology and other innovations to monitor, coordinate and manage care.

The effect of coordination reforms on institutional liability

If the various research and institutional initiatives under PPACA succeed, within a few years ACOs will be successfully formed, comprehensive patient bundling will be implemented in many hospitals, and salary-based payment systems will become widespread. These reforms will do several things at once: they will move more physicians from solo or small group practices into a salaried position in a group model or a hospital; they will shift power toward enterprises that can buy and coordinate the technologies—from electronic health records (EHRs) to case management strategies—to meet the demands of the federal government; and they will therefore turn more physicians into agents of institutional providers and no longer independent contractors. While the health reform measures in the PPACA based on payment reform begin with Medicare providers and beneficiaries, it is predictable that institutional providers will create a system for all patients, private pay and Medicare, for efficiency and consistency reasons.

The liability result is clear if these various reforms, incentives, and forces converge. First, institutional providers will become liable for patient injury, as well as the physicians causing patient injury directly, since agency law will carry liability upstream from agent to principal. Physicians will be much more integrated in the system, whether or not they are salaried, and any argument of independent contractor status will evaporate.

Second, even if ACOs and other entities operate without a hospital as part of the organization, they are now health care providers, subject to liability just as a hospital or managed care organization is, on both vicarious liability and direct negligence principles.

Third, corporate negligence principles are likely to apply to integrated organizations that manage care, whether a patient home, an ACO, or some other delivery form that the PPACA creates. The law of corporate negligence is a malpractice doctrine that spells out the duties owed by a hospital to its patients to keep them safe, or face tort liability. The now-classic statement of this doctrine is found in *Thompson v. Nason Hospital*.[22] *Thompson* combines duties that can be found in isolation in the case law of other jurisdictions. Corporate negligence thus includes four hospital duties: (1) a duty to use reasonable care in the maintenance of safe and adequate facilities and equipment; (2) a duty to select and retain only competent physicians; (3) a duty to oversee all persons who practice medicine within its walls as to patient care; and (4) a duty to formulate, adopt, and enforce adequate rules and policies to ensure quality care for the patients.[23]

The courts are willing to look beyond the hospital form in deciding whether a health care entity might be liable for corporate negligence. For example, in *Gianquitti v. Atwood Medical Associates, LTD*[24] the court held that a professional medical-group practice that provides on-call medical care to its patients if and when they are hospitalized could be liable for corporate negligence if it lacked a formal backup system. In another case, *Davis v. Gish*[25], the court noted the kinds of activities that would turn a professional group or a physicians' practice group into an entity subject to corporate negligence. The entity would, like an HMO, "involve themselves daily in decisions affecting their subscriber's medical care. These decisions may, among others, limit the length of hospital stays, restrict the use of specialists, prohibit or limit post-hospital care, restrict access to therapy, or prevent rendering of emergency room care."[26] The entity must have general responsibility "for arranging and coordinating the total health care of its patients." It must take "an active role in patients' care." All these actions are those that an accountable care organization or an integrated practice would undertake.

Today most physician groups or physician office-based practices would not be said to possess such responsibility. But the entities to be fostered by the PPACA and its millions of dollars in demonstration grants and Medicare mandates are far more likely to coordinate care, taking on new responsibilities that will make them appropriate defendants in tort litigation.

Tort reform under the PPACA

Tort reform was never seriously considered as a central part of health care reform, in part because cost savings from reform were not expected to be substantial, and because it is a Democratic bill. The Congressional Budget Office (CBO), in a letter to Senator Orrin Hatch (October 9, 2009), estimated that at most there might be savings of 0.5 per cent in malpractice premium and indirect costs if tort reforms were implemented. Such reforms have typically included caps on noneconomic damages; caps on punitive damages; modification of the "collateral source" rule; more restrictive statute of limitation rules; and replacement of joint-and-several liability with a fair-share rule limiting a defendant's liability to the percentage of the final award that was equal to his or her share of responsibility for the injury. The CBO noted that limiting the rights of injured patients to sue for injuries from medical errors might have an overall negative effect on patient welfare due to the reduction in deterrence. The CBO noted that the studies ranged from an estimate that a 10 per cent reduction in costs would increase the overall mortality rate by 0.2 per cent, to an estimate of no serious adverse outcomes for patient health.

The PPACA provides for state-funded demonstration projects to explore alternative dispute resolution models. The primary liability reform provision in the PPACA is Section 10607, State Demonstration Programs to Evaluate Alternatives to Current Medical Tort Litigation. The PPACA specifies that the models should resolve disputes over patient injuries and promote a reduction in medical errors by collecting patient safety data as to disputes. Second, the model should increase the reliability of dispute resolution, make it more efficient, enhance patient safety "by detecting, analyzing, and helping to reduce medical errors and adverse events"; improve access to insurance; inform patients about their choices; and allow patients to opt out at any time from the alternative process. This is a modest approach to U.S. tort reform, since it leaves the existing system intact and allows patients to opt out of any alternative system that is developed as a demonstration project.

Health courts have been proposed in a flurry of recent academic writing as an administrative solution that balances the need for compensation of patients for their medical injuries and the need to improve accountability and the efficiency of the current liability system.[27] Such a reform would create a system of administrative compensation for medical injuries, with five essential elements. First, special judges would make the decision. Second, the standard of care would be broader than negligence, with a test of "avoidability." Third, compensation criteria are based on evidence, grounded in experts' interpretations of the leading scientific literature, and *ex ante* determinations about the preventability of common medical adverse events. Fourth, this knowledge would be converted to decision aids that allow quick decisions for certain types of injury. Fifth, guidelines would also help the judges decide about damages.

Conclusion

The passage of the PPACA in 2010 is likely to revolutionize the practice of medicine or patient safety in the United States over the next 10 years. In the patient safety area, its primary goal is to fund billions of dollars in research in comparative effectiveness, best practice, and system integration. Linkage of such research findings with payment reforms in other sections of PPACA means that the fragmented American system is likely to develop integration through electronic medical records, accountable care organizations, and other system reforms in response to both data and dollars. It may well revolutionize patient safety, at the cost of a loss of some physician autonomy.

Notes

1 L.T. Kohn, J.M. Corrigan, and M.S. Donaldson (eds.), Committee on Quality of Health Care in America, Institute of Medicine, *To Err Is Human: Building a Safer Health System*, Washington, D.C.: National Academy Press, 2000, pp. 26–27 (hereafter cited as IOM Report). Online. Available HTTP: http://www.nap.edu/books/0309068371/html/.

2 See, generally, B. Furrow, "Regulating Patient Safety: Toward a Federal Model of Medical Error Reduction," 12 *Widener Law Review* 1 (2005).

3 A useful summary of the legislation can be found at http://dpc.senate.gov/healthreformbill/healthbill53.pdf.

4 M.N. Marshall *et al.*, "The Public Release of Performance Data: What Do We Expect to Gain? A Review of the Evidence," 283 *Journal of the American Medical Association* 1866 (2000).

5 Ashish K. Jha, Zhonghe Li, John Orav, and Arnold Epstein, "Care in U.S. Hospitals—The Hospital Quality Alliance Program," 353 *New England Journal of Medicine* 265, 272 (2005).

6 See Department of Veterans Affairs, Veterans Health Administration, Directive No. 2005-049, "Disclosure of Adverse Events to Patients," 2005. Online. Available HTTP http://www.sorryworks.net/pdf/VA_Link.pdf.

7 Joint Commission on Accreditation of Healthcare Organizations, "Revisions to Joint Commission Standards in Support of Patient Safety and Medical/Health Care Error Reduction," RI.1.2.2 (2001). Online. Available HTTP http://www.dcha.org/JCAHORevision.htm.

8 40 Pa. Stat. Ann. § 131.308(a).

9 Ibid. § 131.308(c).

10 Ibid. § 131.308(b).

11 See, generally, A. Milstein and T.H. Lee, "Comparing Physicians on Efficiency," 357 *New England Journal of Medicine* 264 (2007).

12 R.M. Werner and D.A. Asch, "The Unintended Consequences of Publicly Reporting Quality Information," 293 *Journal of the American Medical Association* 1239 (2005). See also Mark A. Hall and Carl E. Schneider, "Patients as Consumers: Courts, Contracts, and the New Medical Marketplace," 106 *Michigan Law Review* 643 (2008).

13 D.B. Mukamel, D.L. Weimer, and J. Zwanziger., "Quality Report Cards, Selection of Cardiac Surgeons, and Racial Disparities: A Study of the Publication of the New York State Cardiac Surgery Reports," 41 *Inquiry* 435, 443 (Winter 2004/2005); Z.G. Turi, "The Big Chill—The Deleterious Effects of Public Reporting on Access to Health Care for the Sickest Patients," 45 *Journal of the American College of Cardiology* 1766 (2005); J.H. Hibbard *et al.*, "Does

Publicizing Hospital Performance Stimulate Quality Improvement Efforts?" 22 *Health Affairs* 84 (2003).

14 L.L. Leape and D.M. Berwick, "Five Years After *To Err Is Human*: What Have We Learned?" 293 *Journal of the American Medical Association* 2384, 2388 (2005).

15 H. Morreim, *Holding Health Care Accountable: Law and the New Medical Marketplace*, Oxford, Oxford University Press 2001.

16 See, for example, Thomas H. Lee, "Pay for Performance, Version 2.0," 357 *New England Journal of Medicine* 531 (2007).

17 Press Release, Centers for Medicare and Medicaid Services, Office of Public Affairs, *Eliminating Serious, Preventable, and Costly Medical Errors—Never Events* (May 18, 2006) [hereinafter CMS Press Release]. Online. Available HTTP http://www.cms.hhs.gov/apps/media/press/release.asp?Counter=1863.

18 See National Quality Forum. Online. Available HTTP http://www. qualityforum.org/projects/completed/sre/ (accessed March 5, 2009).

19 Minn. Stat. Ann. § 144.7065.

20 CMS Press Release. Online. Available HTTP http://www.cms.gov/Hospital QualityInits/downloads/HospitalRHQDAPU200808.pdf.

21 See, generally, Centers for Medicare & Medicaid Services, *Rewarding Superior Quality Care: The Premier Hospital Quality Incentive Demonstration Fact Sheet*, 2004. Online. Available HTTP http://www.allhealth.org/BriefingMaterials/Hospital PremierFS200602-175.pdf.

22 591 A.2d 703 (Pennsylvania, 1991).

23 Ibid. at 707.

24 973 A.2d 580 (Rhode Island, 2009).

25 2007 WL 5007253 (Pennsylvania Common Pleas Court, 2007).

26 Ibid. at 835.

27 The health courts proposal is presented in M.M. Mello, D.M. Studdert, A.B. Kachalia, and T.A. Brennan, "'Health Courts' and Accountability for Patient Safety," 84 *Milbank Quarterly* 459, 460–461 (2006).

15 Responding to patient harm
Patient safety initiatives in Australia

Merrilyn Walton

Introduction

While the publication of the Quality in Australian Health Care Study in the *Medical Journal of Australia* in 1995[1] was alarming news for many in the health care system, it only confirmed what hundreds of patients had been experiencing over the previous two decades. Patients had been suffering and complaining about adverse events for years, and while their concerns were rarely acknowledged by the health care system, governments did respond to community concerns about inadequate redress for complaints by establishing complaint commissions; the first was established in New South Wales in 1984, followed by Victoria in 1988. All states in Australia now have complaint commissions which receive and investigate and conciliate health care complaints, giving patients an alternative route to the more traditional and costly litigation route.

Since these early days of inadequate information to patients about medical mistakes the Australian health care system has moved towards a more open and transparent system; one which values honest communications with patients and their carers about adverse events and recognises that improvements can only be made with deeper understanding of the underlying causes of them. This journey has been and still is a difficult one. Since 2000 there have been three major commissions of inquiries in Australia;[2] all describe and analyse the multiple system failures and departure from accepted professional standards. These Inquiries are important because they help clarify the problems associated with the environment in which patients are treated and in which health professionals work. They were the catalyst for the establishment of a more accountable and transparent health system. We now have quality and safety commissions in most states and territories, patient safety education and training is being incorporated into health education programmes and curricula, incident reporting is mandated and national standards have been endorsed for areas such as Open Disclosure, health care associated infections, patient identification, clinical handover, medications and falls. Significant improvements have been made in complaint management, incident monitoring and investigation of the root causes of systemic problems in the health system.

Governance initiatives

A major initiative taken by the Commonwealth Government as a result of the findings of the 1995 Quality in Australian Health Care Study was to establish the Australian Council for Safety and Quality (January 2000) as the organisation to lead development of national strategies to improve the safety of patient care. Now, ten years later, with a new name and additional resources, the Australian Commission on Safety and Quality in Health Care (ACSQHC) has obtained national consensus in areas such as accreditation, clinical handover, credentialing for health professionals, falls prevention, health-care associated infections, medication safety, Open Disclosure, patient identification, and recognising and responding to patients who are clinically deteriorating. Like the state-based quality and safety agencies,[3] a main role is to provide infrastructure capable of sustaining improvements designed to reduce errors.

Health ministers use the national and state bodies as the main vehicle for patient safety; many initiatives focus on building frameworks and developing national standards. High level frameworks describe the patient safety context, content and structures necessary to achieve the best patient care outcomes. These frameworks ensure that local health care facilities apply standardised guidelines and protocols that describe the best approach to be taken in particular areas. As a foundation, frameworks describe the relevant patient safety principles and concepts. A framework provides a macro analysis of what must be done or included to improve patient safety and allows the development of specific programmes moving from macro understanding of patient safety to locally developed programmes designed to reduce errors and improve quality.

Following the success of the National Patient Safety Education Framework developed by the former Commission in 2005, the Australian health ministers in 2009 asked the ACSQHC to develop a national safety and quality framework to '*guide action to improve safety and quality of the care provided in all health care settings over the next decade*'. They wanted the framework to be the basis of strategic and operational safety and quality plans; one that could provide a mechanism for refocusing improvement activities, reviewing investments for safety and quality, and designing goals for health service improvement. They see it as a potential vehicle for consumers, clinicians, managers and researchers to contribute to safety and quality improvement.[4]

Frameworks and national standards which are subject to extensive consultation in the community and the health system have strengthened the role of patients in health care delivery. Yet while many health care services are examining whether their services are patient centred, there remains a wide gap between the reality and the rhetoric. Patient centred care has been a term used in health care for decades, but without deep understanding of what the term implies. Most health care services are not patient centred; rather, they are organised and operate to meet the needs of the organisation and health care providers.

In Australia two distinct institutional management pathways exist in relation to adverse events in health care – the complaint commissions, which examine complaints about patient care concerning named institutions and individual health providers, and the safety and quality agencies, which focus on system-wide problems. While patient safety overwhelmingly is concerned with the underlying factors that contribute to health care errors, there is wide acceptance in Australia that this does not mean that individuals are not professionally responsible and accountable for their actions. The safety of the community requires that we inquire into and make changes that improve the system of health care; the indicator of a problem may be the unsupervised junior doctor who makes a serious medication error, causing a death or serious morbidity. The main cause of the error is not the individual junior doctor (we expect them to be inexperienced) but the system that permits junior doctors to be unsupervised. Contrasting with this is the death of a woman from an undiagnosed infection after an epidural as a result of poor infection control procedures. The main factor here may relate to the professional conduct of the clinician, who is professionally accountable for his or her failure to comply with appropriate infection control procedures; there may also be broader system issues related to training and availability of sterilising equipment.

Another national initiative by the Australian health ministers that will impact on patient safety is their agreement to create a single national registration and accreditation system for the ten main health professions. The establishment of the Australian Health Practitioners Registration Agency on 1 July 2010 provided a one stop shop for health professionals and consumers about registration and complaints. The National Registration and Accreditation Scheme is the primary organisation for establishing registration and accreditation standards for all health professions. The scheme consists of a Ministerial Council, an independent national agency with an Agency Management Committee, national profession-specific boards supported by a national office. The Ministerial Council appointed the members of the ten national boards on 31 August 2009. The national boards had their first meeting on 20 September 2009 and the scheme was fully operational on 1 July 2010.

Educating the health care workforce

In 2005 the Australian health ministers endorsed the Australian Patient Safety Education Framework (APSEF), which describes the knowledge, skills and behaviours required by all health care workers in all health care settings to keep patients safe. The realisation by safety and quality commissions and some universities that we have failed to adequately prepare health professionals for twenty-first-century medicine and health care has stimulated the focus on patient safety education generally. Competencies described in the APSEF are now mandated learning outcomes required by the Australian

Medical Council for medical school accreditation. This means that medical schools seeking accreditation will be required to demonstrate in the curriculum where and how they teach students about patient safety.

Notwithstanding the following efforts of governments and educational institutions, patient safety education and training remain underdeveloped in many educational settings. The following case examples show where patient safety education is occurring. Junior doctors are inexperienced and must practise under supervision, but workforce pressures and shortages mean that often they are unsupervised. Research shows that junior doctors are associated with adverse events either by omission or commission – they failed to do the right thing at the right time or they did the wrong thing. The publication of the Australia Curriculum Framework for Junior Doctors[5] fills the knowledge gap in educational outcomes for junior doctors, as well as integrating patient safety principles and concepts into the learning outcomes covering clinical medicine, procedures, communication and professionalism. Medical students are also targeted – the WHO Patient Safety Curriculum Guide for Medical Schools[6] provides comprehensive curriculum with topics selected from the Australian Patient Safety Education Framework. This comprehensive curriculum includes step by step tutorials on how to teach as well as what to teach. The specialist colleges are also responding to the demand for access to patient safety knowledge and skills training. In 2009 the College of Physicians integrated patient safety concepts into its new curriculum.

While many health profession faculties are beginning to include patient safety concepts in their curricula, patient safety education and training present significant challenges; the lack of patient safety capacity in the universities and the main training hospitals is a significant one. Many senior clinicians remain wary of disclosing the existence of medical errors and consequently do not teach students how to prevent them. What is taught in the classroom can be easily undone by a senior and respected clinician belittling the importance of teamwork, of patient engagement and other areas traditionally seen by medicine as 'soft'. There is plenty of evidence demonstrating that these areas are highly relevant in minimising adverse outcomes. The 'hidden culture' is a powerful reminder of the existing cultural barriers we need to overcome before our health system is transformed into a patient centred health care system.

New knowledge and skills are required of health professionals: they need to be skilled communicators; a major component of health care is verbal instruction and communication with patients and between the multitudes of health care workers involved in caring for them. They also need to know how to identify, prevent and manage adverse events and near misses, how to use evidence and information, and how to be workplace teachers and learners.[7]

A major obstacle facing many patient safety programmes is the perception (real or otherwise) that acknowledging errors to one another as well as to patients will lead to increased risk of litigation. States and territory governments[8] in Australia have enacted legislation providing qualified privilege or legal immunity to quality assurance committees as incentives to discuss and analyse adverse events in the knowledge that any information or documentation will not be legally available to patients, their lawyers or the media. These laws are designed to keep confidential information created during quality assurance committees; activities designed to improve the quality and safety of health care. While the laws differ in the jurisdictions, their intention is similar; to encourage health professionals to discuss their mistakes and facilitate an understanding of why and how they occurred, and identify improvements as a result of their findings. The laws provide for:[9]

- the confidentiality of some documents;
- proceedings and records of the committee or activity;
- the protection of those documents and proceedings from being used in legal actions;
- the protection from legal liability for present and former members of health care quality committees who were acting in good faith in carrying out their responsibilities.

Clinicians fear that without qualified privilege any documents they produce during the meeting will be available under Freedom of Information laws or discoverable in legal proceedings. They also fear having to give evidence in civil proceedings about a committee's deliberations or in relation to legal action concerning them. How the media would portray an incident if information about an incident were available to it is also a concern.

Committees who apply for qualified privilege have obligations in relation to record keeping and de-identified reports to ministers of health or other appropriate agencies. Examples of quality improvement committees which have used qualified privilege include infection control; data about hospital acquired infections and comparisons against best practice (benchmarks) rates of infection; surgical mortality and morbidity meetings; deaths under anaesthetic committees; surgical deaths committees.

Open Disclosure

The *Open Disclosure Standard: A National Standard for Open Communication in Public and Private Hospitals, Following an Adverse Event in Health Care*[10] was nationally endorsed in 2003 following extensive consultation coordinated by Standards Australia, which also hosted the national stakeholder committee selected to develop the standards. The momentum to implement Open Disclosure (OD) in Australia has been maintained. In addition to national guidelines most states and territories have developed state Open Disclosure Guidelines consistent with the national standard. New South Wales also embarked on an extensive training programme for health professionals on Open Disclosure. The Australian Commission on Safety and Quality commissioned an evaluation of the OD standard which was published in 2007, but this needs to be supplemented by rigorous research to find out whether Open Disclosure is meeting the expectations of the community and is reducing litigation as suggested.

What is Open Disclosure in the Australian context?

Open Disclosure is the open discussion of incidents that result in harm to a patient while receiving health care.[11] The fears expressed earlier about open discussion during quality improvement activities also apply to Open Disclosure associated with patient harm. A significant impediment to honesty with patients after an adverse event identified by health professionals has been the fear that their honesty will lead to a claim of medical negligence or a complaint to the registration authority, complaint commission or hospital management. The dilemma that honesty (a good deed) has the potential to result in a perceived punitive result (legal/complaint) was extensively debated during the development of the OD standards, and while we do not yet have the evidence that OD prevents litigation, the structure and managerial support of OD have enabled health professionals to feel supported during the process of disclosure.

Most groups in Australia – general community, patient advocate groups, medical defence organisations, health professionals, professional associations and health departments – recognise that unless we know the causes of adverse events we are unlikely to make the improvements necessary to prevent them recurring. Honesty has always been an ethical obligation of health professionals but one they were finding hard to meet; the OD process recognises that ethical obligation by creating a detailed process to follow that involves the appropriate clinicians, hospital management and the patients and/or their carers.

The OD standards are underpinned by the following eight principles[12] – ones that recognise the complexity and dynamic nature of health care as well as the interests of the different parties:

1   *Openness and timeliness of communication*: when things go wrong, the patient and their support person should be provided with information about what happened, in an open and honest manner at all times. The Open Disclosure process is fluid and may involve the provision of ongoing information.
2   *Acknowledgement*: all adverse events should be acknowledged to the patient and their support person as soon as practicable. Health care organisations should acknowledge when an adverse event has occurred and initiate the Open Disclosure process.
3   *Expression of regret*: as early as possible, the patient and their support person should receive an expression of regret for any harm that resulted from an adverse event.
4   *Recognition of the reasonable expectations of patients and their support person*: the patient and their support person may reasonably expect to be fully

informed of the facts surrounding an adverse event and its consequences, treated with empathy, respect and consideration, and provided with support in a manner appropriate to their needs.

5   *Staff support*: health care organisations should create an environment in which all staff are able and encouraged to recognise and report adverse events and are supported through the Open Disclosure process.

6   *Integrated risk management and systems improvement*: investigation of adverse events and outcomes are to be conducted through processes that focus on the management of risk (see AS/NZS 4360). Outcomes of investigations are to focus on improving systems of care and will be reviewed for their effectiveness.

7   *Good governance*: Open Disclosure requires the creation of clinical risk and quality improvement processes through governance frameworks, where adverse events are investigated and analysed to find out what can be done to prevent their recurrence.

8   *Confidentiality*: policies and procedures are to be developed by health care organisations with full consideration of the patient's, carer's and staff's privacy and confidentiality, in compliance with relevant law, including Commonwealth and State/Territory privacy and health records legislation.

A detailed flow chart of the OD process can be found in the OD Standards and accessed at http://www.health.qld.gov.au/patientsafety/od/documents/odst.pdf.

Legal issues associated with Open Disclosure

During the drafting of the OD standards there was substantial discussion about the legal context for implementing OD. Hospitals and health professionals were unwilling to expose themselves to costly litigation. We knew that OD would be yet another guideline that stays in the cupboard unless there was some understanding of the implications of OD in the context where no plans were afoot to change the laws relating to negligence. At the end of extensive debate it was agreed by the expert committee that legal issues were not a barrier to the OD standards being implemented. In my experience many health professionals misunderstand the law, and when fully informed about a legal principle or obligation individual personal anxieties are reduced. This is particularly the case in relation to disciplinary law and medical negligence.

The national OD standards, as a result of the above concerns, include a range of legal caveats aimed at clarifying any legal uncertainties associated with OD. First, organisations are required to know and observe any legal requirements, including any insurance obligations before they create training tools or implement the standard. The hospital workforce comprises many diverse groups who may have other legal and administrative obligations apart from those to the patients. Some health professionals such as doctors have statutory duties emanating from their registration; hospital managers may have duties associated with their employment contracts. Since an incident concerning a patient is likely to involve a number of different groups, it is probable that there will be times where there are multiple duties and obligations – to the patient, the organisation and/or the professional registration authority. States and territory laws which need to be taken into account when implementing OD standards also vary.

The Standards give the following instructions to health care clinicians and managers when giving information to a patient or their carer:[13]

1   acknowledge that an adverse event has occurred;
2   acknowledge that the patient is unhappy with the outcome;
3   express regret for what has occurred;
4   provide *known* clinical facts and discuss ongoing care (including any side effects to look out for);
5   indicate that an investigation is being, or will be, undertaken to determine what happened and prevent such an adverse event happening again;
6   agree to provide feedback information from the investigation when available; and provide contact details of a person or persons within the health care organisation whom the patient can contact to discuss ongoing care.
7   Health care professionals need to be aware of the risk of making an admission of liability during the Open Disclosure process. In any discussion with the patient and their support person during the Open Disclosure process, the health care professional should take care not to

•   state or agree that they are liable for the harm caused to the patient;
•   state or agree that another health care professional is liable for the harm caused to the patient; or
•   state or agree that the health care organisation is liable for the harm caused to the patient.

The Standards require that clinicians and managers record facts rather than opinions because the OD process is available to third party access. Any email or written communications and documents that are generated as a result of the OD process may later be discoverable in legal proceedings, complaint commission investigations or, in the case of public hospitals, in any Freedom of Information application. The Standards also cover the situation in relation to legal professional privilege, qualified privilege legislation, Freedom of Information legislation, privacy and confidentiality legislation, defamation and insurance law, including notification requirements.

The main findings of the evaluation of the OD Standards in Australia[14] revealed that consumers and health professions approved the OD process, with staff reporting feeling more comfortable about discussing matters that were too difficult in the past, and consumers liking being told what happened. But the evaluation also revealed continued uncertainties about the type of incident that triggers the OD process, the impact on the reputation of the organisation, the legal and insurance implications and whether colleagues will support those carrying out OD. Notwithstanding these findings, staff said they were willing to integrate OD more consistently into everyday clinical practice.

Community engagement

The health system in Australia, while including consumers on advisory committees, has yet to discover effective ways for engaging with the community. Consumer membership on registration boards, Area Health Service committees and others has been a feature for decades, but there is no evidence that their voice has made an impact on service delivery. The complaint commissions were the first to advocate the concept of patient rights, stemming from the consumer rights movement in the United States during the 1970s. The acceptance by the health system of the unintended harm to patients as a result of their health care has enabled a shift in the way patients are perceived by health professionals; many no longer view patients merely as passive recipients of care but as partners in achieving the best outcomes possible.

Education and service delivery frameworks mentioned earlier now take into account the voice and experience of patients, but with a different focus from earlier attempts to engage with consumers, who as members of committees were relatively powerless to effect change or have their voice heard. By using patient experiences of care, patients are better able to interact and engage with health care professionals at the service delivery level, where it counts.

The patient's experience of their care is one of the three dimensions in the National Safety and Quality Framework.[15] Health care rights are included in the framework, as are access to quality health care, access to health information, care and treatment coordinated by people who work in partnerships, appropriate treatment if harmed, including an apology and full explanation of what happened; care and treatment is to be based on the best knowledge and evidence; clinical outcomes are to be used to build an evidence base to improve care; there is acceptance by governments and health care managers of their responsibility for their safety; money is spent efficiently; and, finally, if something goes wrong action will be taken to prevent it happening to someone else.

The Australian Charter of Patient Rights,[16] published by the ACSQHC and endorsed by all Health Ministers in July 2008, was developed in collaboration with the Australian Consumers Health Forum and other organisations. Training resources have been developed to assist health facilities to embed the Charter into their organisations. The Charter is set out in Figure 15.1.

AUSTRALIAN CHARTER OF HEALTHCARE RIGHTS

The Australian Charter of Healthcare Rights describes the rights of patients and other people using the Australian health system. These rights are essential to make sure that, wherever and whenever care is provided, it is of high quality and is safe.

The Charter recognises that people receiving care and people providing care all have important parts to play in achieving healthcare rights. The Charter allows patients, consumers, families, carers and services providing health care to share an understanding of the rights of people receiving health care. This helps everyone to work together towards a safe and high quality health system. A genuine partnership between patients, consumers and providers is important so that everyone achieves the best possible outcomes.

Guiding Principles

These three principles describe how this Charter applies in the Australian health system.

1 Everyone has the right to be able to access health care and this right is essential for the Charter to be meaningful.

2 The Australian Government commits to international agreements about human rights which recognise everyone's right to have the highest possible standard of physical and mental health.

3 Australia is a society made up of people with different cultures and ways of life, and the Charter acknowledges and respects these differences.

For further information please visit
www.safetyandquality.gov.au

AUSTRALIANCOMMISSION on
SAFETY and QUALITY in HEALTHCARE

What can I expect from the Australian health system?

MY RIGHTS	WHAT THIS MEANS
Access	
I have a right to health care.	I can access services to address my healthcare needs.
Safety	
I have a right to receive safe and high quality care.	I receive safe and high quality health services, provided with professional care, skill and competence.
Respect	
I have a right to be shown respect, dignity and consideration.	The care provided shows respect to me and my culture, beliefs, values and personal characteristics.
Communication	
I have a right to be informed about services, treatment, options and costs in a clear and open way.	I receive open, timely and appropriate communication about my health care in a way I can understand.
Participation	
I have a right to be included in decisions and choices about my care.	I may join in making decisions and choices about my care and about health service planning.
Privacy	
I have a right to privacy and confidentiality of my personal information.	My personal privacy is maintained and proper handling of my personal health and other information is assured.
Comment	
I have a right to comment on my care and to have my concerns addressed.	I can comment on or complain about my care and have my concerns dealt with properly and promptly.

Figure 15.1 Australian Charter of Healthcare Rights.

The Charter takes into account Australia's international obligations, including the Universal Declaration of Human Rights[17] and the International Covenant on Economic, Social and Cultural Rights.[18] The mechanism for mandating a range of health services in Australia is the responsibility of the federal government via the federally operated and funded system of health delivery known as Medicare. Medicare provides universal access to health care for eligible citizens.

The medicolegal environment

As a result of vociferous lobbying by the insurance industry and medical groups (for different reasons), governments turned their attention to reforming tort laws in Australia in the late 1990s in the belief the country was experiencing an explosion of civil litigation evidenced by the number of high profile public liability cases and escalating costs of professional insurance, particularly for obstetricians. Responding to the perceived crisis the Commonwealth, state and territory governments requested a review of the law of negligence. The review, commonly known as the Ipp Review (the review was headed by the Hon. David Ipp of the NSW Court of Appeal),[19] led to Australia-wide tort reform. But whether the evidence of a litigation explosion ever existed has been questioned. A review of national litigation rates by law professor Ted Wright[20] for the Law Council of Australia of the litigation situation pre and post the Ipp reforms shows that there was no evidence of an increase in cases before the Ipp Review and that since the reforms there has been a noticeable decline in litigation. Legal commentary since the reforms has invariably lamented the lack of evidence supporting an escalation in litigation, adding that more successful claims and reduced insurance profits may have been factors overlooked in any debate and analysis of the environment at the time.

Legislative change in NSW

The medical profession was one of the main lobbyists in the debate encouraging governments to reform the law of negligence. They argued that the medicolegal environment encouraged them to practise defensive medicine, which in turn increased costs and reduced services to high risk patients. At the same time pressure was mounting on health departments and governments to endorse and implement Open Disclosure guidelines to enable health professionals and organisations to implement Open Disclosure with patients who had suffered an adverse event. Clinicians at the time were (and to some extent still are) concerned that if they apologised to a patient their apology would be construed as an admission of liability and later used as evidence in litigation.

The outcome of the review by the NSW government was the proclamation of the Civil Liability Act 2002 (NSW), which limited medical negligence actions as well as addressing the way apologies could be used in legal proceedings. The following provisions[21] have limited the ability of plaintiffs to sue health professions for negligence:

- a limit on the duty of care owed by public authorities;
- the introduction of a modified *Bolam* principle;
- the exclusion of plaintiff's evidence in establishing causation in failure to warn actions;
- the prohibition of damages for the costs of child rearing in wrongful birth actions;
- caps on economic and non-economic damages;
- protection for medical practitioners who administer medical assistance without payment in 'good faith';
- the introduction of a new rule for calculating the limitation period for personal injury claims;
- the prevention of apologies being used as evidence of liability or fault.

The Civil Liability Act 2002 (s68) defines apology to mean 'an expression of sympathy or regret, or of a general sense of benevolence or compassion, in connection with any matter whether or not the apology admits or implies an admission of fault in connection with the matter'. Section 69 amplifies that an apology made by or on behalf of a person in connection with any matter alleged to have been caused by the fault of the person: (1) does not constitute an express or implied admission of fault or liability by the person in connection with that matter, and (2) is not relevant to the determination of fault or liability in connection with that matter. S69 (2) provides that evidence of an apology made by or on behalf of a person in connection with any matter alleged to have been caused by the fault of the person is not admissible in any civil proceedings as evidence of the fault or liability of the person in connection with that matter. Other countries have similar apologies or variants of apologies subject to protection.[22]

Eight years have passed since the reforms to the laws of negligence, yet the medical profession remains as concerned about litigation as ever. Conversations in hospital corridors and operating theatres are still dominated by litigation fears. Salem and Forster[23] in 2009 showed in a study in NSW that GPs remain unaware of the legal reforms and the consequent reduction in their legal liability and continue to practice defensive medicine. Another study in 2008[24] found that general practitioners with previous medicolegal experience believed (more than their colleagues) that the law required them to make perfect decisions and that medicolegal factors made them consider early retirement from medicine. They were also less likely to believe that inadequate communication is a common factor in complaints. If health professionals continue to have inadequate knowledge about the laws governing health care we will continue to have unnecessary cost caused by defensive medicine and unnecessary harm caused by increased prescribing and procedures (caused by defensive medicine). Health professionals require rigorous and timely training in medicolegal aspects of health care so that patient safety becomes the dominant cause of conversation and remedy.

Conclusion

There will not be a hospital or health facility in Australia untouched by the realisation that today's health care is responsible for significant harm to patients. We need to transform the health system and move it to a twenty-first-century model that recognises that patient care today is highly complex, involving multiple professions who are required to work together in teams and potentially dangerous because of the increased technology and drugs available. Patients can no longer be silent or passive; their role is important; their understanding of the risks of health care and the choices they make are important safety measures. Patient safety concepts and principles work at the interface between patients and their health care providers, but laws and regulations play a significant role in patient safety too. They drive change in circumstances where the cultural and professional barriers are resistant and they can provide clear safeguards for everyone – patients, health professionals and health managers alike.

Notes

1 R. Wilson, W.B. Gibberd, B. Harrison, L. Newby and J. Hamilton, 'The Quality in Australian Health Care Study', *Medical Journal of Australia* 163:9, 1995, pp. 458–471. The study showed that 16.6 per cent of admissions were associated with an adverse event (AEs) and that for 8.3 per cent of admissions the AEs were judged to have high preventability.

2 Inquiry into Obstetric and Gynaecological Services at King Edward Memorial Hospital (WA), 2001; Campbelltown and Camden Hospital inquiry (NSW), 2002; Special Commission of Inquiry into the delivery of patient care within the NSW Public Health System (NSW), 2007.

3 The names of the state-based safety organisations are as follows: Queensland Health Patient Safety and Quality Executive Committee, the Victorian Quality Council, the NSW Clinical Excellence Commission, Office of Quality and Safety in Healthcare (Western Australian), the South Australian Safety and Quality Council.

4 Australian Commission on Safety and Quality in Health Care, 'The National Safety and Quality Framework', in Australian Commission on Safety and Quality in Health Care (ed.), Sydney, Commonwealth Government, 2009.

5 I. Graham, A. Gleason, G. Keogh, D. Paltridge, I. Rogers and M. Walton, 'Australian Curriculum Framework for Junior Doctors', *Medical Journal of Australia* 186:7, 2007, pp. S14–S19.

6 World Health Organisation, *Patient Safety Curriculum Guide for Medical Schools*, Geneva, WHO, 2009. Online. Available HTTP http://www.who.int/patient safety/education/curriculum/background/en/index.html.

7 M.M. Walton and S.L. Elliot, 'Improving Safety and Quality: How Can Education Help?', *Medical Journal of Australia* 184 (10 suppl), 2006, pp. S60–S64.

8 Health Act 1993 (ACT), Health Administration Act 1982 (NSW) (ss.20D-20K), Health Services Act 1991 (Qld) (ss. 30-38), Health Commission Act

1976 (SA) (s. 64D), Health Act 1997 (Tas), HealthServices Act 1988 (Vic) (s. 139), Health Services (Quality Improvement) Act 1994 (WA) and Health Insurance Act 1973 (Cth) (Part VC).

 9 Australian Council on Safety and Quality in Health Care, *National Report on Qualified Privilege*, Canberra, Commonwealth of Australia, 2002. Online. Available HTTP http://www.health.gov.au/internet/safety/publishing.nsf/Content/F0FD7442D1F2F8DDCA2571C6000894FF/$File/qual_priv1.pdf.

10 Australian Commission on Safety and Quality in Health Care, 'Open Disclosure Standard', in Commonwealth Department of Health and Aging (ed.), Sydney, Commonwealth of Australia, 2008.

11 Ibid.

12 Ibid.

13 Ibid.

14 R. Iedema, N. Mallock, R. Sorensen, E. Manias, A. Tuckett, A. Williams A *et al.*, 'Evaluation of the Pilot of the National Open Disclosure Standard', in Care ACoSaQiH (ed.), Sydney, Australian Commission on Safety and Quality in Health Care, 2007.

15 Australian Commission on Safety and Quality in Health Care, 'The National Safety and Quality Framework'.

16 Australian Commission on Safety and Quality in Health Care, 'The Australian Charter of Healthcare Rights', in Australian Commission on Safety and Quality in Health Care (ed.), Sydney, Commonwealth of Australia, 2008.

17 United Nations, *Universal Declaration of Human Rights*. Online. Available HTTP http://www.un.org/en/documents/udhr/ (accessed 7 January 2010).

18 Office of the High Commissioner for Human Rights, *International Covenant on Economic, Social and Cultural Rights*. Online. Available HTTP http://www.unhchr.ch/html/menu3/b/a_cescr.htm (accessed 7 January 2010).

19 The Ipp Report can be found at http://revofneg.treasury.gov.au/content/review2.asp.

20 E. Wright, 'National Trends in Personal Injury Litigation: Before and After "Ipp"',. *Torts Law Journal* 14, 2006, p. 233.

21 O. Salem and C. Forster, 'Defensive Mediciane in General Practice: Recent Trends and the Impact of the Civil Liability Act 2002 (NSW)', *Journal of Law and Medicine* 17, 2009, pp. 235–248.

22 Canada and the United States as well as England and Wales have also introduced legislation allowing apologies, but different conditions apply in relation to who is protected and the extent of the apology.

23 Salem and Forster, 'Defensive Medicine in General Practice'.

24 L. Nash, M. Walton, M. Daly, M. Johnson *et al.*, 'GP's Concerns about Medicolegal Issues: How It Afects Their Practice', *Australian Family Physician* 38:12, 2009, pp. 66–70.

Index